D1210735

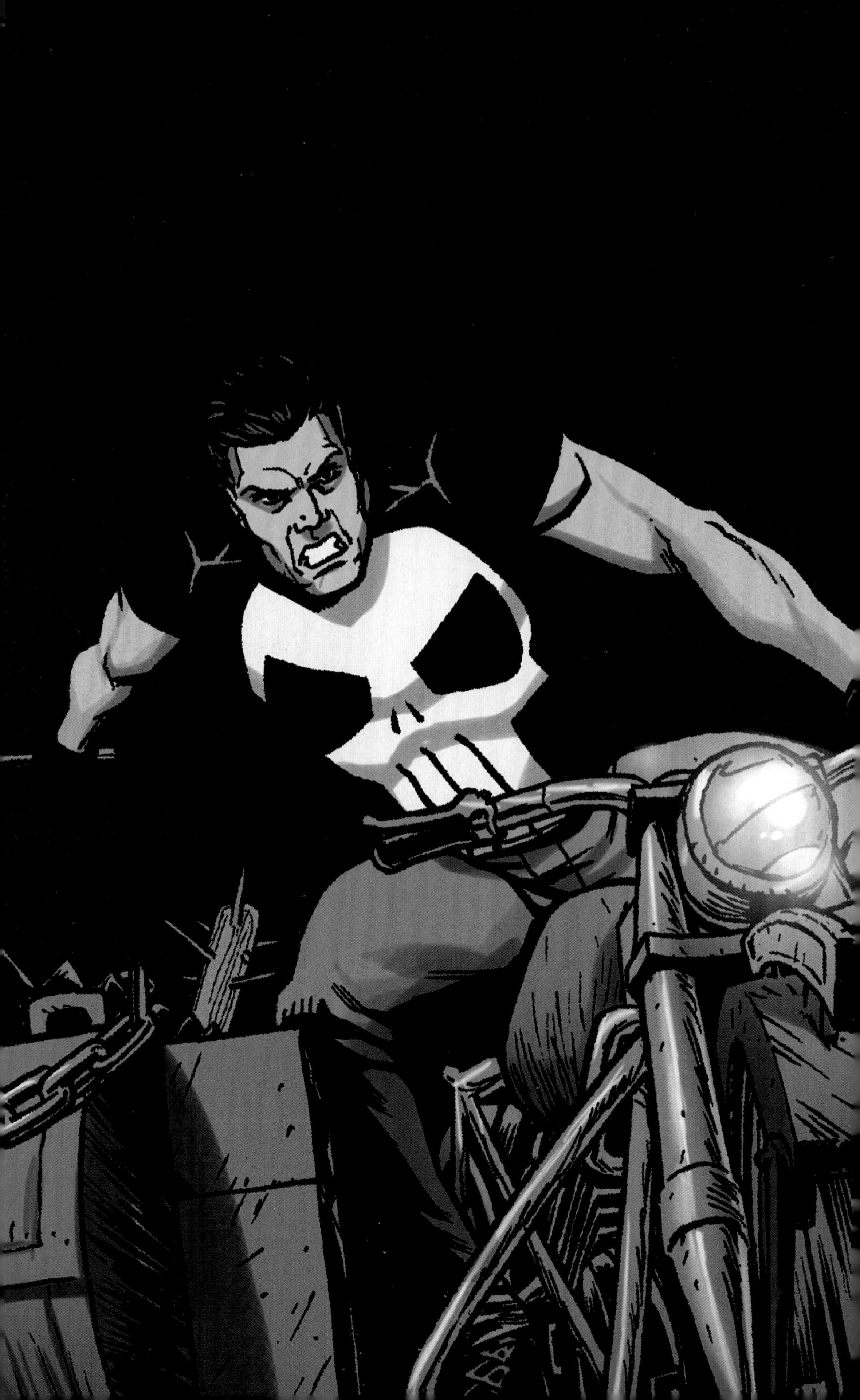

FRANK CASTLE was a decorated Marine, an upstanding citizen and a family man. Then his family was taken from him when they were accidentally killed in a brutal mob hit. From that day, he became a force of cold, calculated retribution and vigilantism. Frank Castle died with his family. Now, there is only...

THE PUNISHER

End of the Line

Becky Cloonan
writer

Matt Horak (Nos. 7, 9-12) with **Steve Dillon** (No. 7) & **Laura Braga** with **Iolanda Zanfardino** (No. 8)
artists

Frank Martin with **Guru-eFX** (No. 10)
color artists

VC's Cory Petit
letterer

Declan Shalvey & **Jordie Bellaire**
cover art

Kathleen Wisneski
assistant editor

Jake Thomas
editor

collection editor: Jennifer Grünwald
assistant editor: Caitlin O'Connell
associate managing editor: Kateri Woody
editor, special projects: Mark D. Beazley

vp production & special projects: Jeff Youngquist
svp print, sales & marketing: David Gabriel
book designer: Adam Del Re

editor in chief: Axel Alonso
chief creative officer: Joe Quesada
president: Dan Buckley
executive producer: Alan Fine

THE PUNISHER VOL. 2: END OF THE LINE. Contains material originally published in magazine form as THE PUNISHER #7-12. First printing 2017. ISBN# 978-1-302-90048-9. Published by MARVEL WORLDWIDE, INC., a subsidiary of MARVEL ENTERTAINMENT, LLC. OFFICE OF PUBLICATION: 135 West 50th Street, New York, NY 10020.

Printed in Canada. DAN BUCKLEY, President, Marvel Entertainment; JOE QUESADA, Chief Creative Officer; TOM BREVOORT, SVP of Publishing; DAVID BOGART, SVP of Business Affairs & Operations, Publishing & Partnership; C.B. CEBULSKI, VP of Brand Management & Development, Asia; DAVID GABRIEL, SVP of Sales & Marketing, Publishing; JEFF YOUNGQUIST, VP of Production & Special Projects; DAN CARR, Executive Director of Publishing Technology; ALEX MORALES, Director of Publishing Operations; SUSAN CRESPI, Production Manager; STAN LEE, Chairman Emeritus. For information regarding advertising in Marvel Comics or on Marvel.com, please contact Vit DeBellis, Integrated Sales Manager, at vdebellis@marvel.com. For Marvel subscription inquiries, please call 888-511-5480. **Manufactured between 5/26/2017 and 6/27/2017 by SOLISCO PRINTERS, SCOTT, QC, CANADA.**

10 9 8 7 6 5 4 3 2 1

THE PUNISHER raided a drug warehouse run
by the mercenary organization CONDOR.
Frank's former commander in the Marines,
Olaf, was working for Condor, but,
tired of being low man on the totem pole,
he directed Frank towards Condor's
main production centers.

The trail ended at EXETER ASYLUM.
In the ensuing bloody battle, Condor's
lead operative Face overdosed on the
dangerous performance-enhancing drug
EMC and lost a hand. D.E.A. Agent Ortiz
was forced to kill her EMC-crazed partner,
and the Punisher was caught in an explosion
underneath the asylum's cemetery.

But you can't keep the
Punisher buried for long...

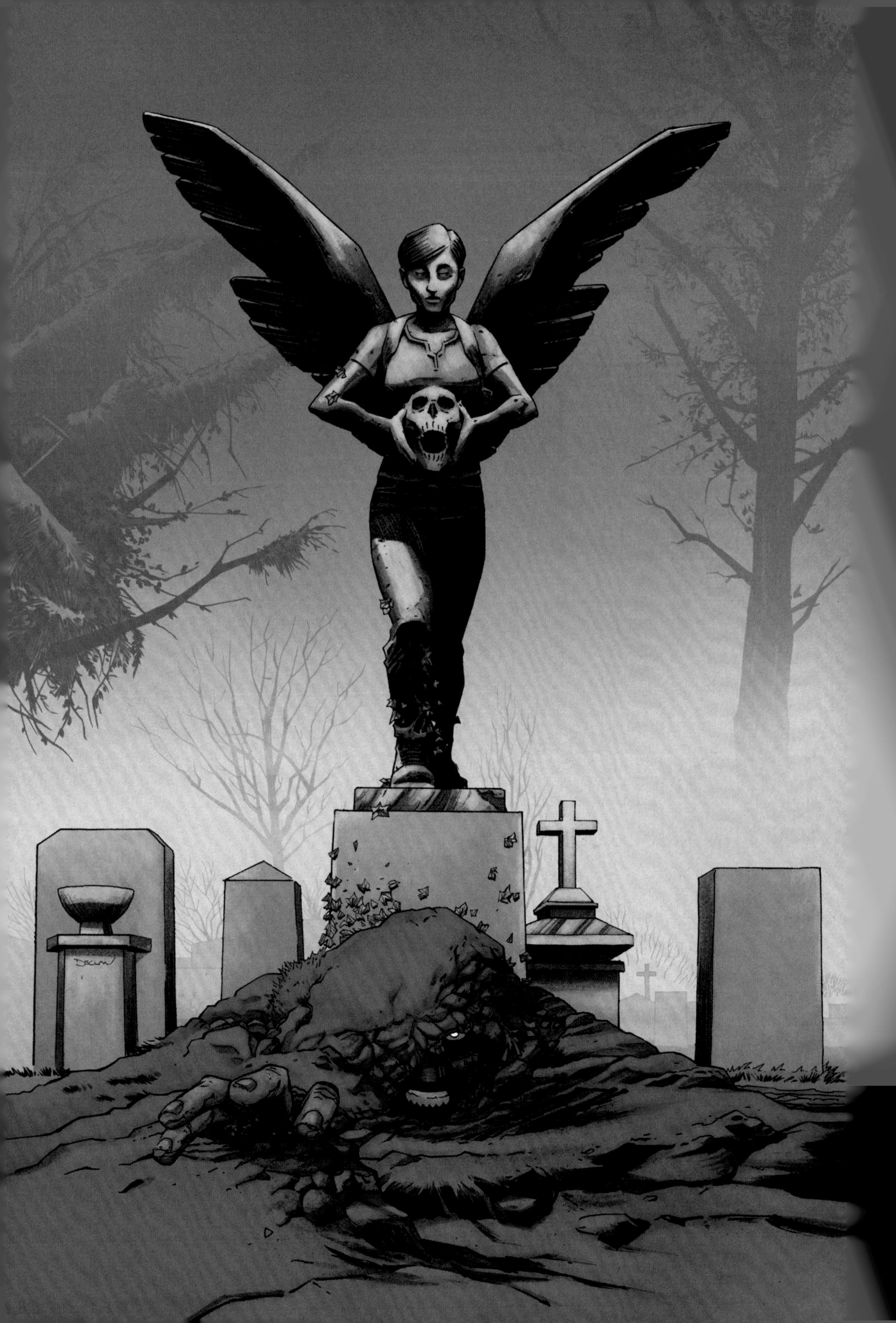

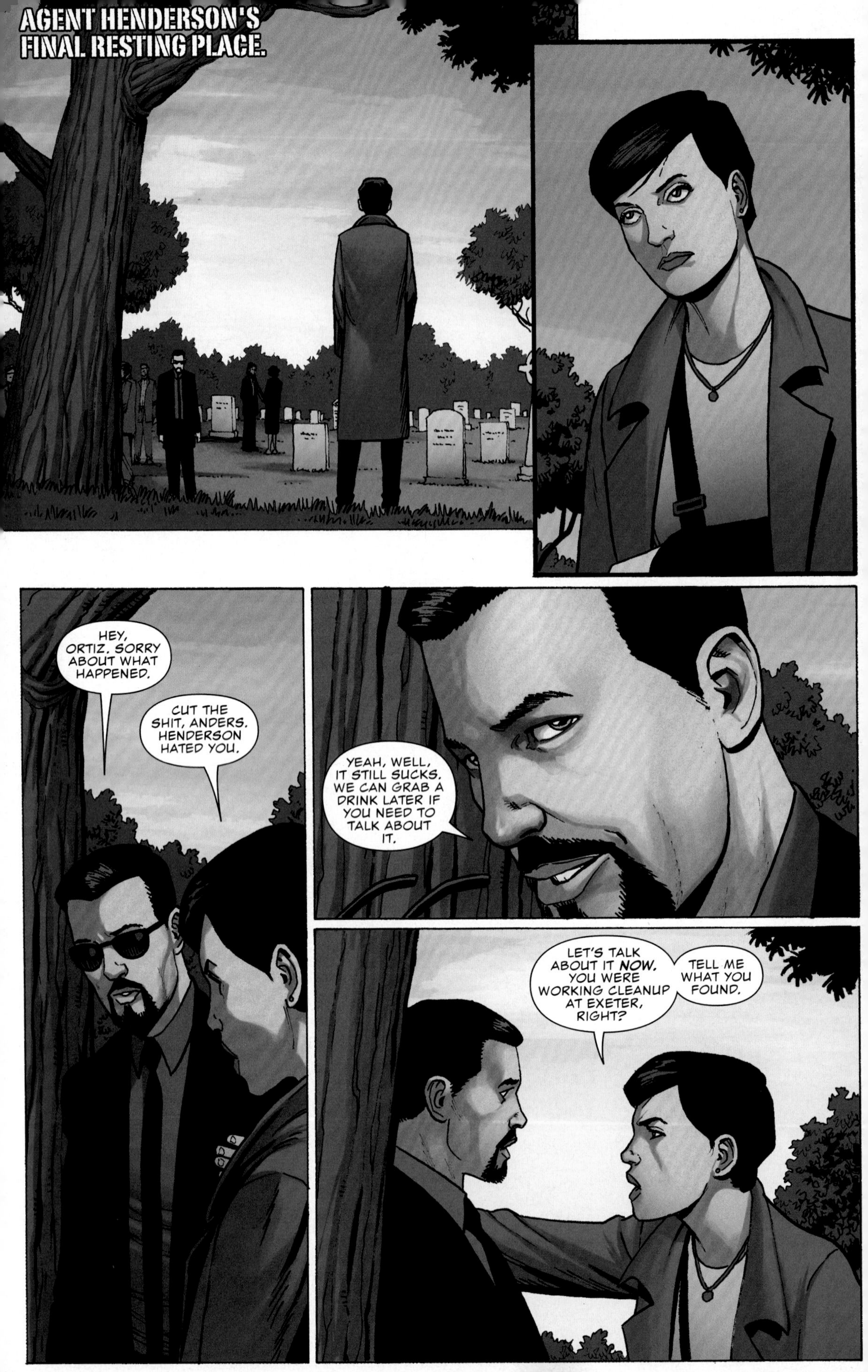
AGENT HENDERSON'S FINAL RESTING PLACE.
HEY, ORTIZ. SORRY ABOUT WHAT HAPPENED.
CUT THE SHIT, ANDERS. HENDERSON HATED YOU.
YEAH, WELL, IT STILL SUCKS. WE CAN GRAB A DRINK LATER IF YOU NEED TO TALK ABOUT IT.
LET'S TALK ABOUT IT NOW. YOU WERE WORKING CLEANUP AT EXETER, RIGHT?
TELL ME WHAT YOU FOUND.

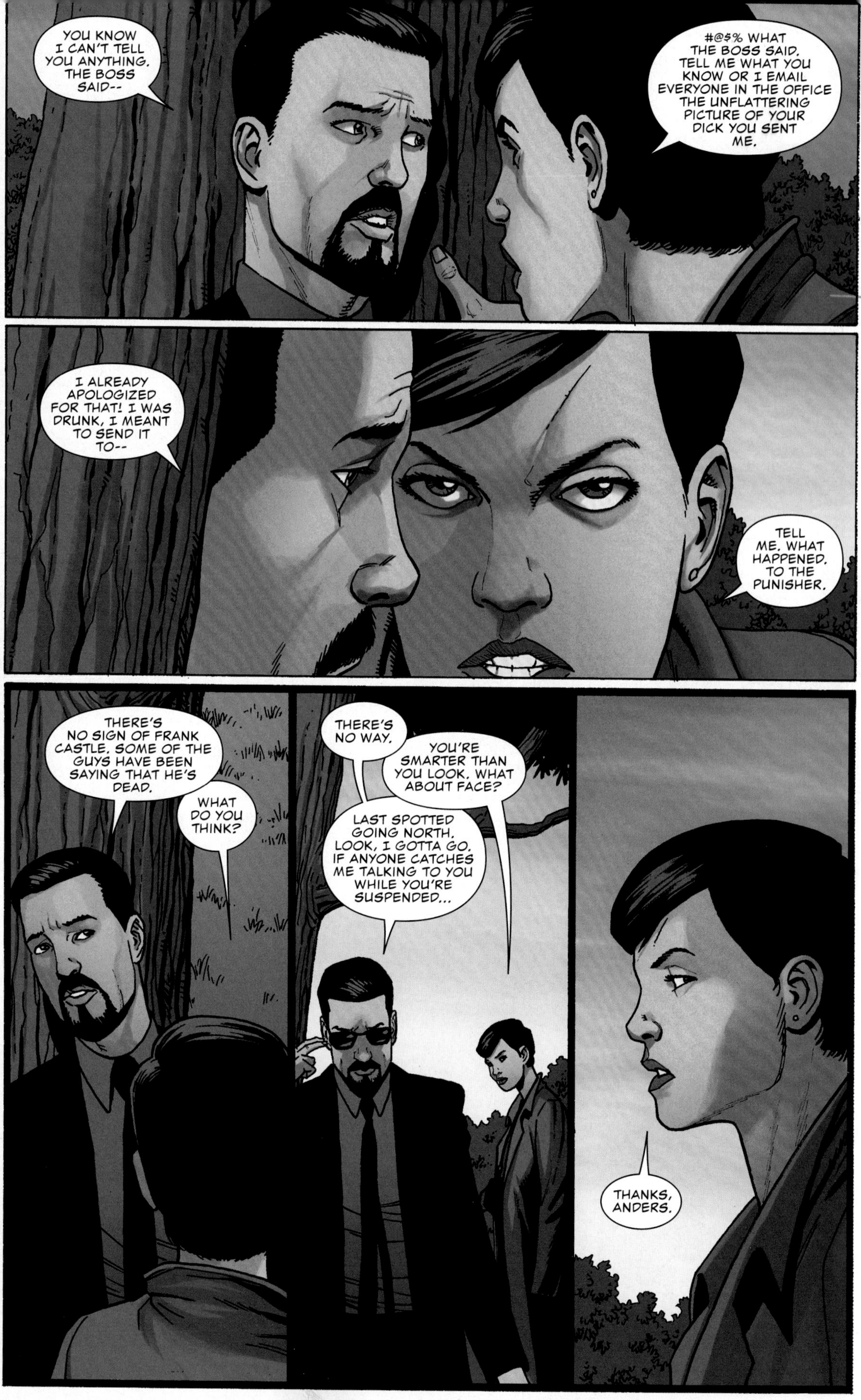
YOU KNOW I CAN'T TELL YOU ANYTHING. THE BOSS SAID--
#@$% WHAT THE BOSS SAID. TELL ME WHAT YOU KNOW OR I EMAIL EVERYONE IN THE OFFICE THE UNFLATTERING PICTURE OF YOUR DICK YOU SENT ME.
I ALREADY APOLOGIZED FOR THAT! I WAS DRUNK, I MEANT TO SEND IT TO--
TELL ME. WHAT HAPPENED. TO THE PUNISHER.
THERE'S NO SIGN OF FRANK CASTLE. SOME OF THE GUYS HAVE BEEN SAYING THAT HE'S DEAD.
WHAT DO YOU THINK?
THERE'S NO WAY.
YOU'RE SMARTER THAN YOU LOOK. WHAT ABOUT FACE?
LAST SPOTTED GOING NORTH. LOOK, I GOTTA GO. IF ANYONE CATCHES ME TALKING TO YOU WHILE YOU'RE SUSPENDED...
THANKS, ANDERS.

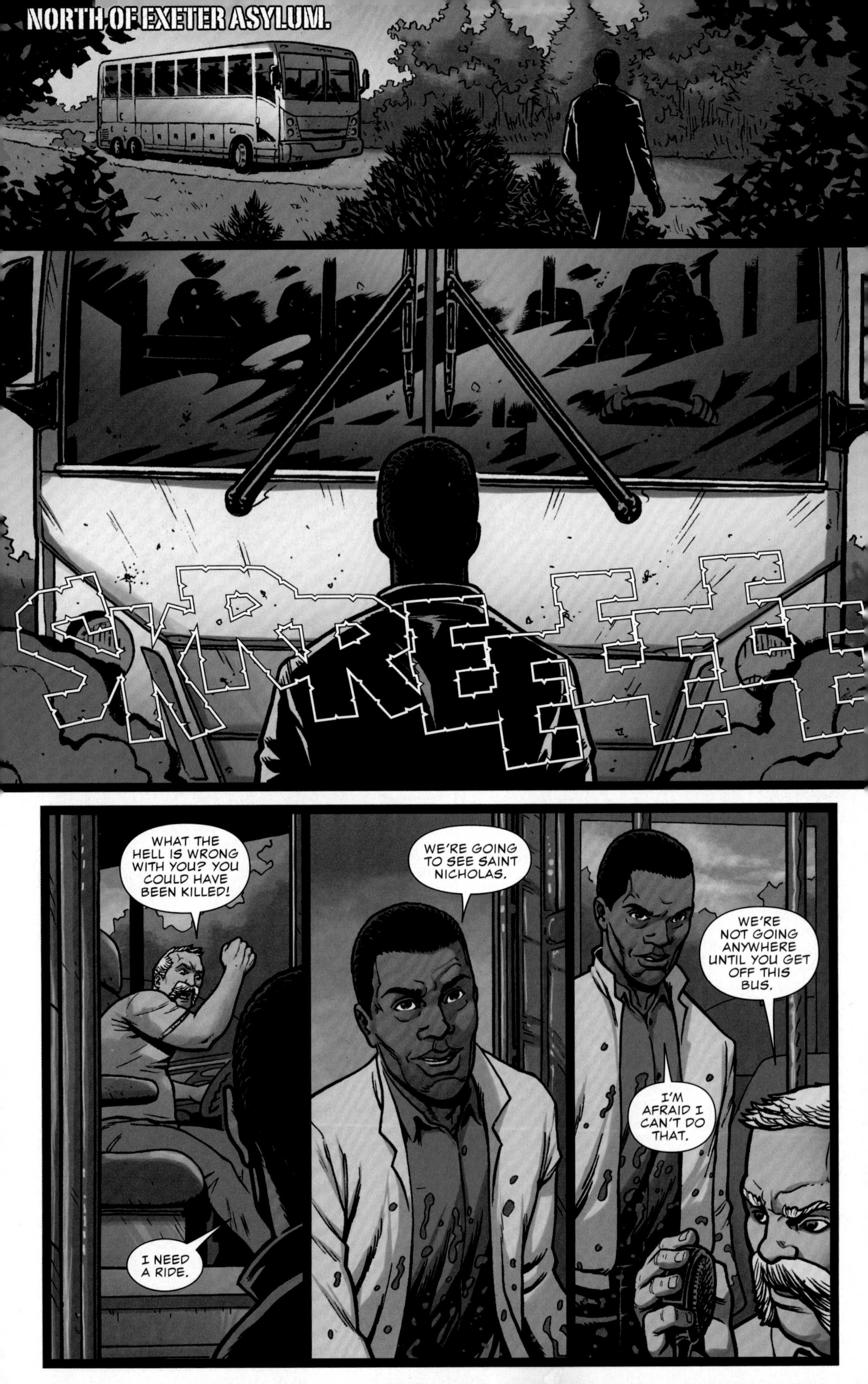
NORTH OF EXETER ASYLUM.
SKREEEEE
WHAT THE HELL IS WRONG WITH YOU? YOU COULD HAVE BEEN KILLED!
I NEED A RIDE.
WE'RE GOING TO SEE SAINT NICHOLAS.
WE'RE NOT GOING ANYWHERE UNTIL YOU GET OFF THIS BUS.
I'M AFRAID I CAN'T DO THAT.

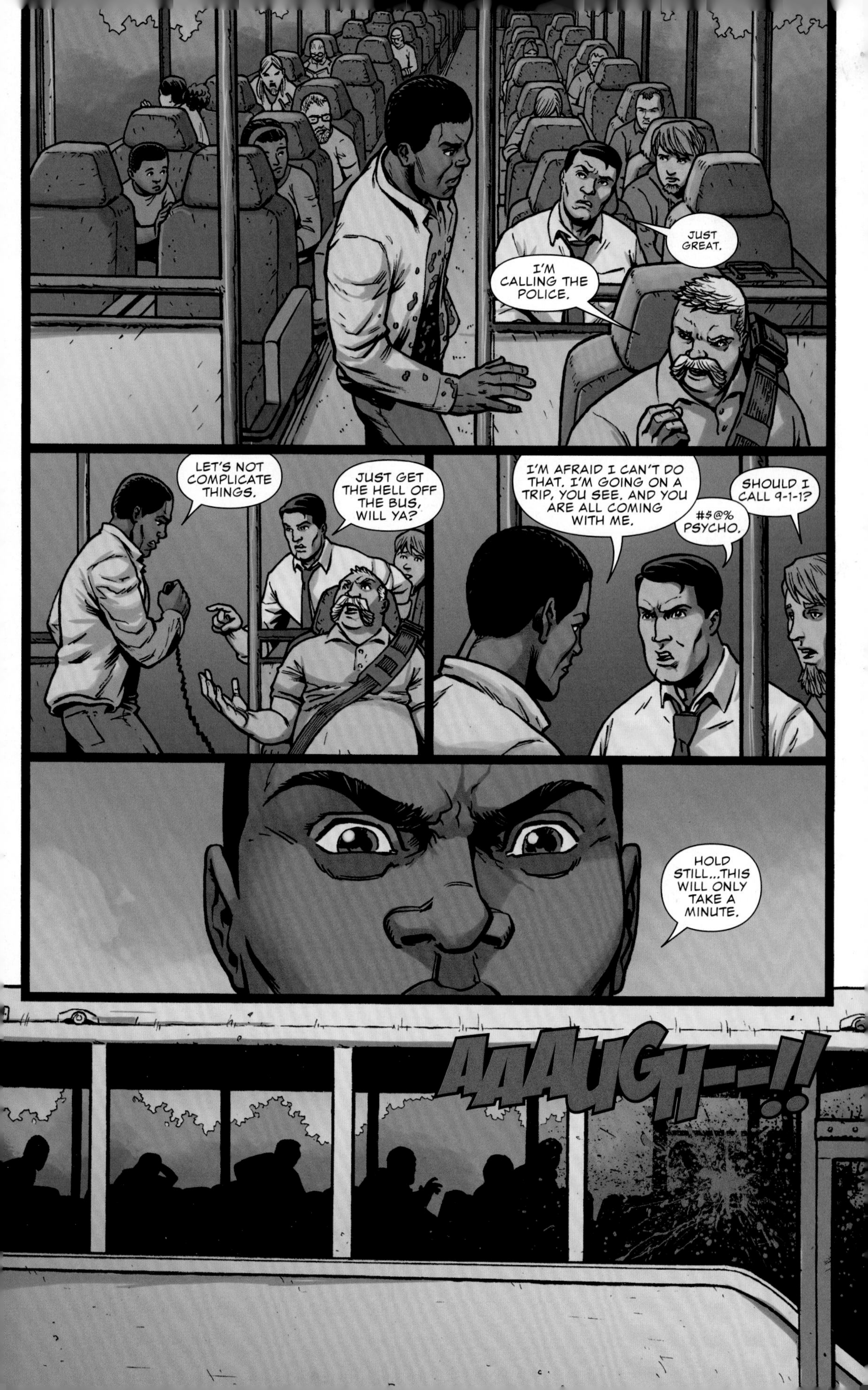
I'M CALLING THE POLICE.
JUST GREAT.
LET'S NOT COMPLICATE THINGS.
JUST GET THE HELL OFF THE BUS, WILL YA?
I'M AFRAID I CAN'T DO THAT. I'M GOING ON A TRIP, YOU SEE. AND YOU ARE ALL COMING WITH ME.
#$@% PSYCHO.
SHOULD I CALL 9-1-1?
HOLD STILL...THIS WILL ONLY TAKE A MINUTE.
AAAAUGH--!!

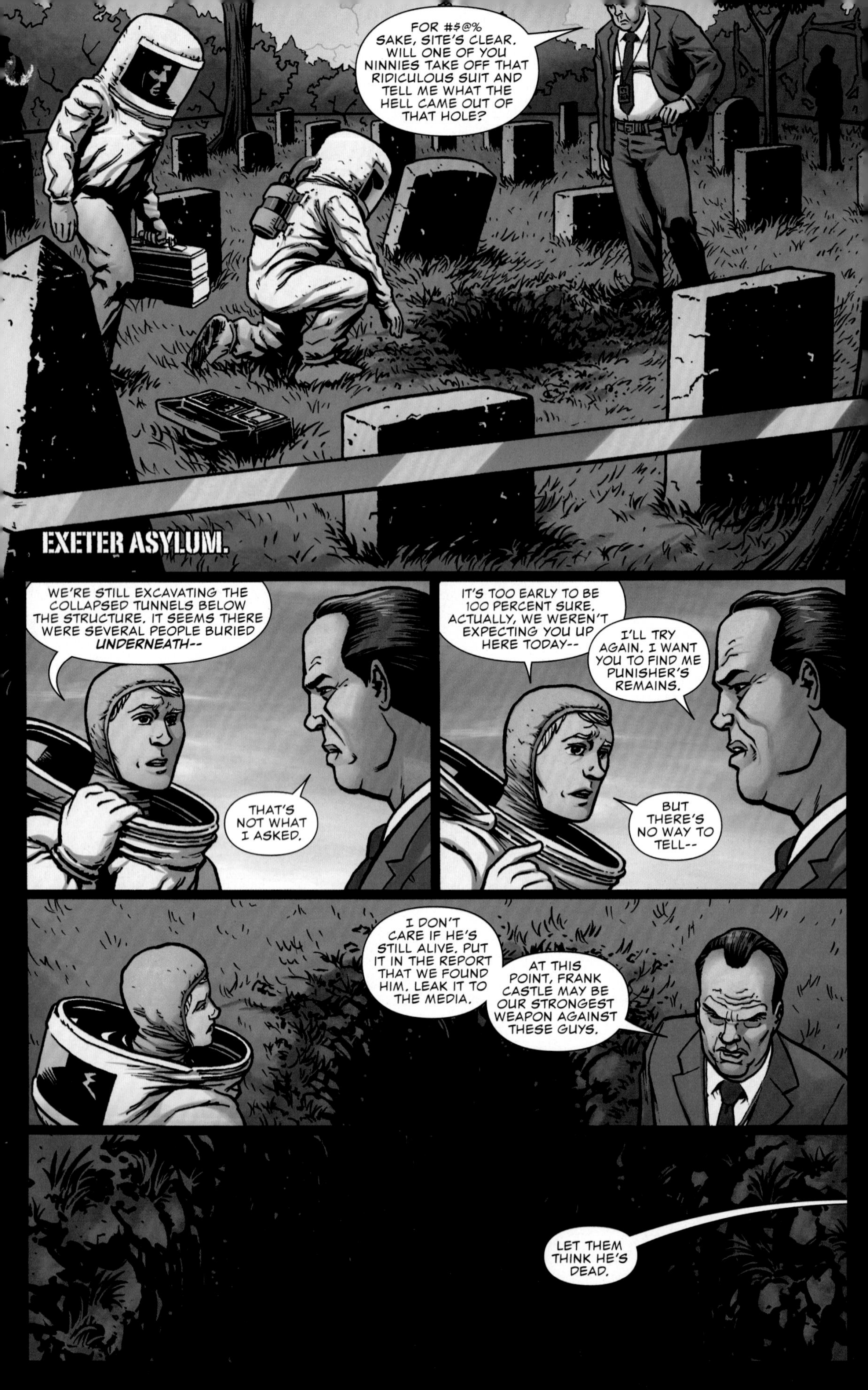
FOR #$@% SAKE, SITE'S CLEAR. WILL ONE OF YOU NINNIES TAKE OFF THAT RIDICULOUS SUIT AND TELL ME WHAT THE HELL CAME OUT OF THAT HOLE?
EXETER ASYLUM.
WE'RE STILL EXCAVATING THE COLLAPSED TUNNELS BELOW THE STRUCTURE. IT SEEMS THERE WERE SEVERAL PEOPLE BURIED UNDERNEATH--
THAT'S NOT WHAT I ASKED.
IT'S TOO EARLY TO BE 100 PERCENT SURE. ACTUALLY, WE WEREN'T EXPECTING YOU UP HERE TODAY--
I'LL TRY AGAIN. I WANT YOU TO FIND ME PUNISHER'S REMAINS.
BUT THERE'S NO WAY TO TELL--
I DON'T CARE IF HE'S STILL ALIVE. PUT IT IN THE REPORT THAT WE FOUND HIM. LEAK IT TO THE MEDIA.
AT THIS POINT, FRANK CASTLE MAY BE OUR STRONGEST WEAPON AGAINST THESE GUYS.
LET THEM THINK HE'S DEAD.

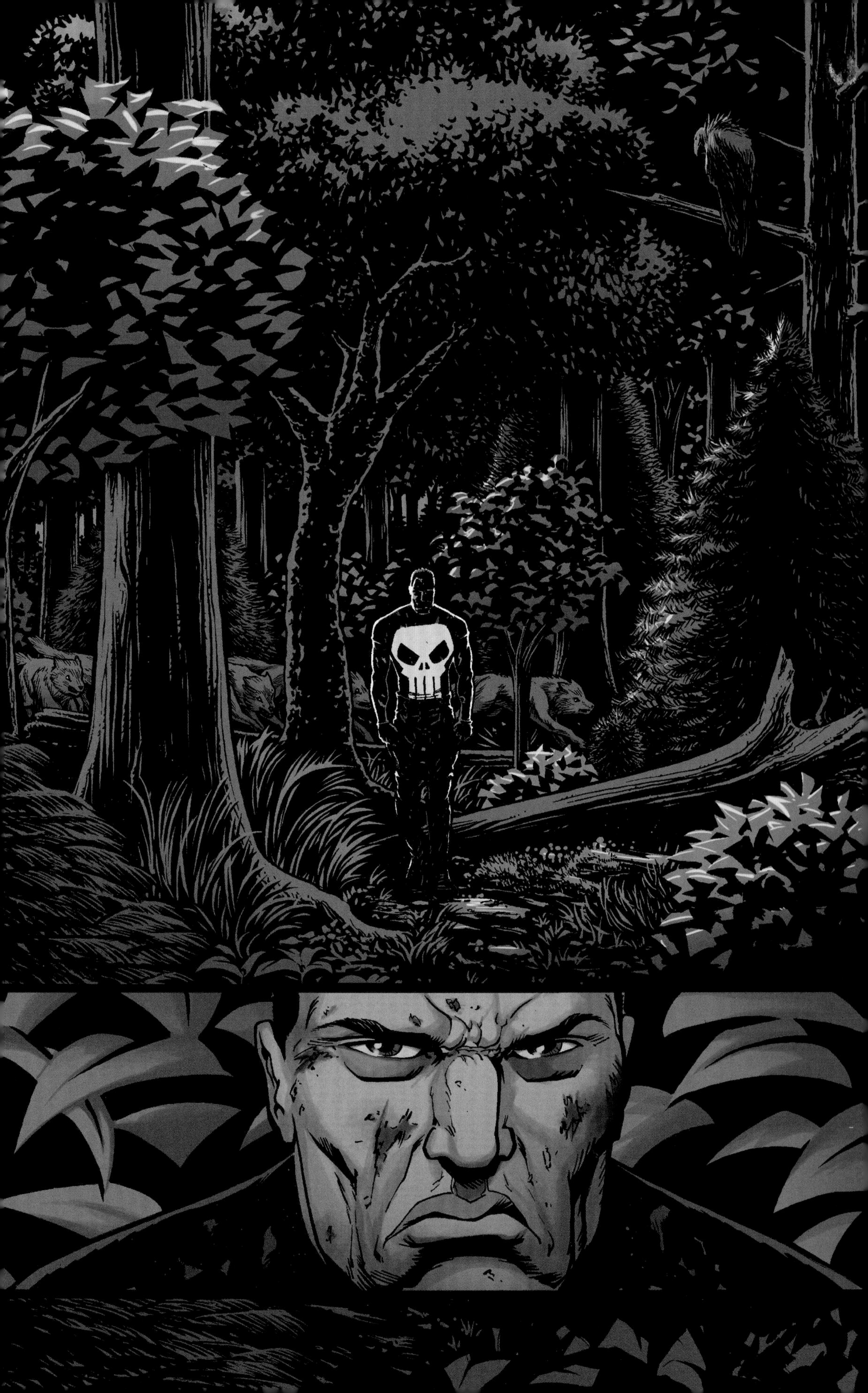

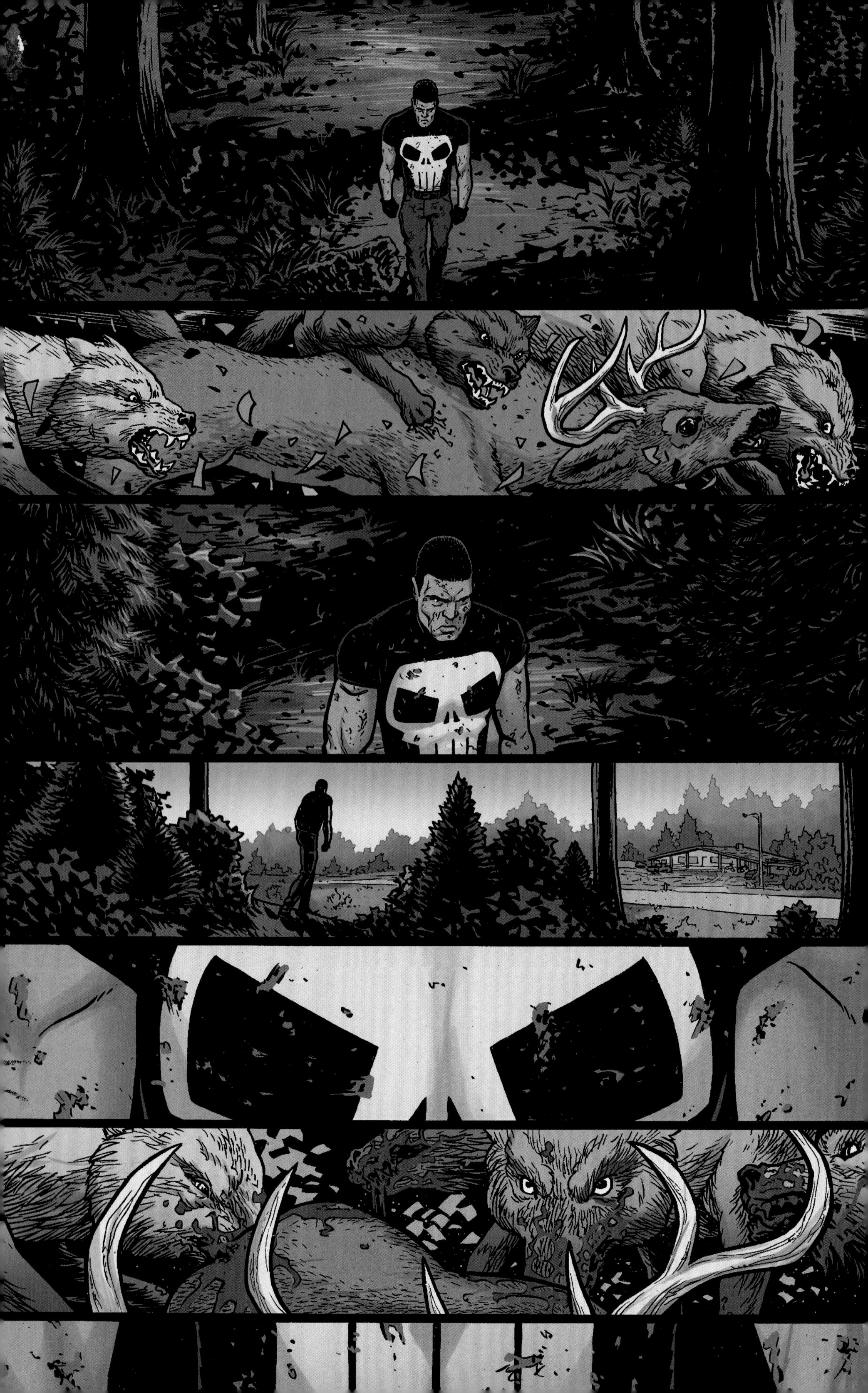

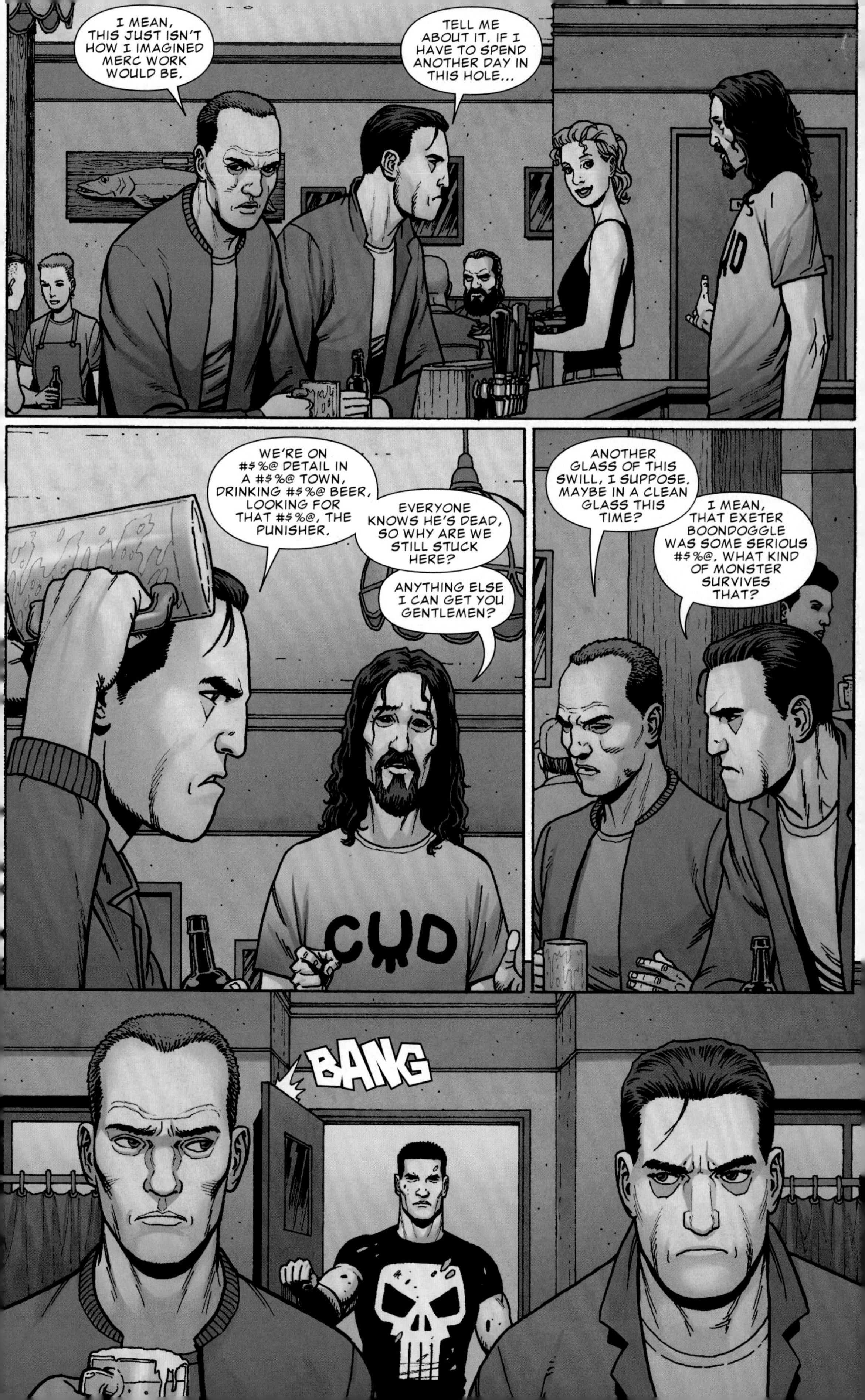

I MEAN, THIS JUST ISN'T HOW I IMAGINED MERC WORK WOULD BE.
TELL ME ABOUT IT. IF I HAVE TO SPEND ANOTHER DAY IN THIS HOLE...
WE'RE ON #$%@ DETAIL IN A #$%@ TOWN, DRINKING #$%@ BEER, LOOKING FOR THAT #$%@, THE PUNISHER.
EVERYONE KNOWS HE'S DEAD, SO WHY ARE WE STILL STUCK HERE?
ANYTHING ELSE I CAN GET YOU GENTLEMEN?
CUD
ANOTHER GLASS OF THIS SWILL, I SUPPOSE. MAYBE IN A CLEAN GLASS THIS TIME?
I MEAN, THAT EXETER BOONDOGGLE WAS SOME SERIOUS #$%@. WHAT KIND OF MONSTER SURVIVES THAT?
BANG

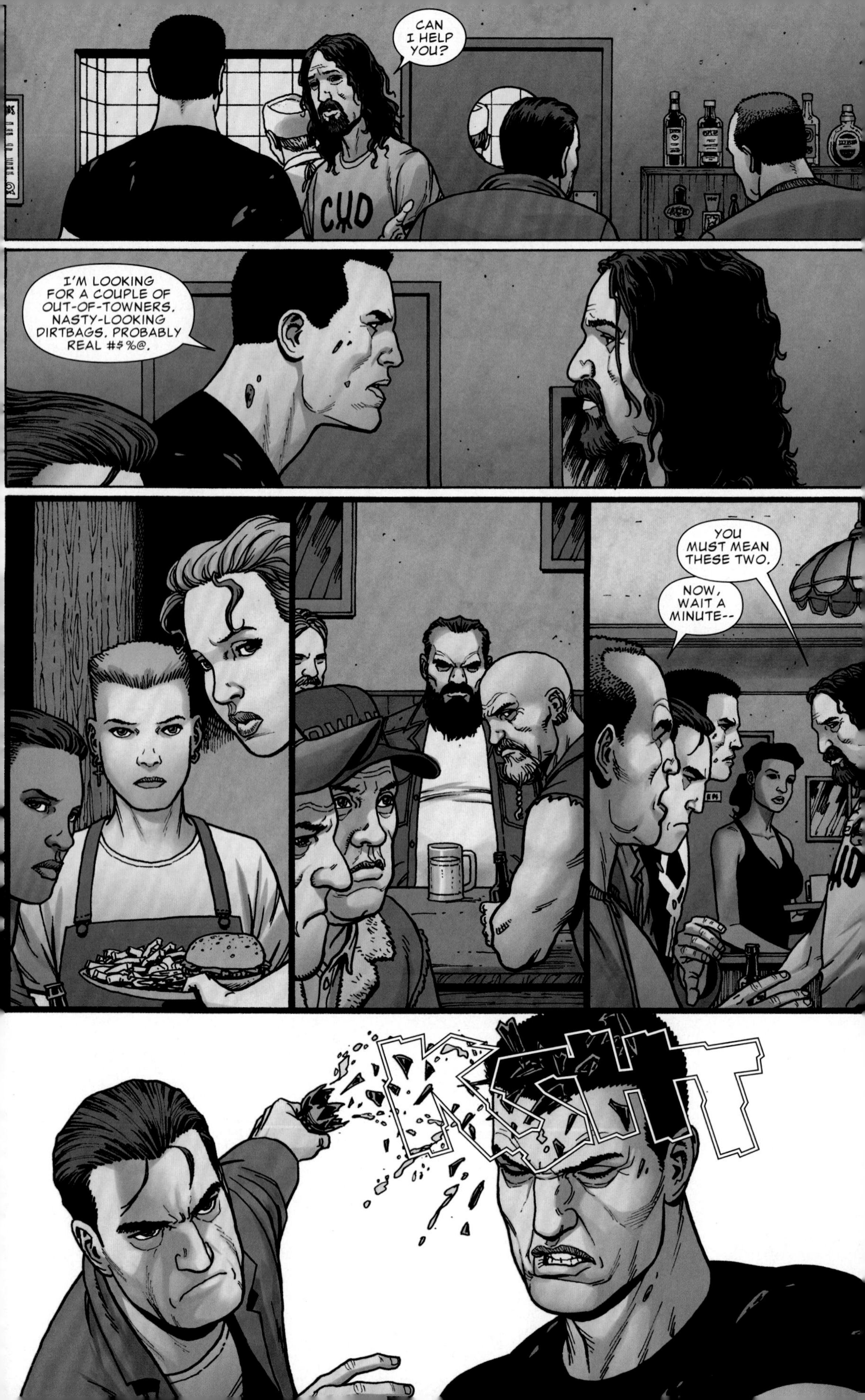
CAN I HELP YOU?
I'M LOOKING FOR A COUPLE OF OUT-OF-TOWNERS. NASTY-LOOKING DIRTBAGS. PROBABLY REAL #$%@.
YOU MUST MEAN THESE TWO.
NOW, WAIT A MINUTE--
KSSH

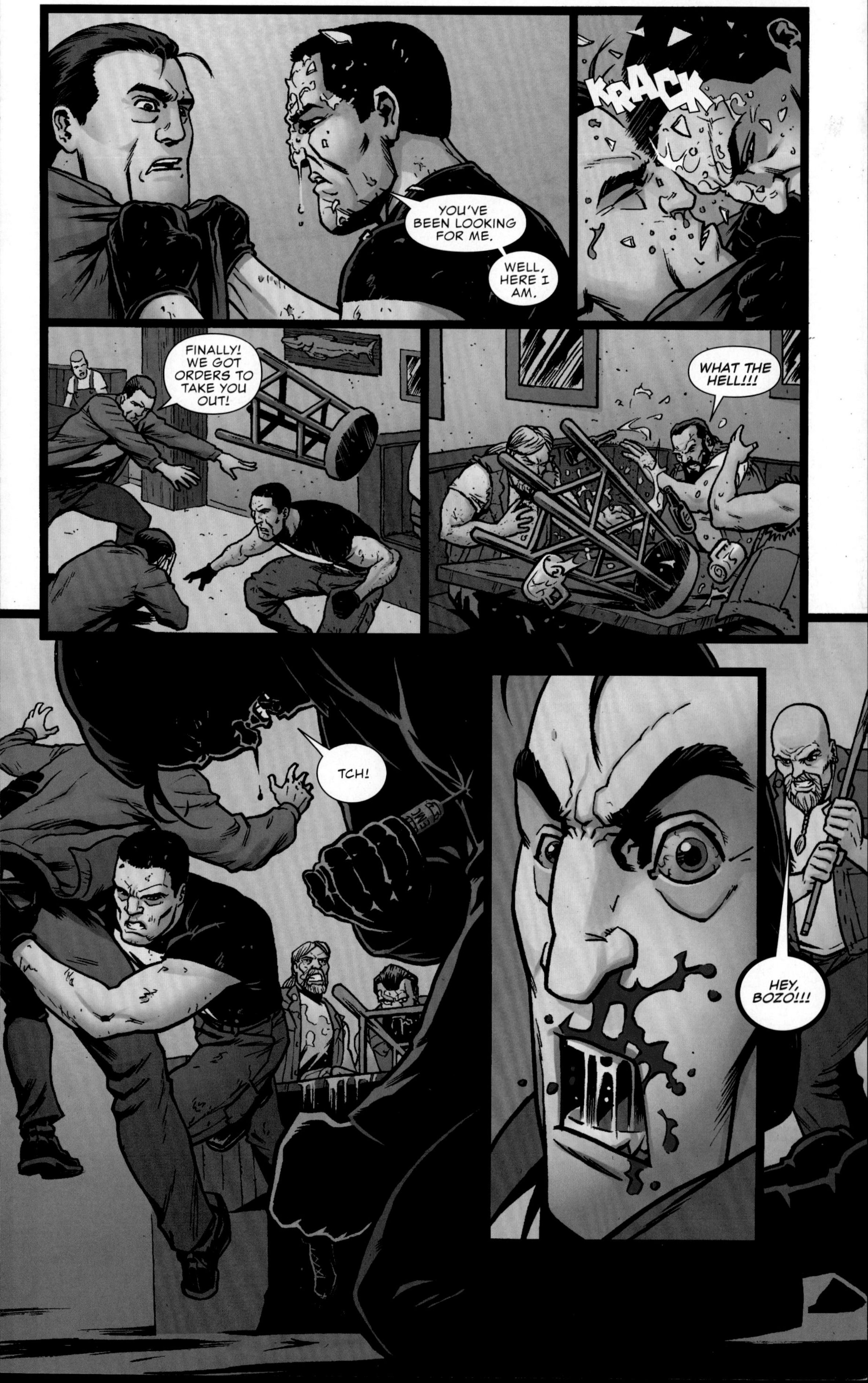

YOU'VE BEEN LOOKING FOR ME.
WELL, HERE I AM.
KRACK
FINALLY! WE GOT ORDERS TO TAKE YOU OUT!
WHAT THE HELL!!!
TCH!
HEY, BOZO!!!

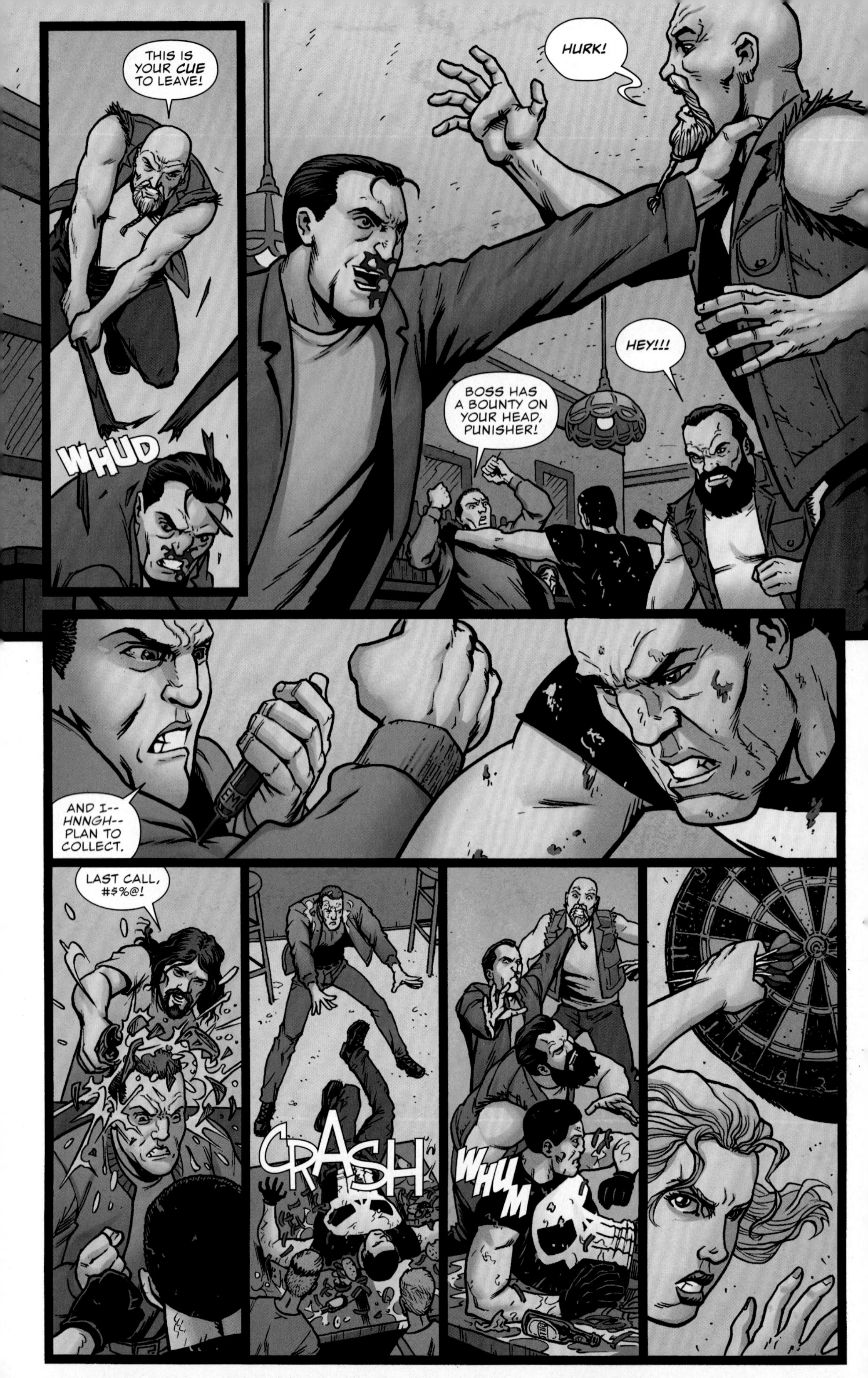
THIS IS YOUR CUE TO LEAVE!
WHUD
HURK!
HEY!!!
BOSS HAS A BOUNTY ON YOUR HEAD, PUNISHER!
AND I-- HNNGH-- PLAN TO COLLECT.
LAST CALL, #$%@!
CRASH
WHUM

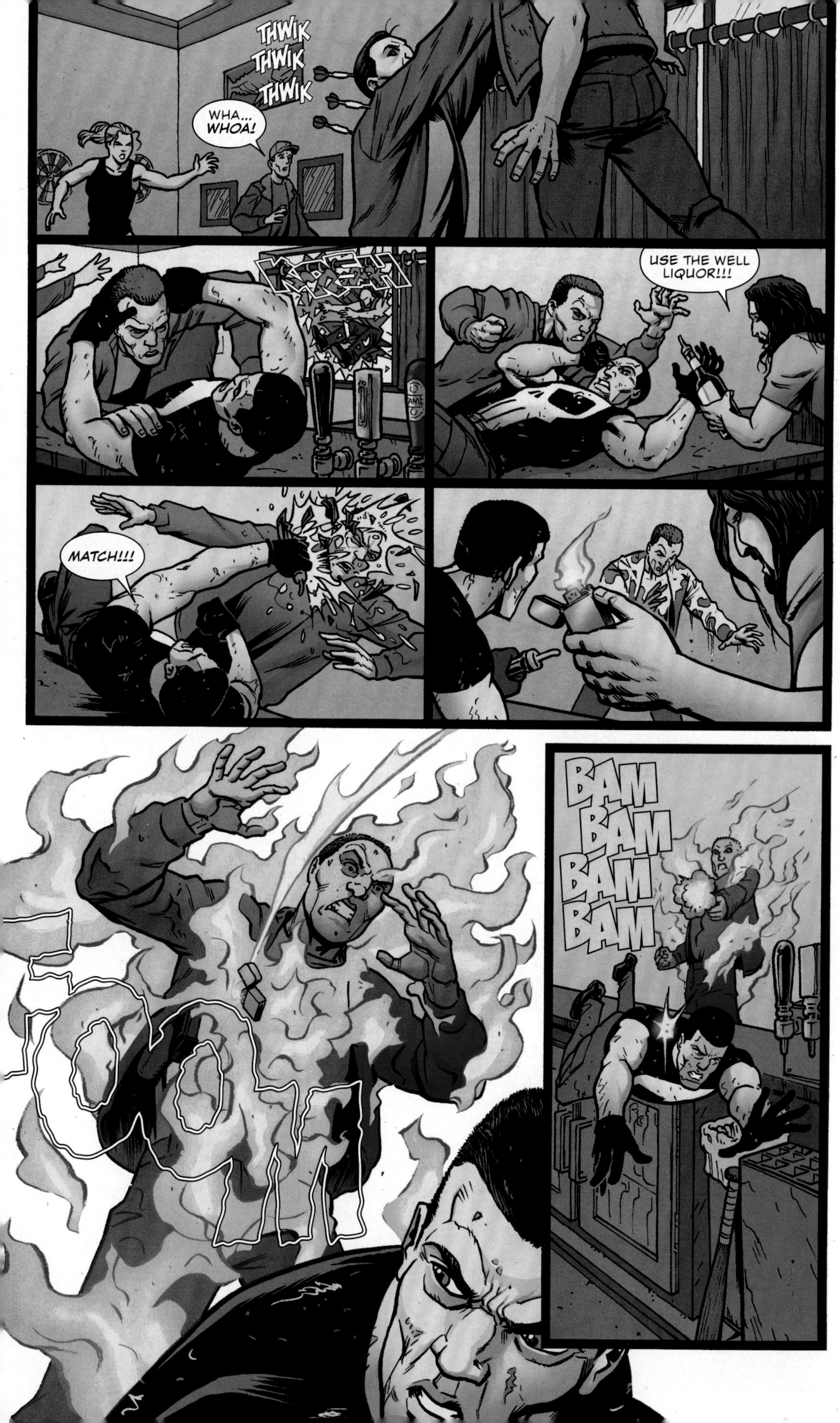
THWIK
THWIK
THWIK
WHA... WHOA!
USE THE WELL LIQUOR!!!
MATCH!!!
BAM
BAM
BAM
BAM

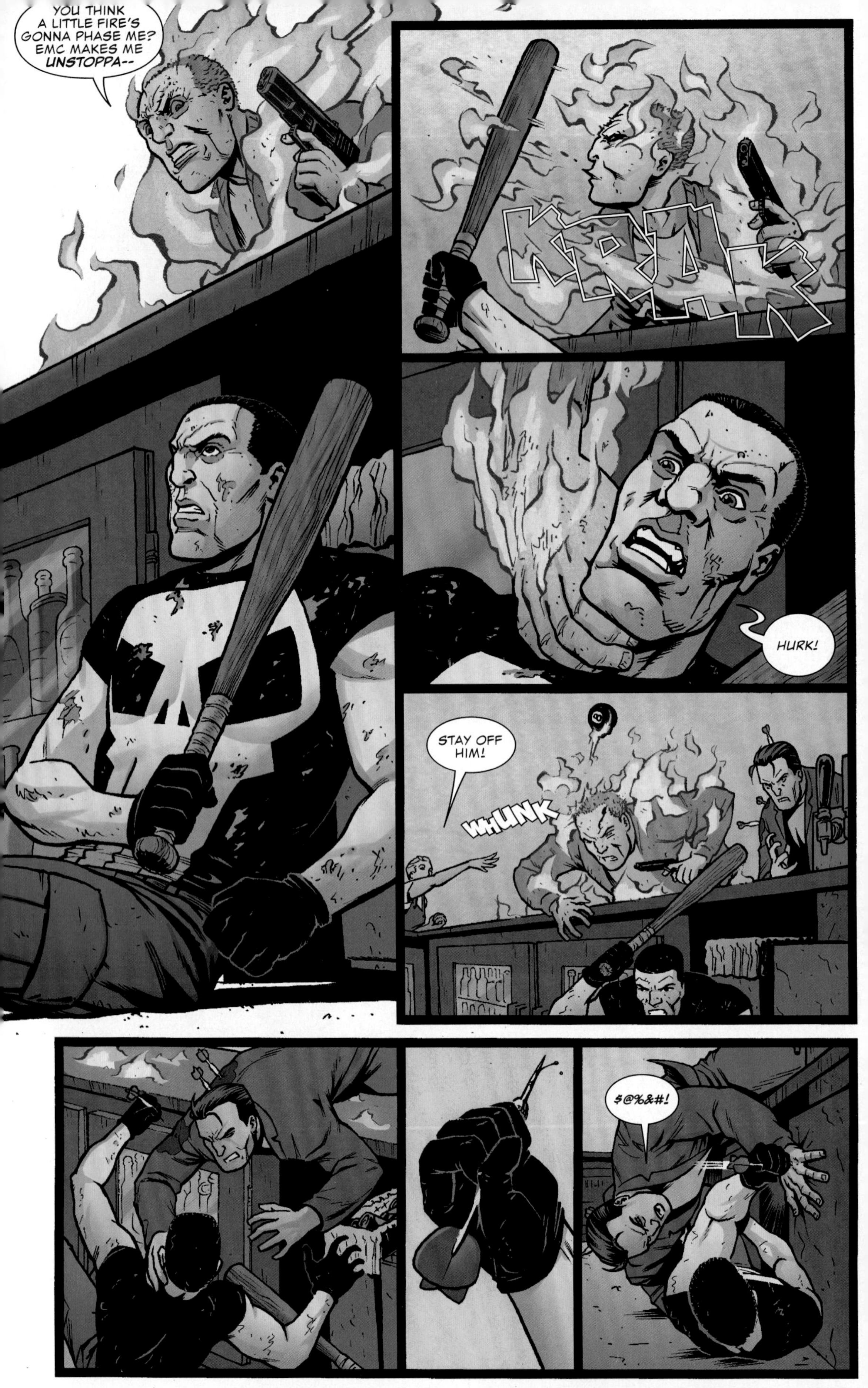
YOU THINK A LITTLE FIRE'S GONNA PHASE ME? EMC MAKES ME UNSTOPPA--
KRAK
HURK!
STAY OFF HIM!
WHUNK
$@%&#!

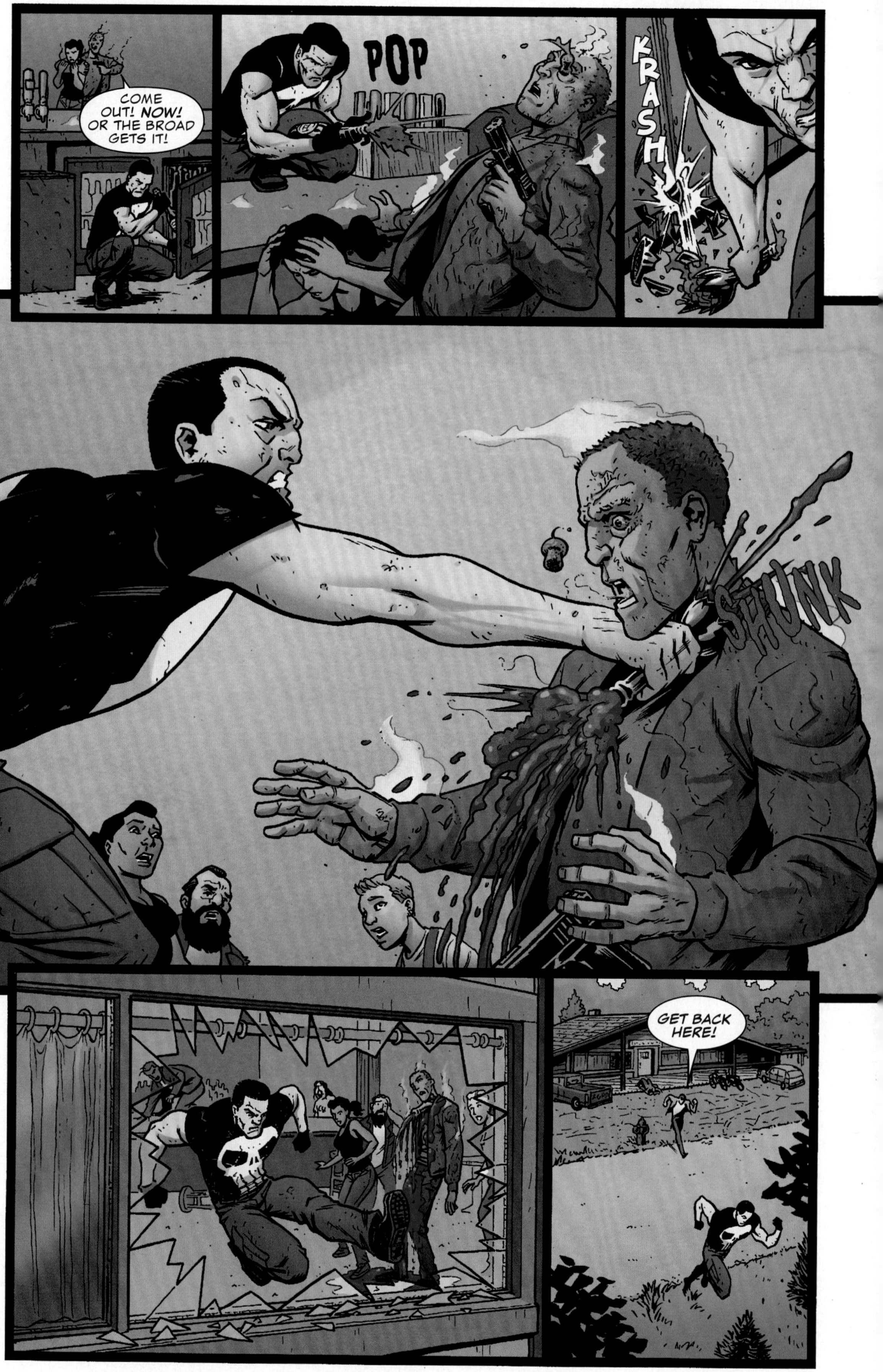
COME OUT! NOW! OR THE BROAD GETS IT!
POP
KRASH
SHUNK
GET BACK HERE!

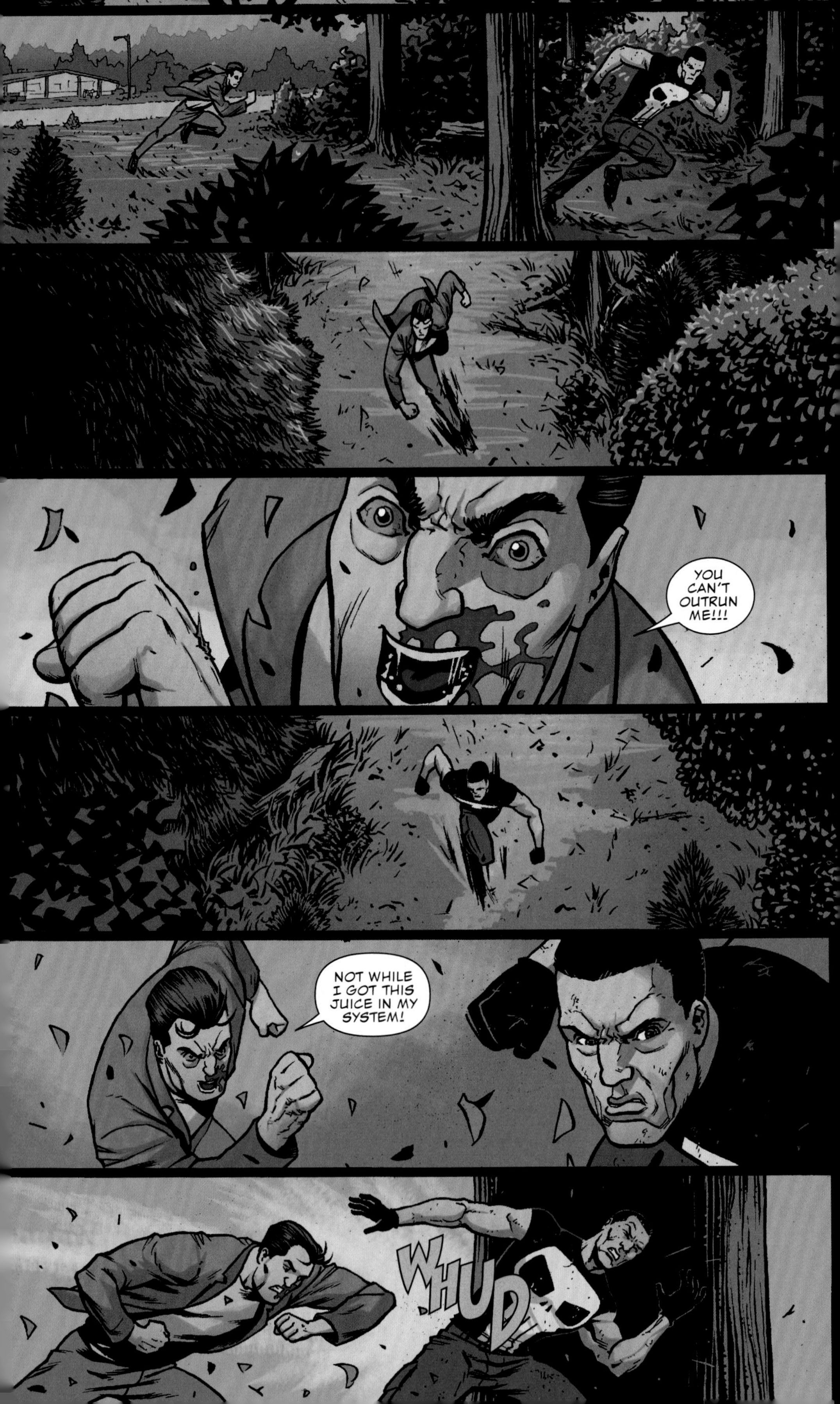
YOU CAN'T OUTRUN ME!!!
NOT WHILE I GOT THIS JUICE IN MY SYSTEM!
WHUD

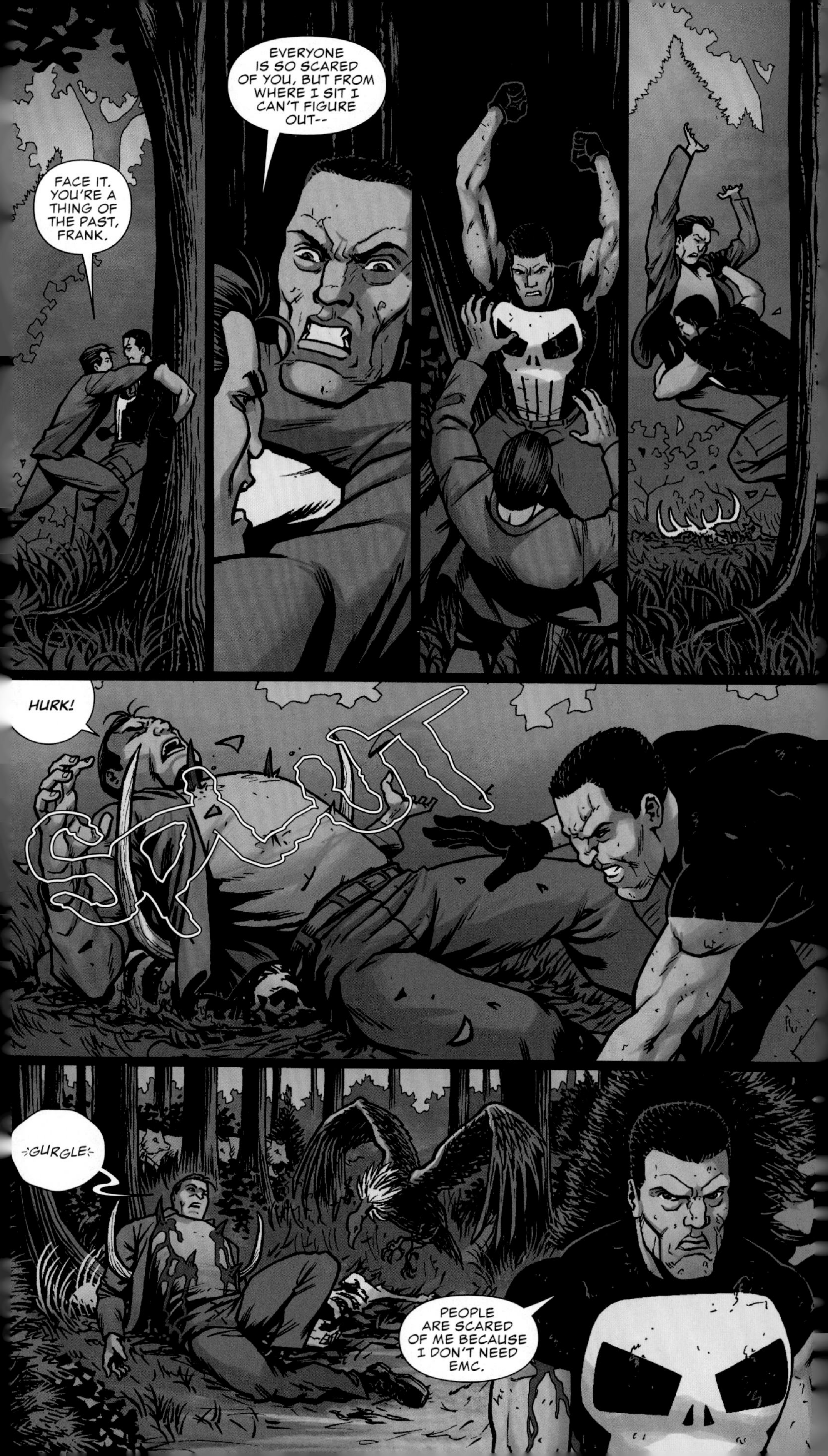
FACE IT, YOU'RE A THING OF THE PAST, FRANK.
EVERYONE IS SO SCARED OF YOU, BUT FROM WHERE I SIT I CAN'T FIGURE OUT--
HURK!
SPLUT
-GURGLE-
PEOPLE ARE SCARED OF ME BECAUSE I DON'T NEED EMC.

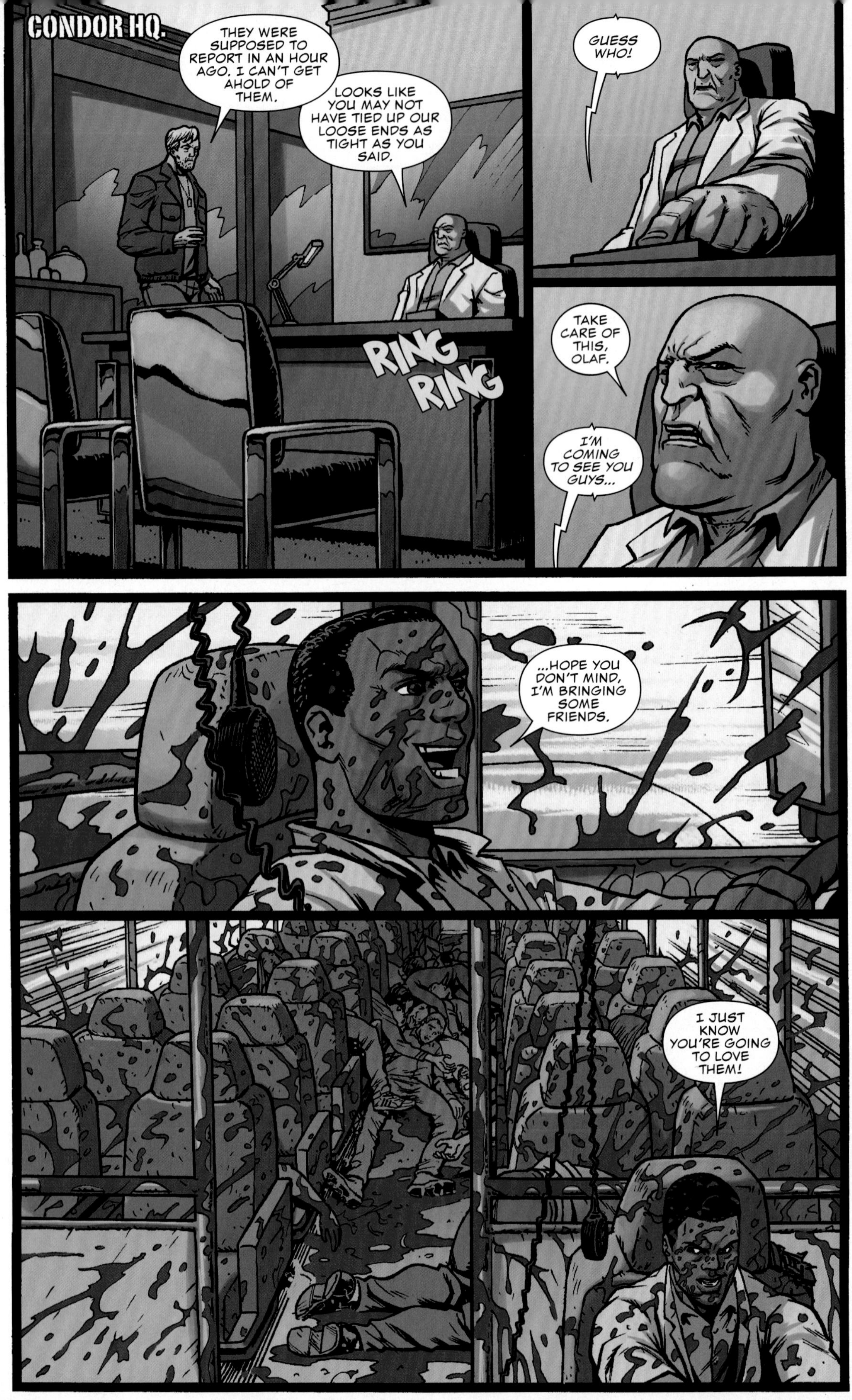
CONDOR HQ.
THEY WERE SUPPOSED TO REPORT IN AN HOUR AGO. I CAN'T GET AHOLD OF THEM.
LOOKS LIKE YOU MAY NOT HAVE TIED UP OUR LOOSE ENDS AS TIGHT AS YOU SAID.
RING RING
GUESS WHO!
TAKE CARE OF THIS, OLAF.
I'M COMING TO SEE YOU GUYS...
...HOPE YOU DON'T MIND, I'M BRINGING SOME FRIENDS.
I JUST KNOW YOU'RE GOING TO LOVE THEM!

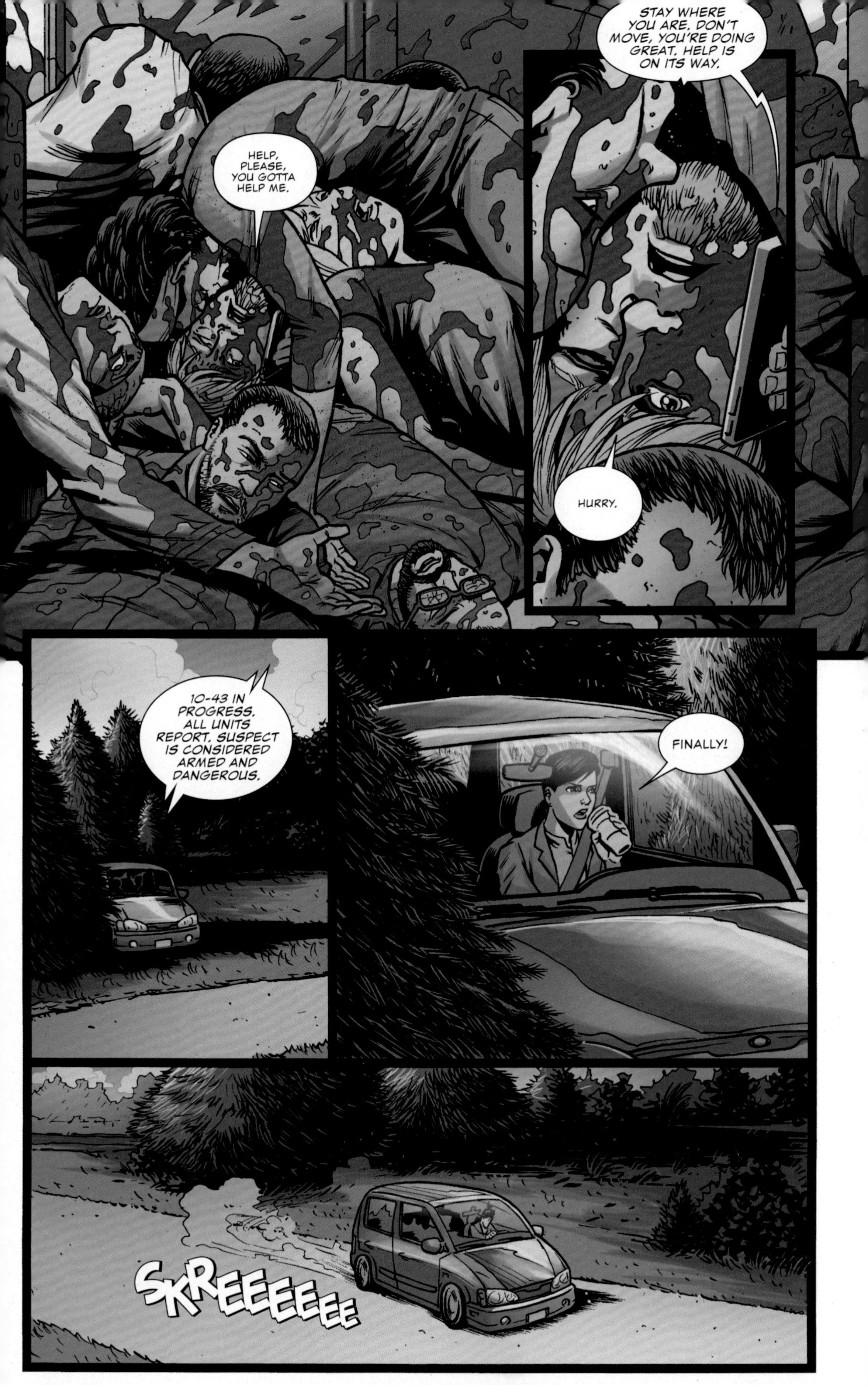
HELP, PLEASE, YOU GOTTA HELP ME.
STAY WHERE YOU ARE. DON'T MOVE, YOU'RE DOING GREAT. HELP IS ON ITS WAY.
HURRY.
10-43 IN PROGRESS. ALL UNITS REPORT. SUSPECT IS CONSIDERED ARMED AND DANGEROUS.
FINALLY!
SKREEEEEEE

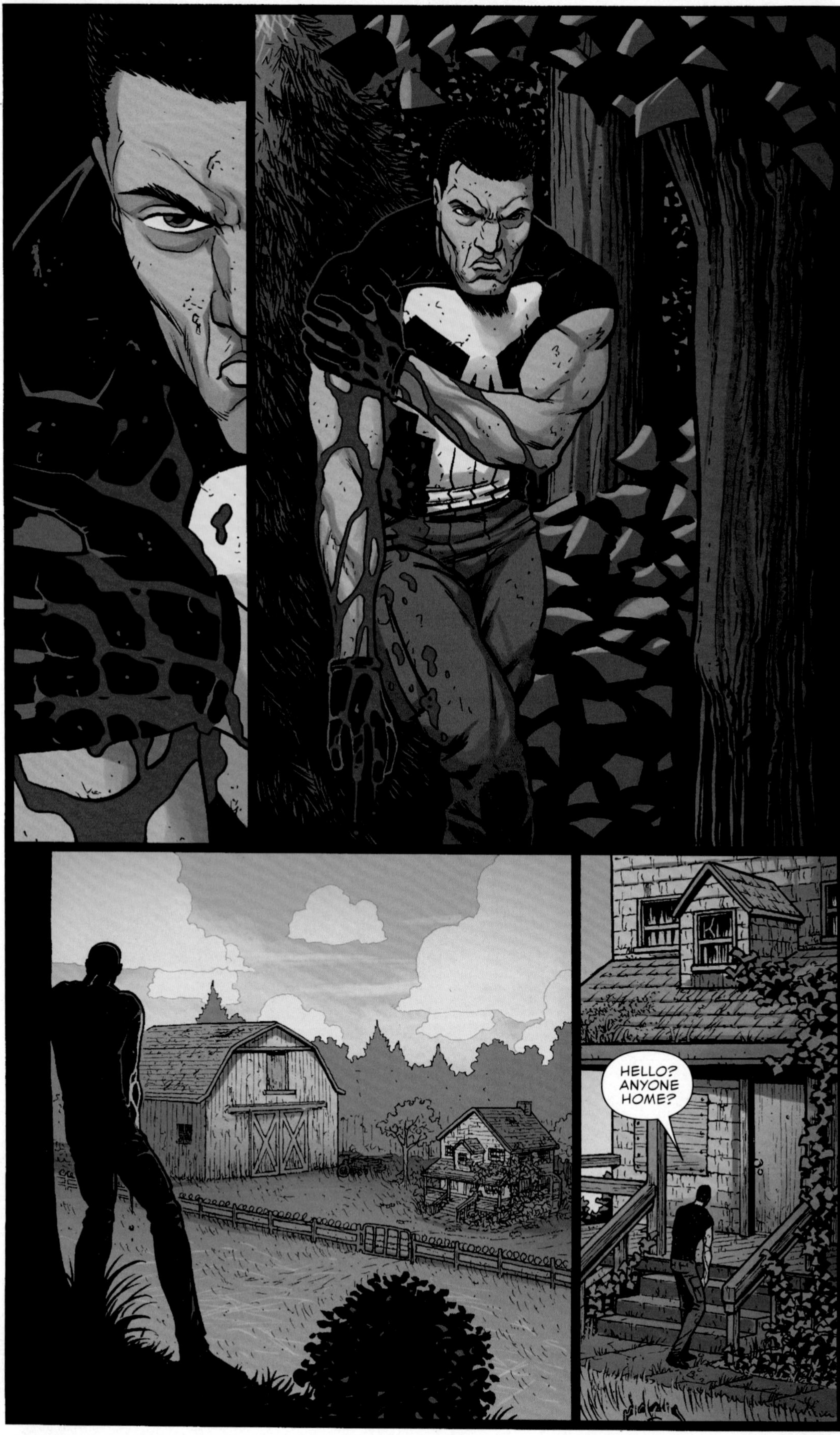
HELLO? ANYONE HOME?

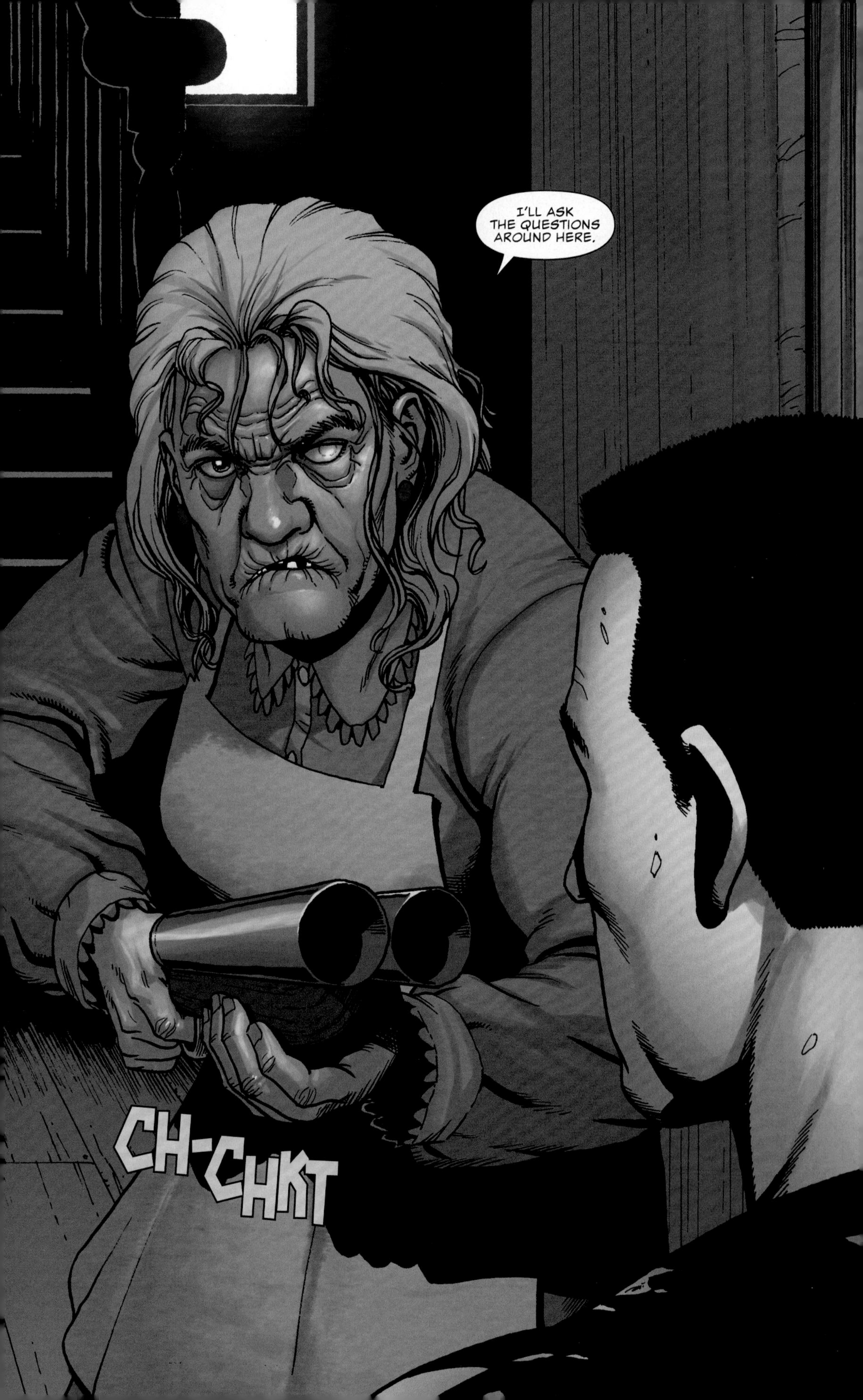
I'LL ASK THE QUESTIONS AROUND HERE.
CH-CHKT

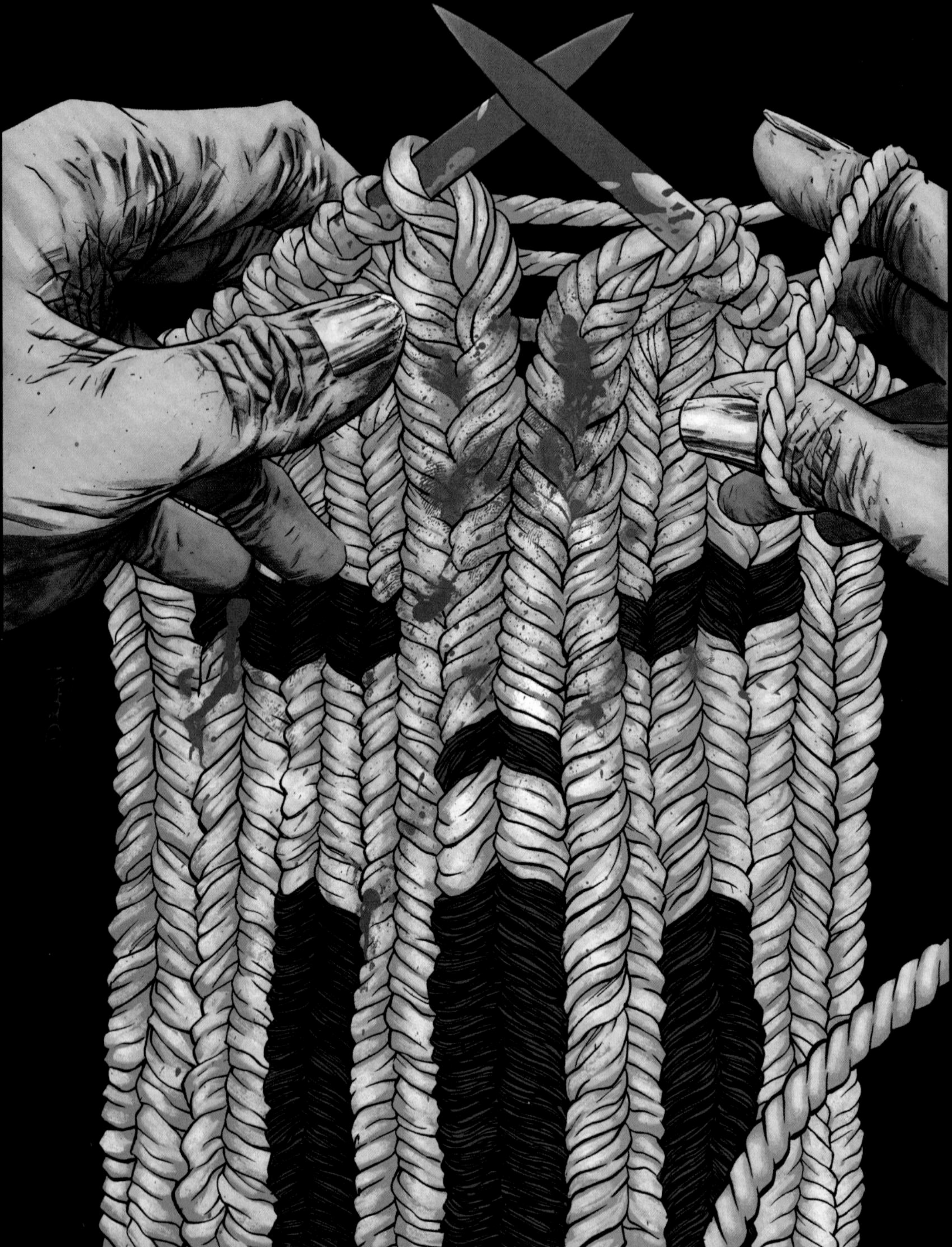

8

GIVE ME ONE GOOD REASON I SHOULDN'T SEND YOU STRAIGHT TO HELL.

NO OFFENSE, MA'AM, BUT I'VE BEEN TO HELL.

IT'S NOTHING I COULDN'T HANDLE.

ARMY?

SPECIAL FORCES.

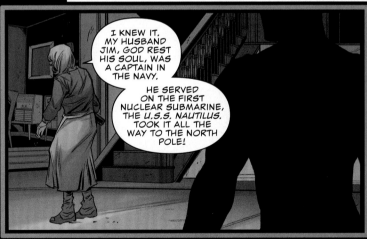

I KNEW IT. MY HUSBAND JIM, GOD REST HIS SOUL, WAS A CAPTAIN IN THE NAVY.

HE SERVED ON THE FIRST NUCLEAR SUBMARINE, THE U.S.S. NAUTILUS. TOOK IT ALL THE WAY TO THE NORTH POLE!

WELL, DON'T JUST STAND THERE, WIPE YOUR FEET AND COME ON IN.

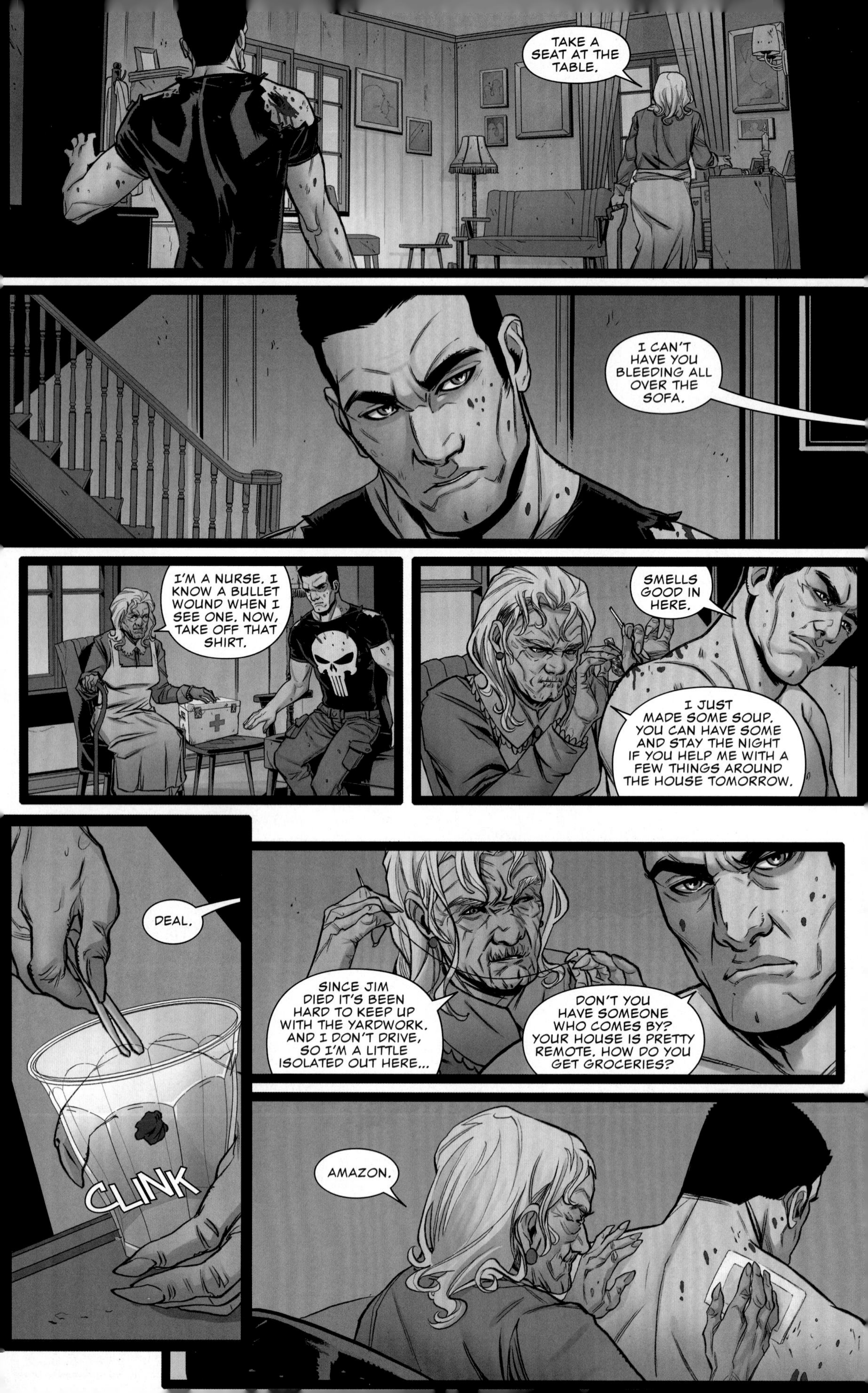
TAKE A SEAT AT THE TABLE.
I CAN'T HAVE YOU BLEEDING ALL OVER THE SOFA.
I'M A NURSE. I KNOW A BULLET WOUND WHEN I SEE ONE. NOW, TAKE OFF THAT SHIRT.
SMELLS GOOD IN HERE.
I JUST MADE SOME SOUP. YOU CAN HAVE SOME AND STAY THE NIGHT IF YOU HELP ME WITH A FEW THINGS AROUND THE HOUSE TOMORROW.
DEAL.
CLINK
SINCE JIM DIED IT'S BEEN HARD TO KEEP UP WITH THE YARDWORK. AND I DON'T DRIVE, SO I'M A LITTLE ISOLATED OUT HERE...
DON'T YOU HAVE SOMEONE WHO COMES BY? YOUR HOUSE IS PRETTY REMOTE. HOW DO YOU GET GROCERIES?
AMAZON.

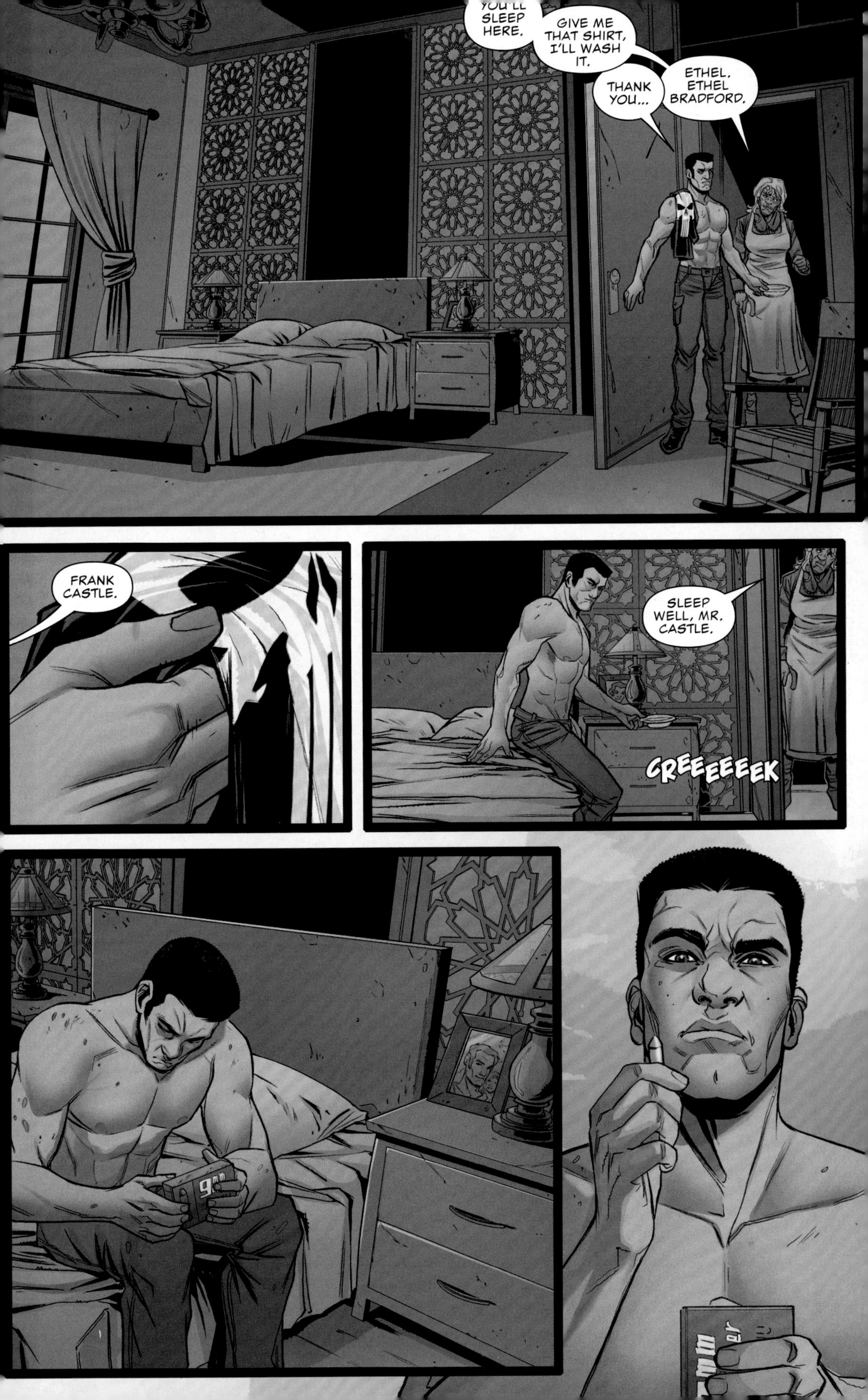
YOU'LL SLEEP HERE.
GIVE ME THAT SHIRT, I'LL WASH IT.
THANK YOU...
ETHEL. ETHEL BRADFORD.
FRANK CASTLE.
SLEEP WELL, MR. CASTLE.
CREEEEEEK

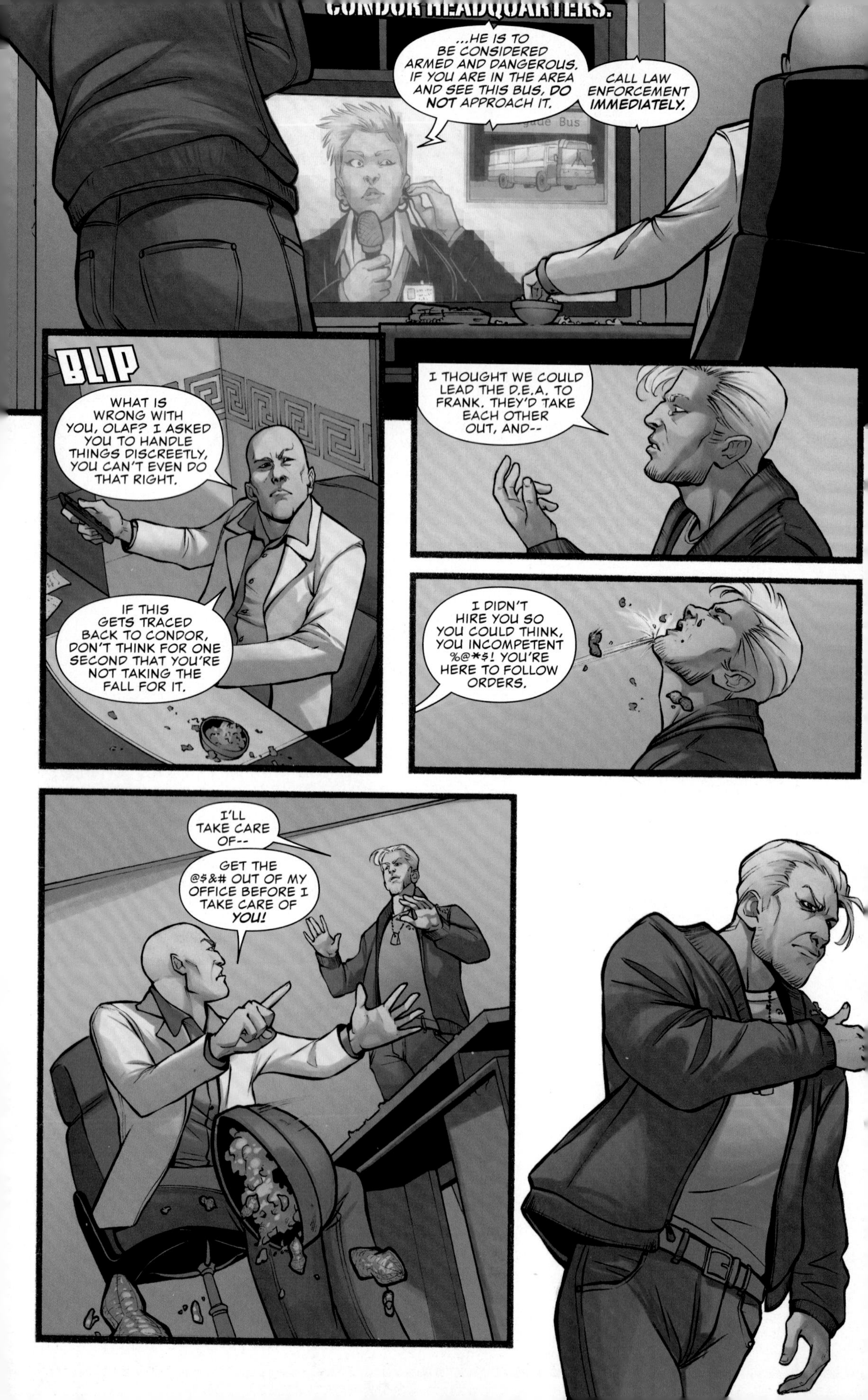
CONDOR HEADQUARTERS.
...HE IS TO BE CONSIDERED ARMED AND DANGEROUS. IF YOU ARE IN THE AREA AND SEE THIS BUS, DO NOT APPROACH IT.
CALL LAW ENFORCEMENT IMMEDIATELY.
BLIP
WHAT IS WRONG WITH YOU, OLAF? I ASKED YOU TO HANDLE THINGS DISCREETLY, YOU CAN'T EVEN DO THAT RIGHT.
IF THIS GETS TRACED BACK TO CONDOR, DON'T THINK FOR ONE SECOND THAT YOU'RE NOT TAKING THE FALL FOR IT.
I THOUGHT WE COULD LEAD THE D.E.A. TO FRANK. THEY'D TAKE EACH OTHER OUT, AND--
I DIDN'T HIRE YOU SO YOU COULD THINK, YOU INCOMPETENT %@*$! YOU'RE HERE TO FOLLOW ORDERS.
I'LL TAKE CARE OF--
GET THE @$&# OUT OF MY OFFICE BEFORE I TAKE CARE OF YOU!

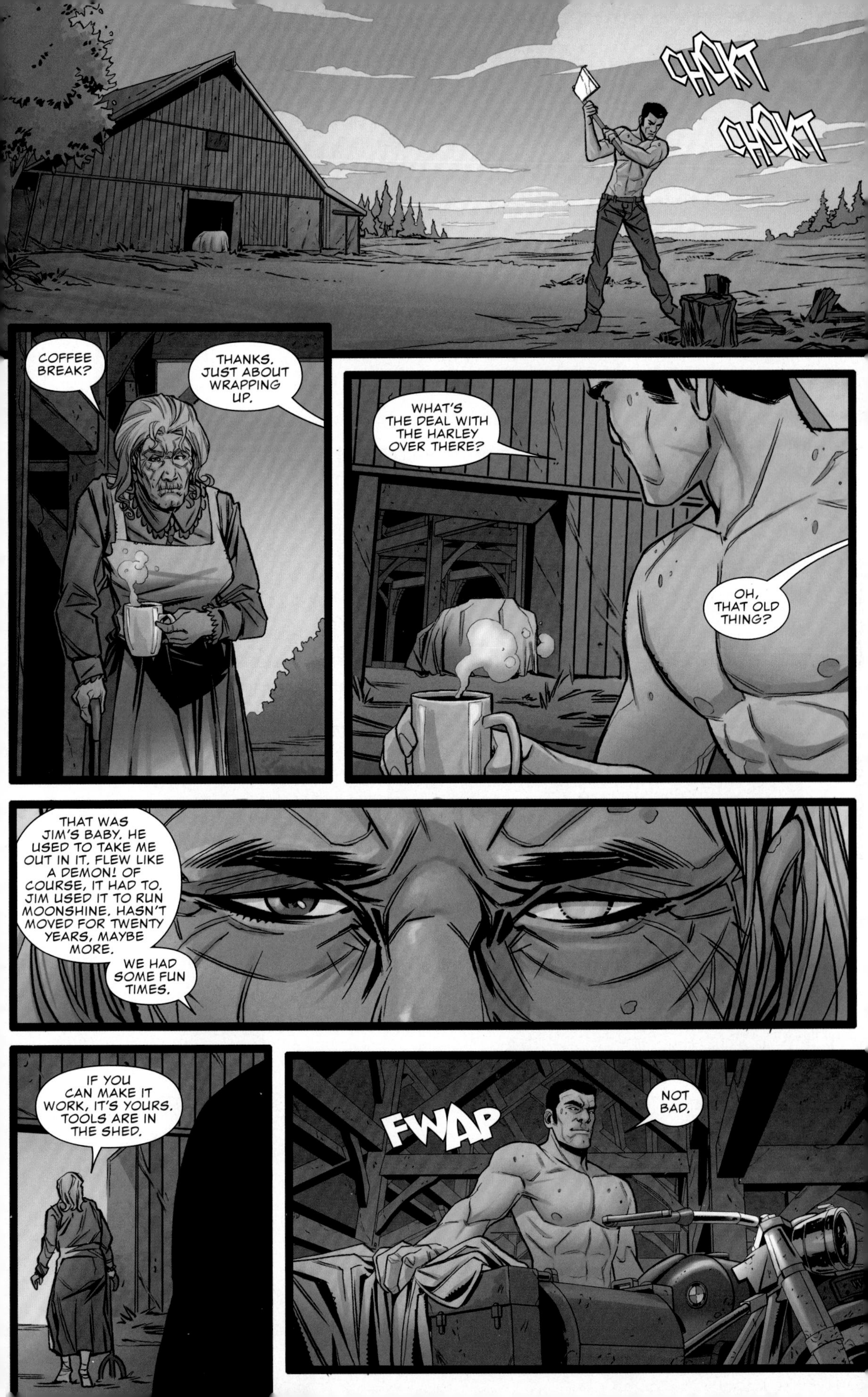
CHOKT
CHOKT
COFFEE BREAK?
THANKS. JUST ABOUT WRAPPING UP.
WHAT'S THE DEAL WITH THE HARLEY OVER THERE?
OH, THAT OLD THING?
THAT WAS JIM'S BABY. HE USED TO TAKE ME OUT IN IT. FLEW LIKE A DEMON! OF COURSE, IT HAD TO. JIM USED IT TO RUN MOONSHINE. HASN'T MOVED FOR TWENTY YEARS, MAYBE MORE.
WE HAD SOME FUN TIMES.
IF YOU CAN MAKE IT WORK, IT'S YOURS. TOOLS ARE IN THE SHED.
FWAP
NOT BAD.

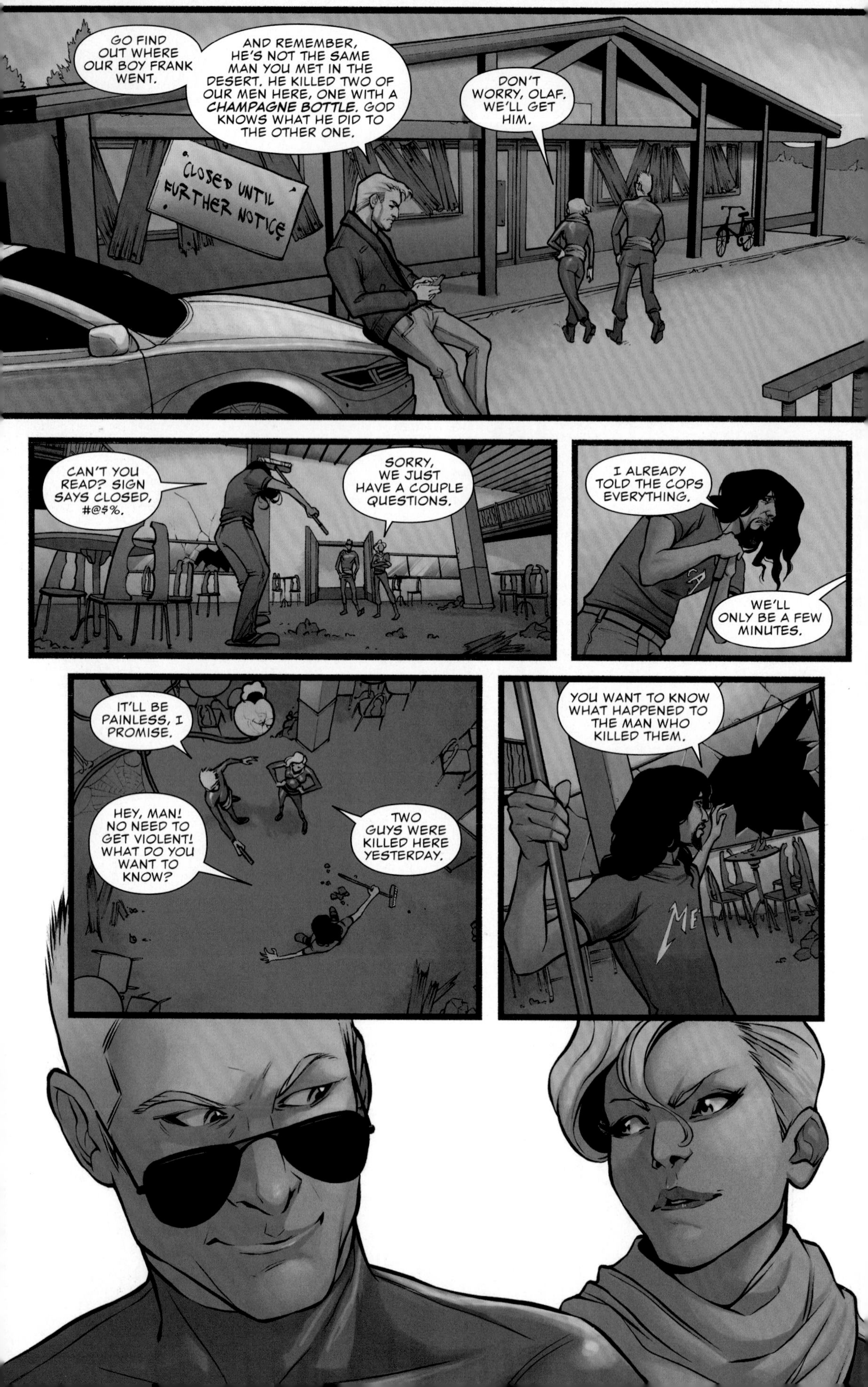
GO FIND OUT WHERE OUR BOY FRANK WENT.
AND REMEMBER, HE'S NOT THE SAME MAN YOU MET IN THE DESERT. HE KILLED TWO OF OUR MEN HERE, ONE WITH A CHAMPAGNE BOTTLE. GOD KNOWS WHAT HE DID TO THE OTHER ONE.
DON'T WORRY, OLAF. WE'LL GET HIM.
CLOSED UNTIL FURTHER NOTICE
CAN'T YOU READ? SIGN SAYS CLOSED, #@$%.
SORRY, WE JUST HAVE A COUPLE QUESTIONS.
I ALREADY TOLD THE COPS EVERYTHING.
WE'LL ONLY BE A FEW MINUTES.
IT'LL BE PAINLESS, I PROMISE.
HEY, MAN! NO NEED TO GET VIOLENT! WHAT DO YOU WANT TO KNOW?
TWO GUYS WERE KILLED HERE YESTERDAY.
YOU WANT TO KNOW WHAT HAPPENED TO THE MAN WHO KILLED THEM.

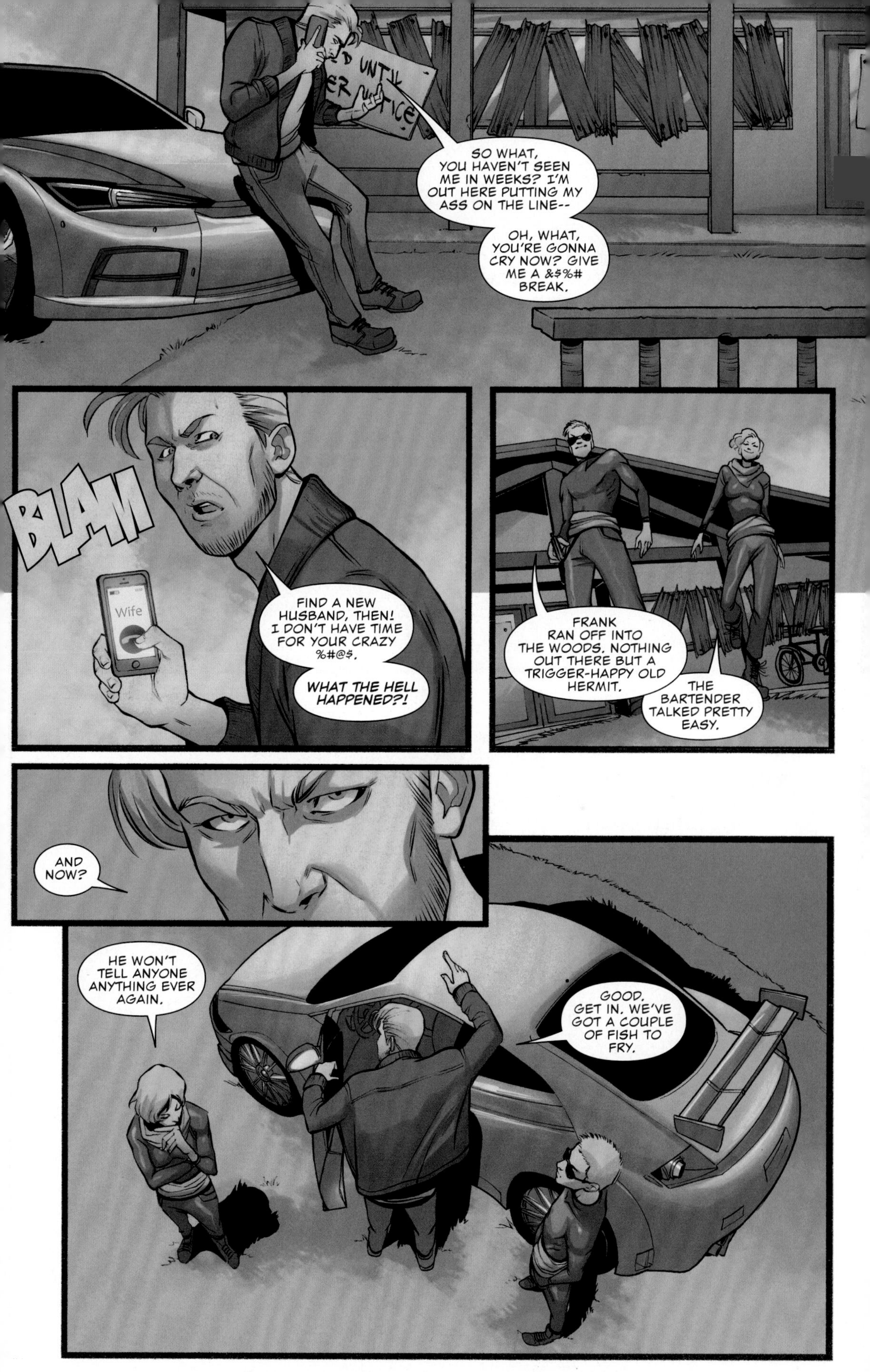
D UNTIL
ER NOTICE
SO WHAT, YOU HAVEN'T SEEN ME IN WEEKS? I'M OUT HERE PUTTING MY ASS ON THE LINE--
OH, WHAT, YOU'RE GONNA CRY NOW? GIVE ME A &$%# BREAK.
BLAM
Wife
FIND A NEW HUSBAND, THEN! I DON'T HAVE TIME FOR YOUR CRAZY %#@$.
WHAT THE HELL HAPPENED?!
FRANK RAN OFF INTO THE WOODS. NOTHING OUT THERE BUT A TRIGGER-HAPPY OLD HERMIT.
THE BARTENDER TALKED PRETTY EASY.
AND NOW?
HE WON'T TELL ANYONE ANYTHING EVER AGAIN.
GOOD. GET IN. WE'VE GOT A COUPLE OF FISH TO FRY.

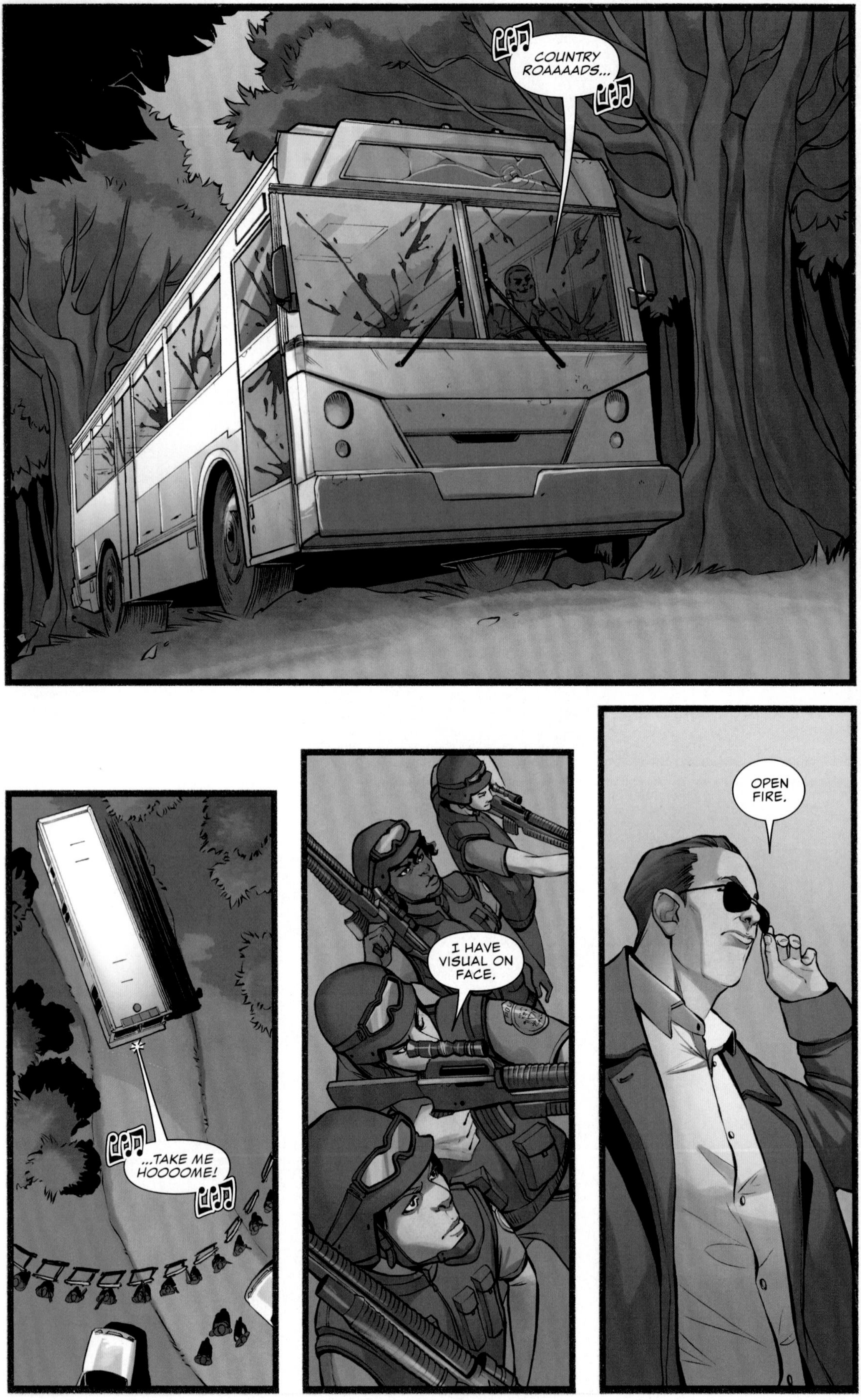
COUNTRY ROAAAADS...
...TAKE ME HOOOOME!
I HAVE VISUAL ON FACE.
OPEN FIRE.

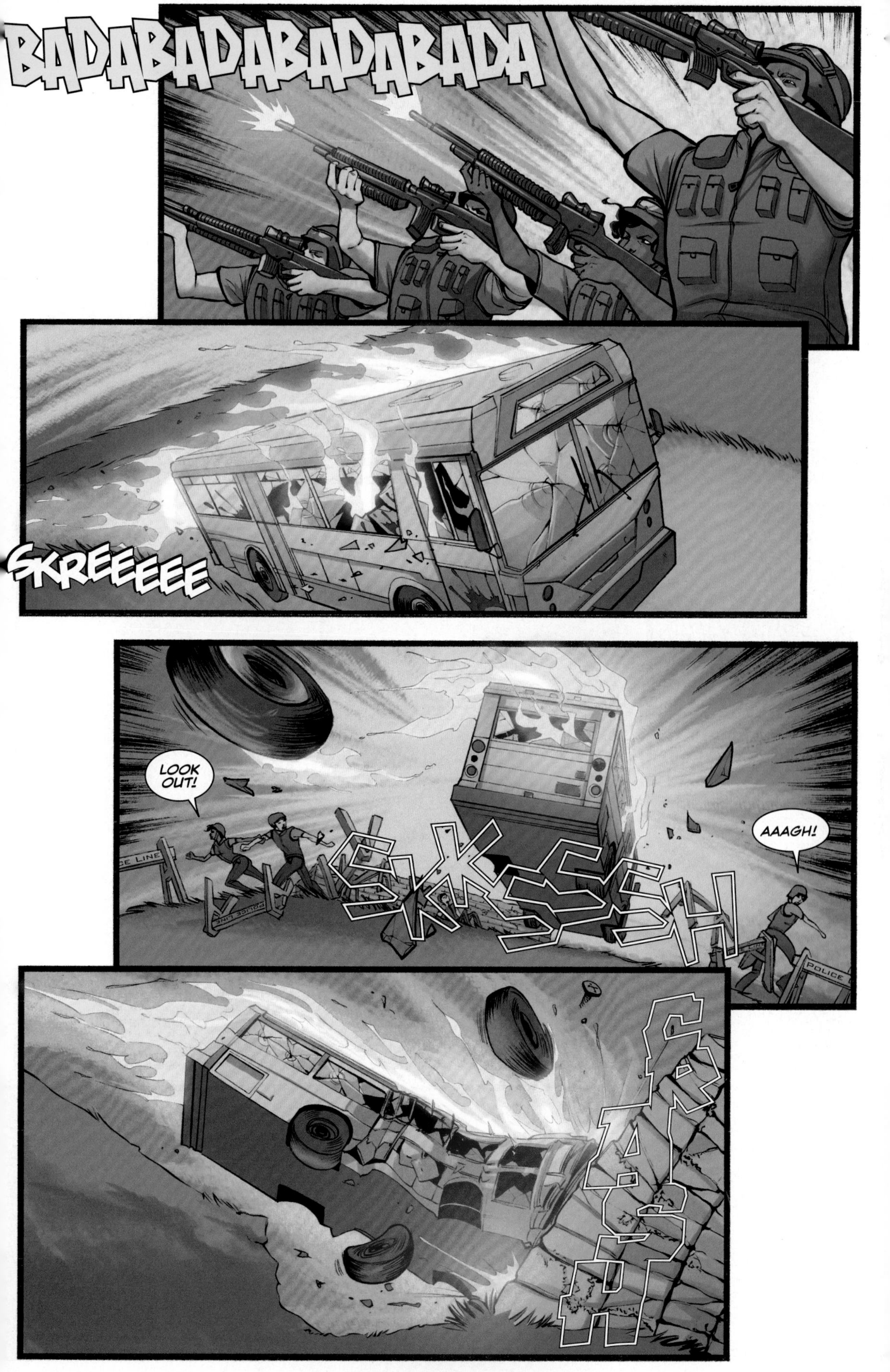
BADABADABADABADA
SKREEEEEE
LOOK OUT!
POLICE LINE
SKSSH
AAAGH!
POLICE
CRASH

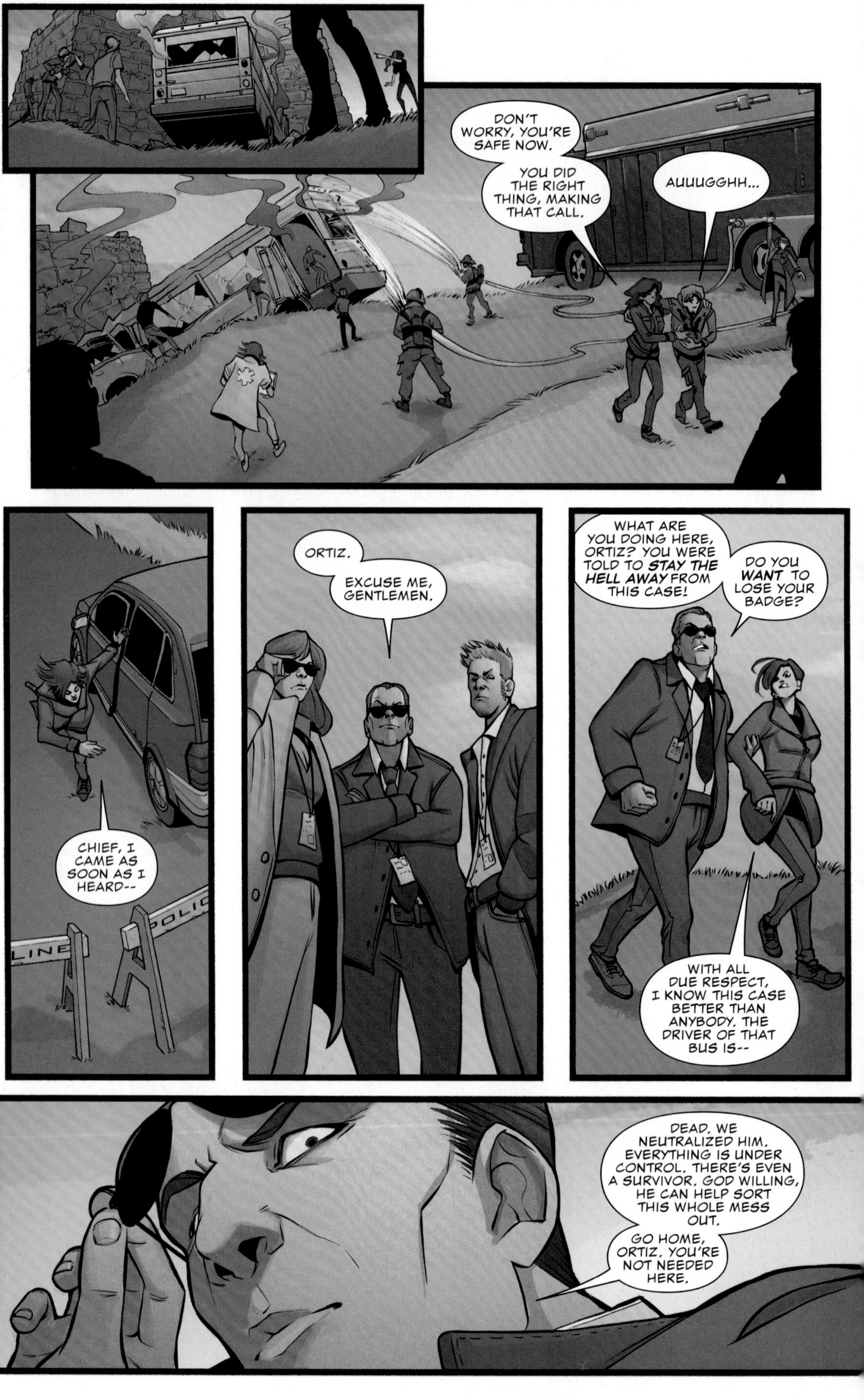
DON'T WORRY, YOU'RE SAFE NOW.
YOU DID THE RIGHT THING, MAKING THAT CALL.
AUUUGGHH...
CHIEF, I CAME AS SOON AS I HEARD--
POLIC
LINE
ORTIZ.
EXCUSE ME, GENTLEMEN.
WHAT ARE YOU DOING HERE, ORTIZ? YOU WERE TOLD TO **STAY THE HELL AWAY** FROM THIS CASE!
DO YOU **WANT** TO LOSE YOUR BADGE?
WITH ALL DUE RESPECT, I KNOW THIS CASE BETTER THAN ANYBODY. THE DRIVER OF THAT BUS IS--
DEAD. WE NEUTRALIZED HIM. EVERYTHING IS UNDER CONTROL. THERE'S EVEN A SURVIVOR. GOD WILLING, HE CAN HELP SORT THIS WHOLE MESS OUT.
GO HOME, ORTIZ. YOU'RE NOT NEEDED HERE.

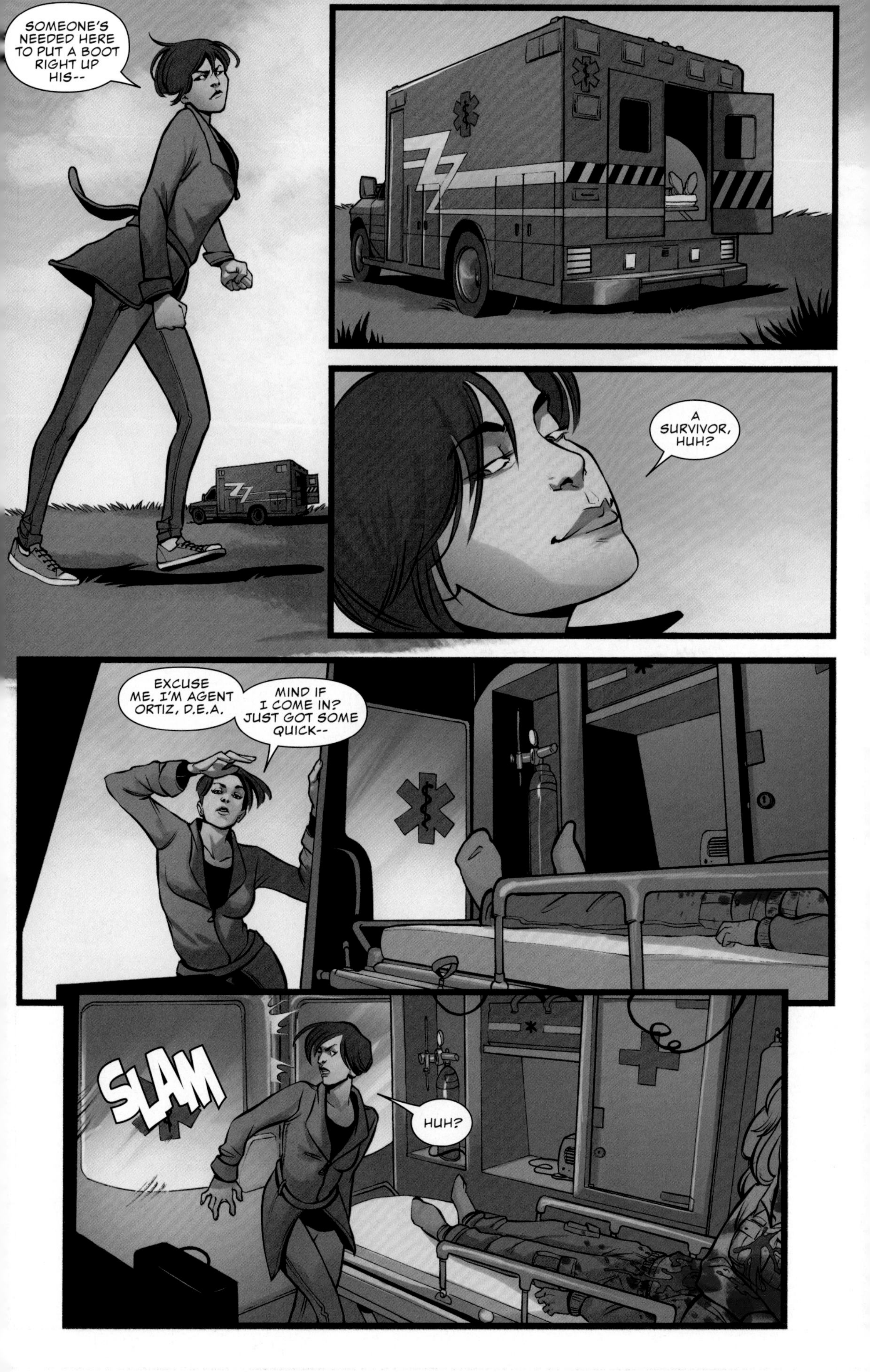
SOMEONE'S NEEDED HERE TO PUT A BOOT RIGHT UP HIS--
A SURVIVOR, HUH?
EXCUSE ME. I'M AGENT ORTIZ, D.E.A.
MIND IF I COME IN? JUST GOT SOME QUICK--
SLAM
HUH?

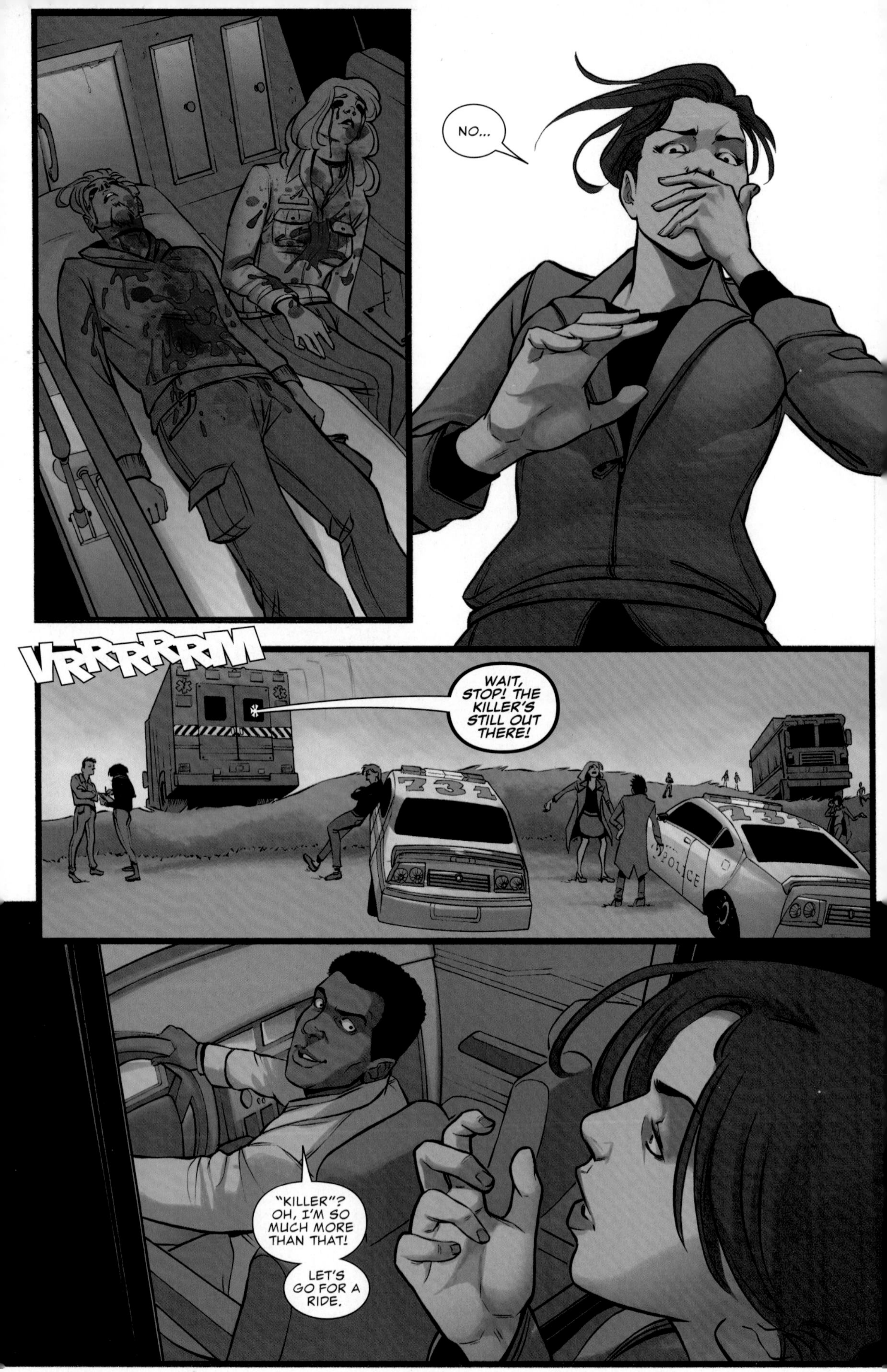
NO...
VRRRRRRM
WAIT, STOP! THE KILLER'S STILL OUT THERE!
731
POLICE
"KILLER"? OH, I'M SO MUCH MORE THAN THAT!
LET'S GO FOR A RIDE.

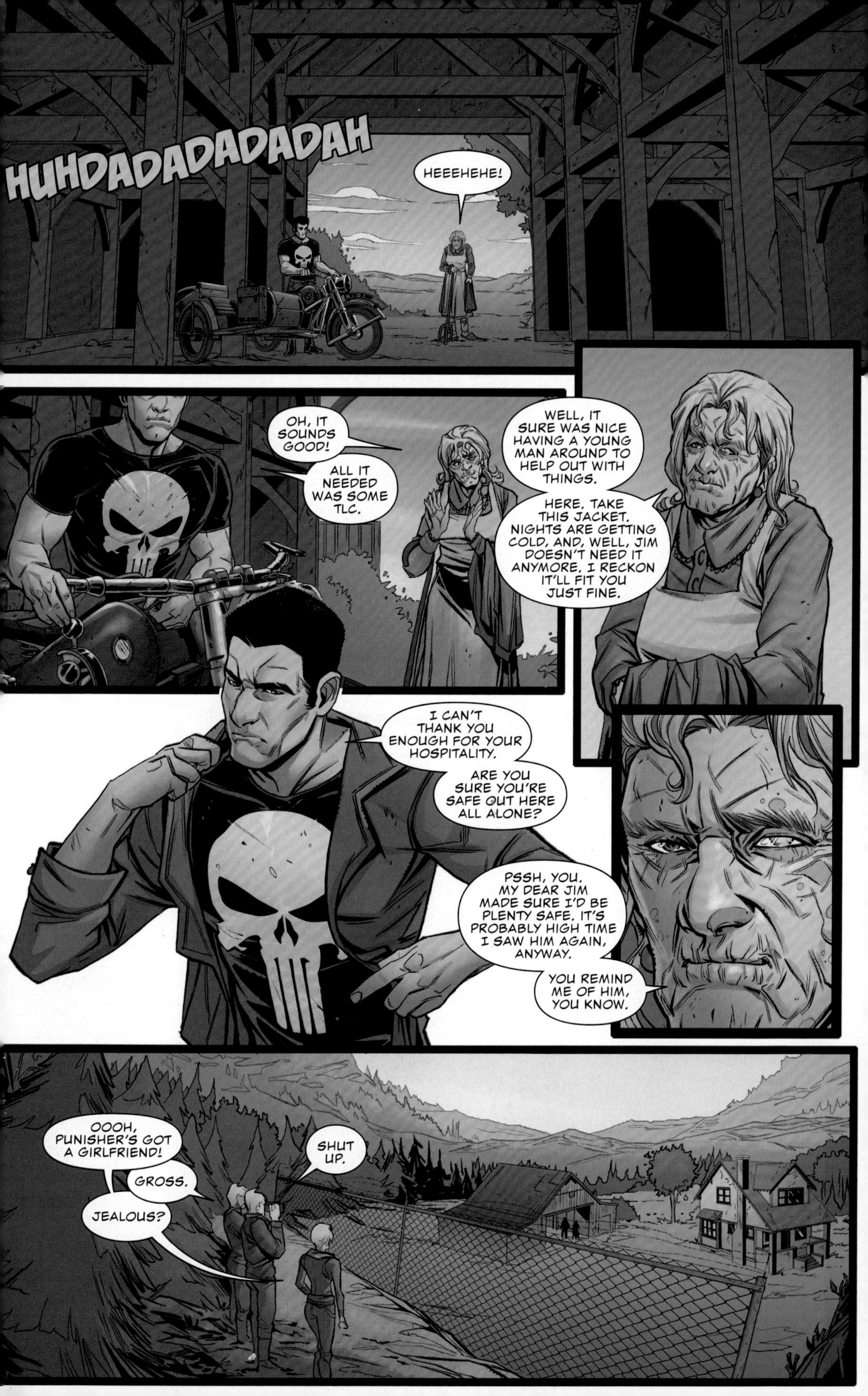

HUHDADADADADAH
HEEEHEHE!
OH, IT SOUNDS GOOD!
ALL IT NEEDED WAS SOME TLC.
WELL, IT SURE WAS NICE HAVING A YOUNG MAN AROUND TO HELP OUT WITH THINGS.
HERE. TAKE THIS JACKET. NIGHTS ARE GETTING COLD, AND, WELL, JIM DOESN'T NEED IT ANYMORE. I RECKON IT'LL FIT YOU JUST FINE.
I CAN'T THANK YOU ENOUGH FOR YOUR HOSPITALITY.
ARE YOU SURE YOU'RE SAFE OUT HERE ALL ALONE?
PSSH, YOU. MY DEAR JIM MADE SURE I'D BE PLENTY SAFE. IT'S PROBABLY HIGH TIME I SAW HIM AGAIN, ANYWAY.
YOU REMIND ME OF HIM, YOU KNOW.
OOOH, PUNISHER'S GOT A GIRLFRIEND!
SHUT UP.
GROSS.
JEALOUS?

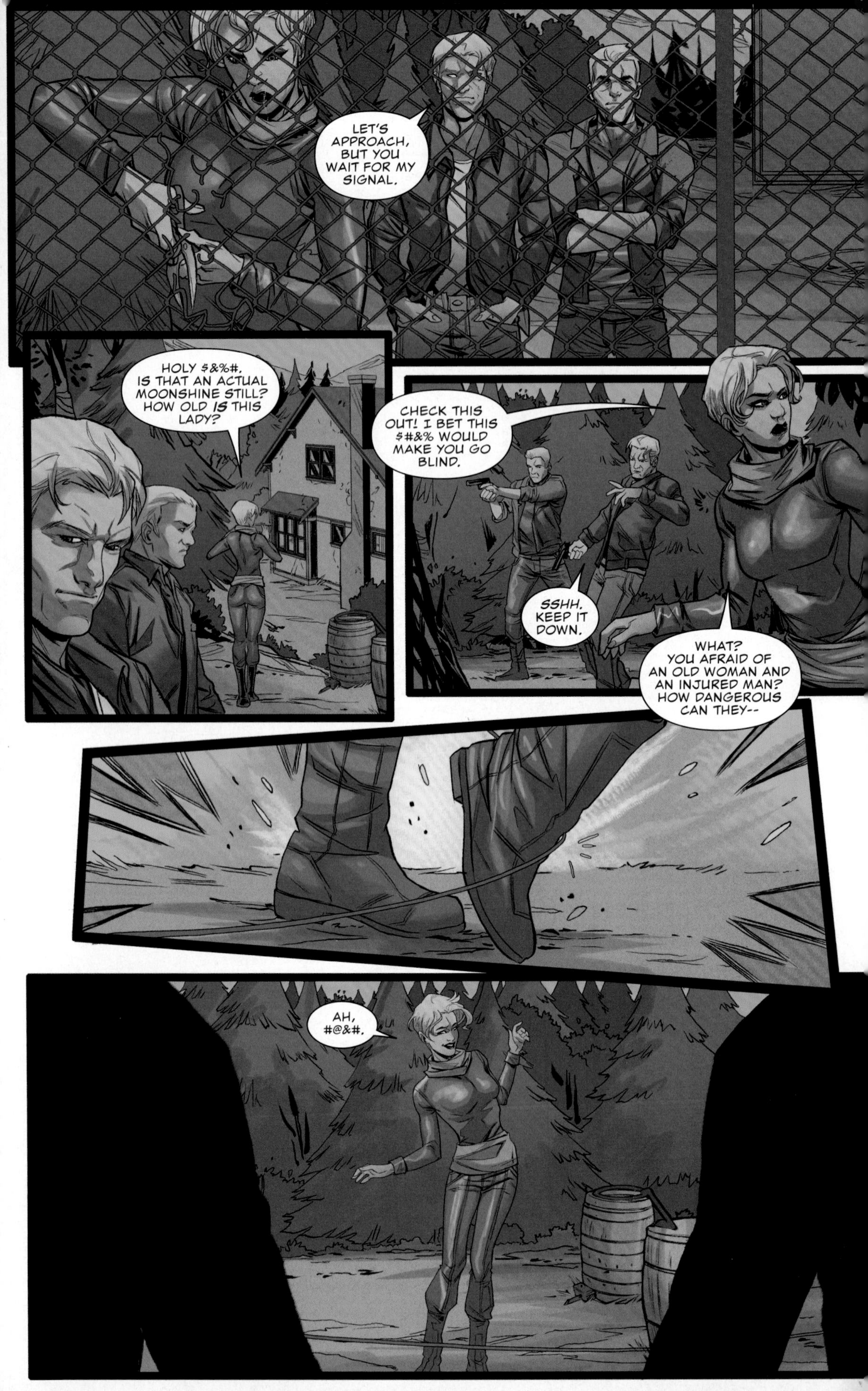
LET'S APPROACH, BUT YOU WAIT FOR MY SIGNAL.
HOLY $&%#. IS THAT AN ACTUAL MOONSHINE STILL? HOW OLD IS THIS LADY?
CHECK THIS OUT! I BET THIS $#&% WOULD MAKE YOU GO BLIND.
SSHH. KEEP IT DOWN.
WHAT? YOU AFRAID OF AN OLD WOMAN AND AN INJURED MAN? HOW DANGEROUS CAN THEY--
AH, #@&#.

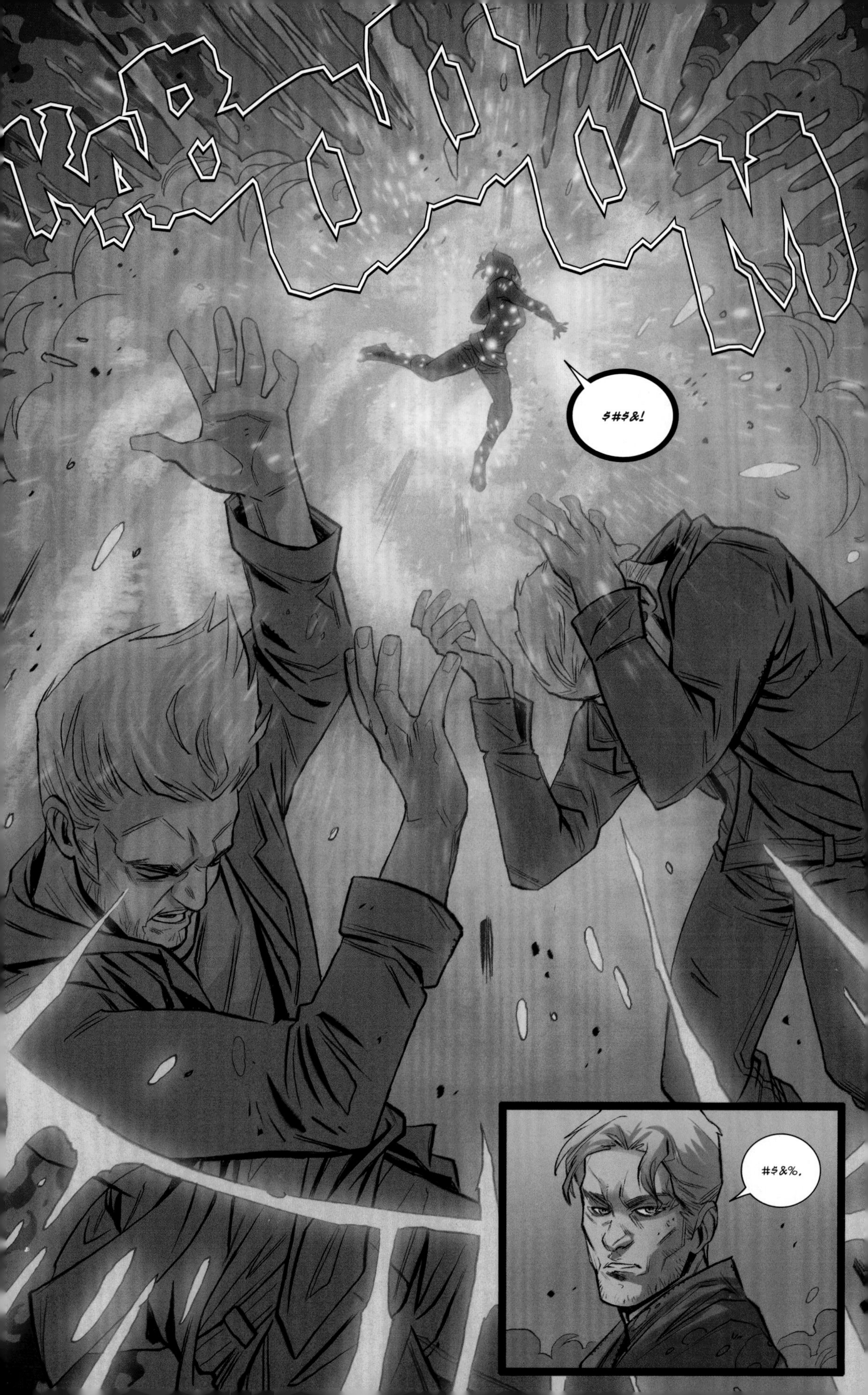
KA-BOOOOM
$#$&!
#$&%.

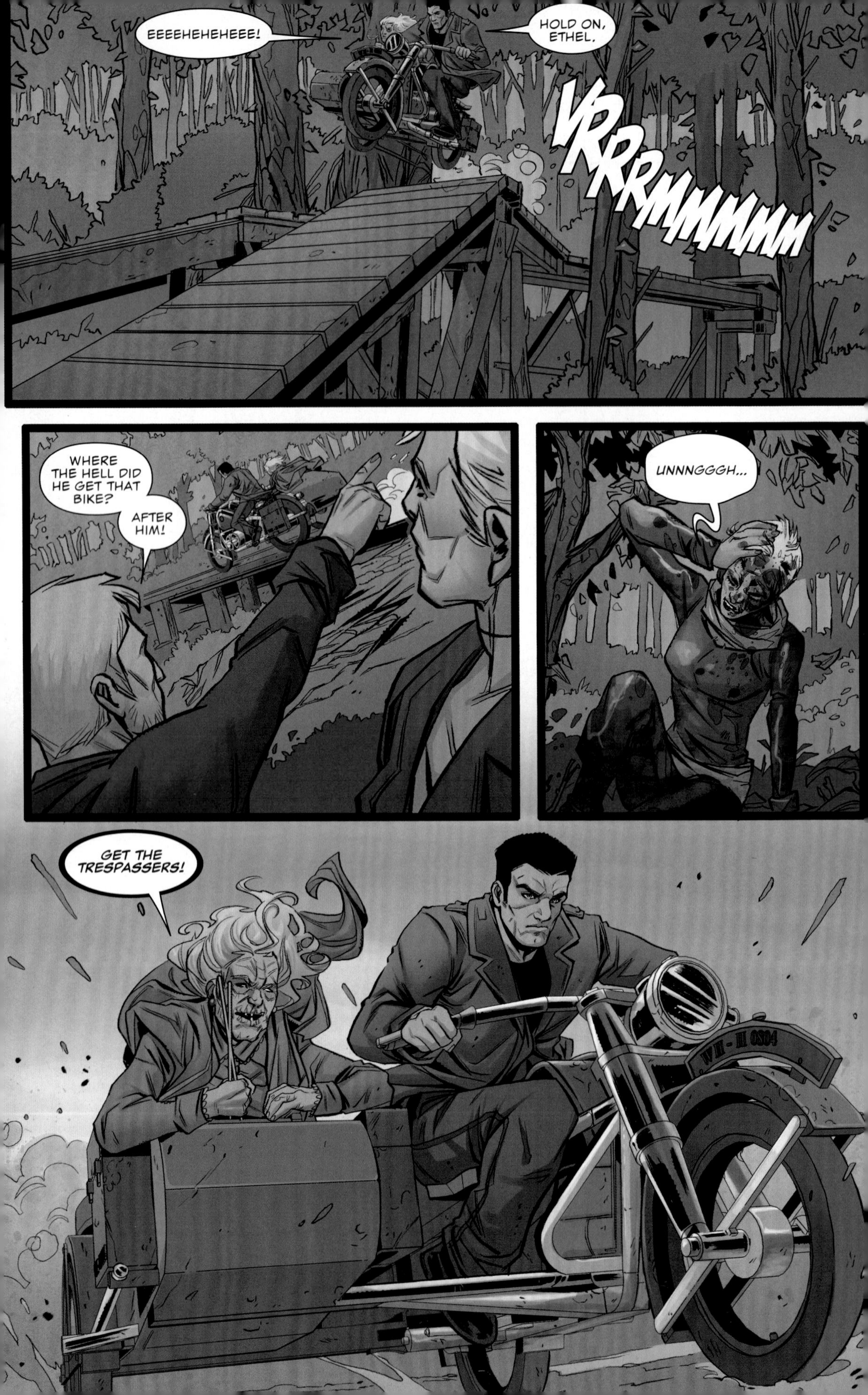
EEEEHEHEHEEE!
HOLD ON, ETHEL.
VRRRMMMMMM
WHERE THE HELL DID HE GET THAT BIKE?
AFTER HIM!
UNNNGGGH...
GET THE TRESPASSERS!
WH - H 0S04

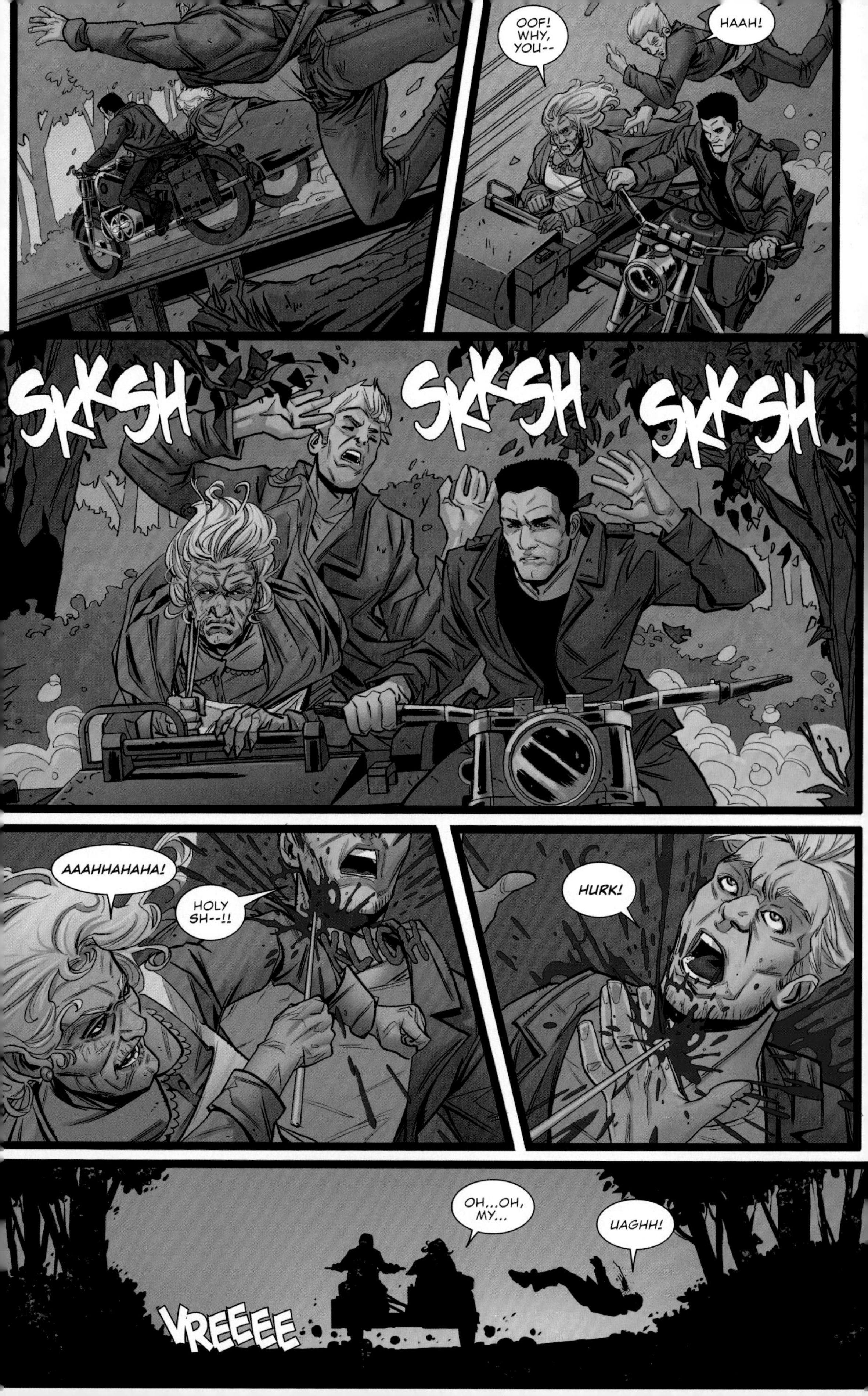
OOF! WHY, YOU--
HAAH!
SKKSH SKKSH SKKSH
AAAHHAHAHA!
HOLY SH--!!
KLICH
HURK!
OH...OH, MY...
UAGHH!
VREEEEE

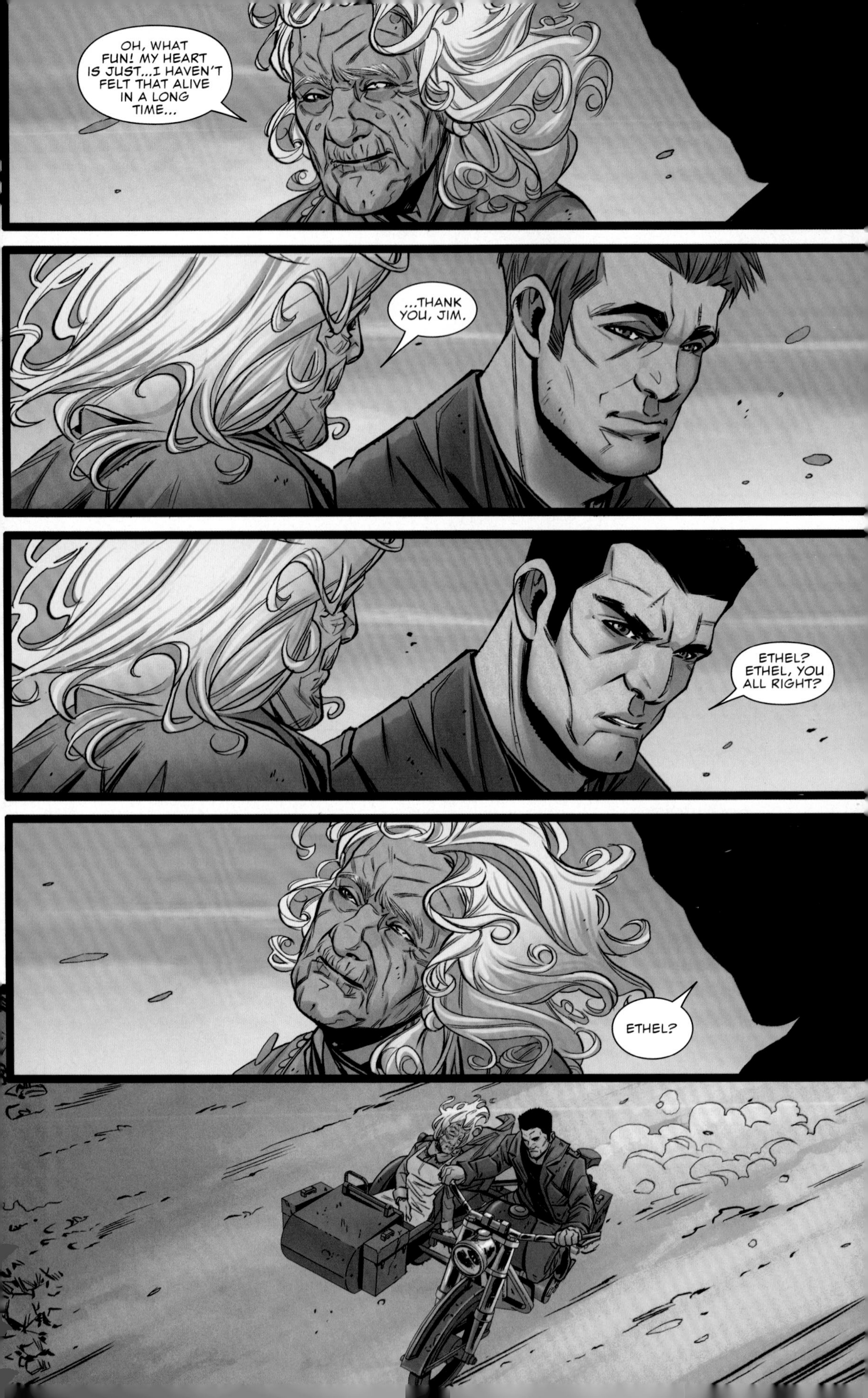
OH, WHAT FUN! MY HEART IS JUST...I HAVEN'T FELT THAT ALIVE IN A LONG TIME...
...THANK YOU, JIM.
ETHEL? ETHEL, YOU ALL RIGHT?
ETHEL?

UGGHHH...

WUH... WHAT THE HELL?!

YOU'RE IN BEAR COUNTRY, AND I'VE OPENED UP YOUR GUTS. YOU DON'T HAVE MUCH TIME, SO I'M ONLY GOING TO ASK YOU ONCE.

WHERE IS CONDOR HEADQUARTERS?

SNIIIIFF SNIFF

HUH? DUDE--NO! NO, I SWEAR!

CRACK

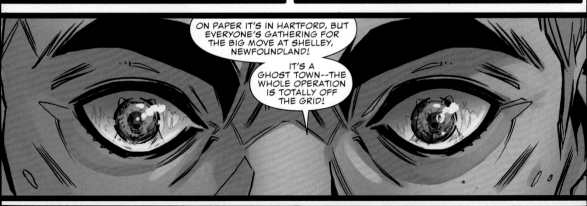

ON PAPER IT'S IN HARTFORD, BUT EVERYONE'S GATHERING FOR THE BIG MOVE AT SHELLEY, NEWFOUNDLAND!

IT'S A GHOST TOWN--THE WHOLE OPERATION IS TOTALLY OFF THE GRID!

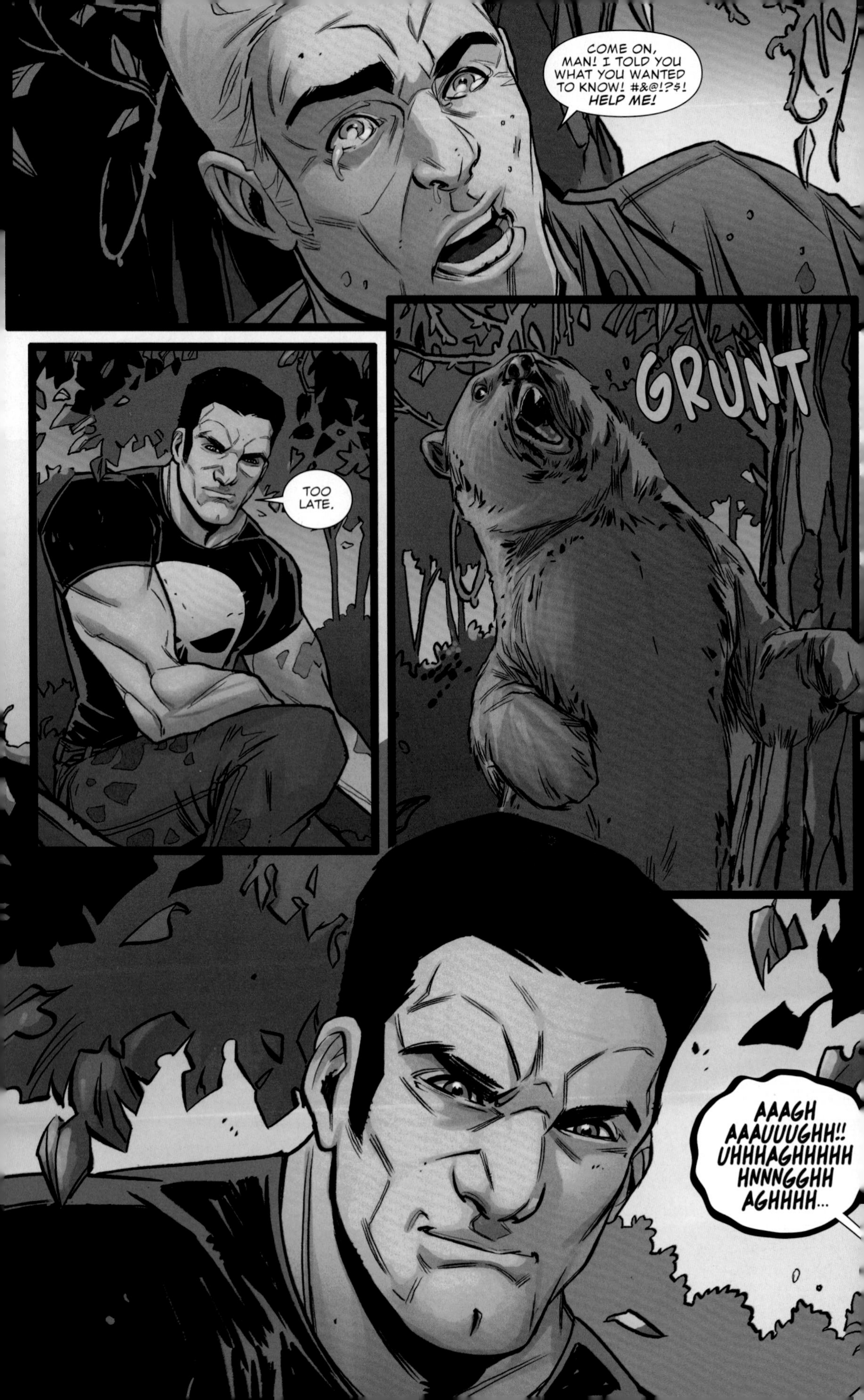
COME ON, MAN! I TOLD YOU WHAT YOU WANTED TO KNOW! #&@!?$! HELP ME!
TOO LATE.
GRUNT
AAAGH AAAUUUGHH!! UHHHAGHHHHH HNNNGGHH AGHHHH...

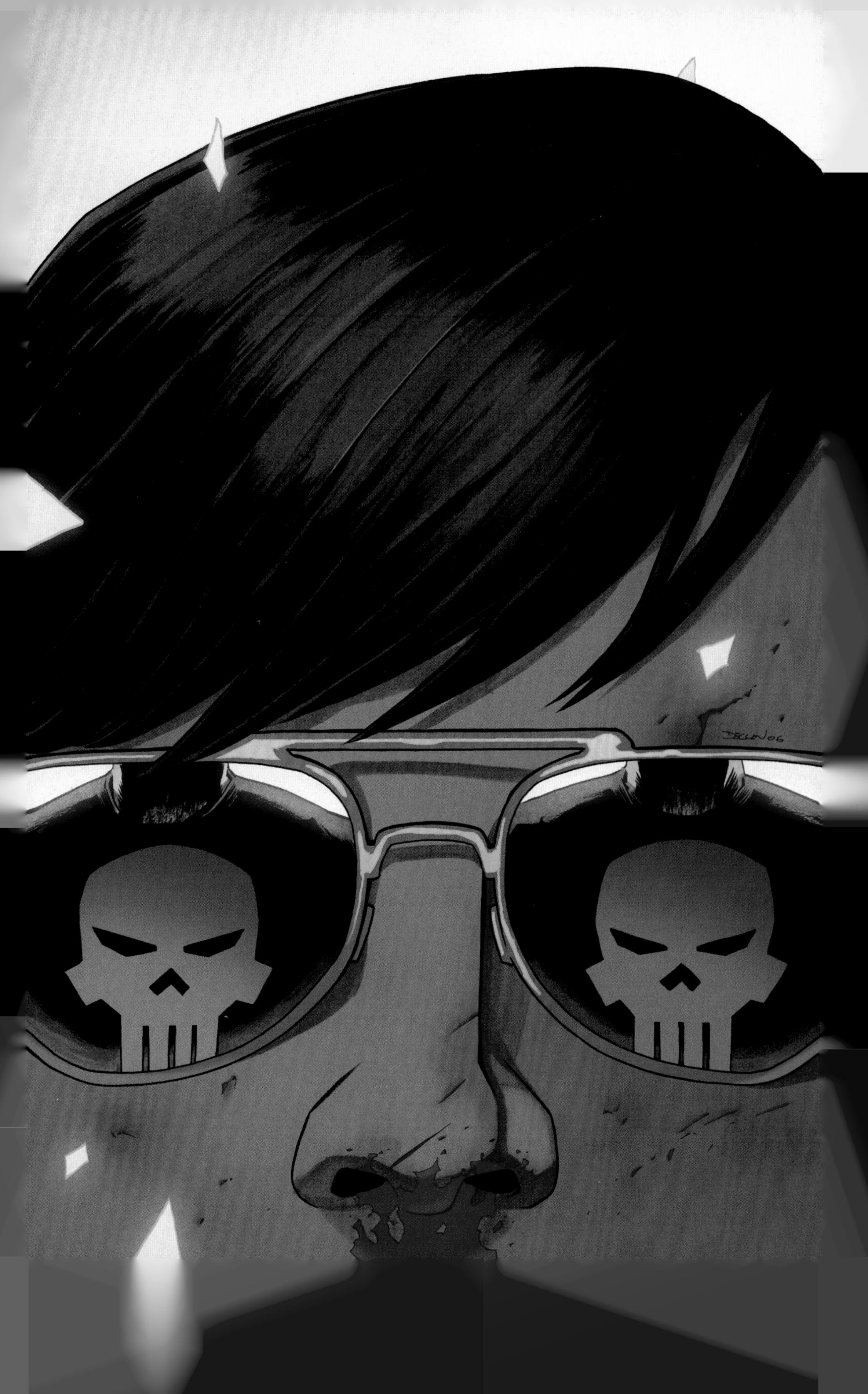

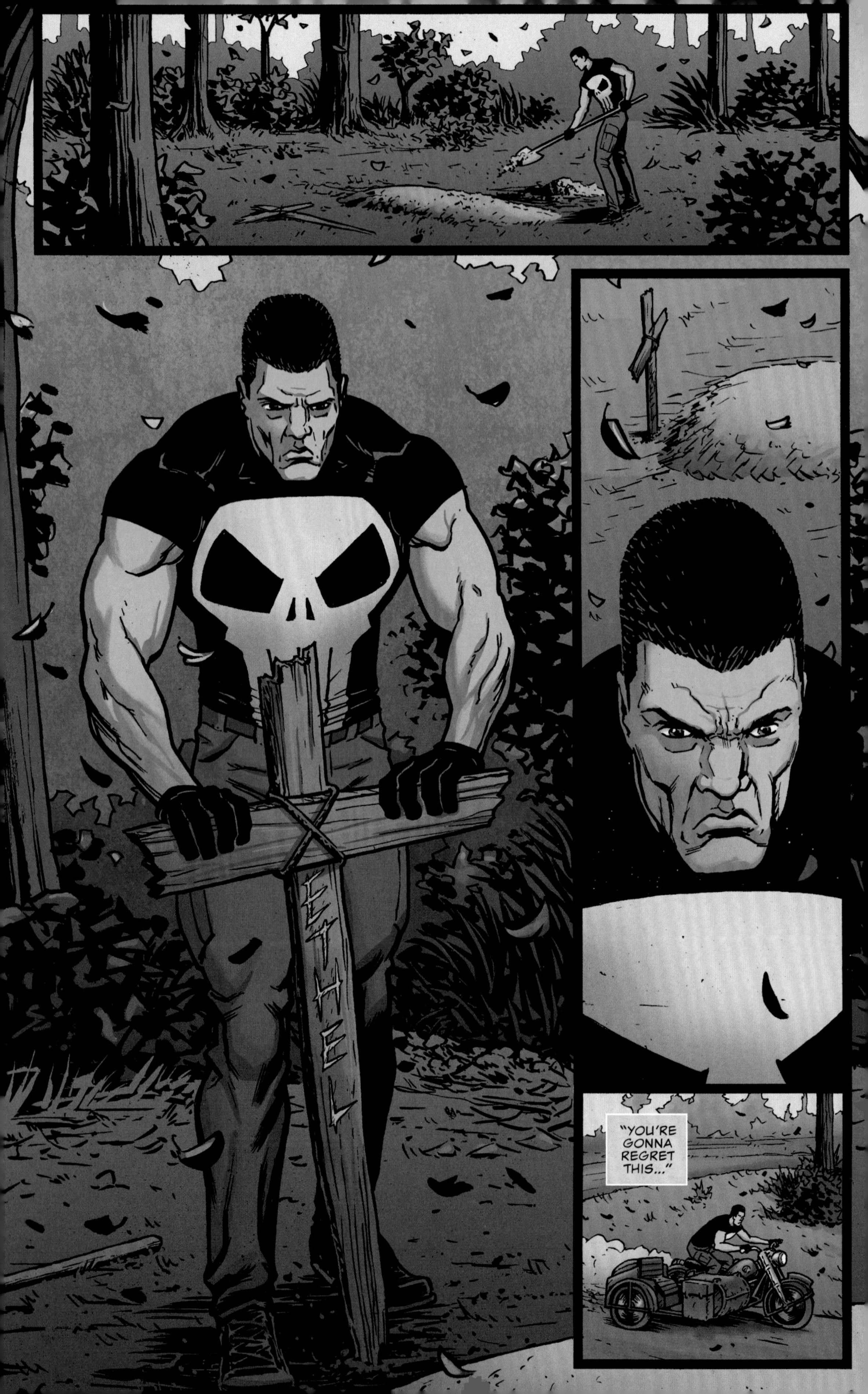
"YOU'RE GONNA REGRET THIS..."

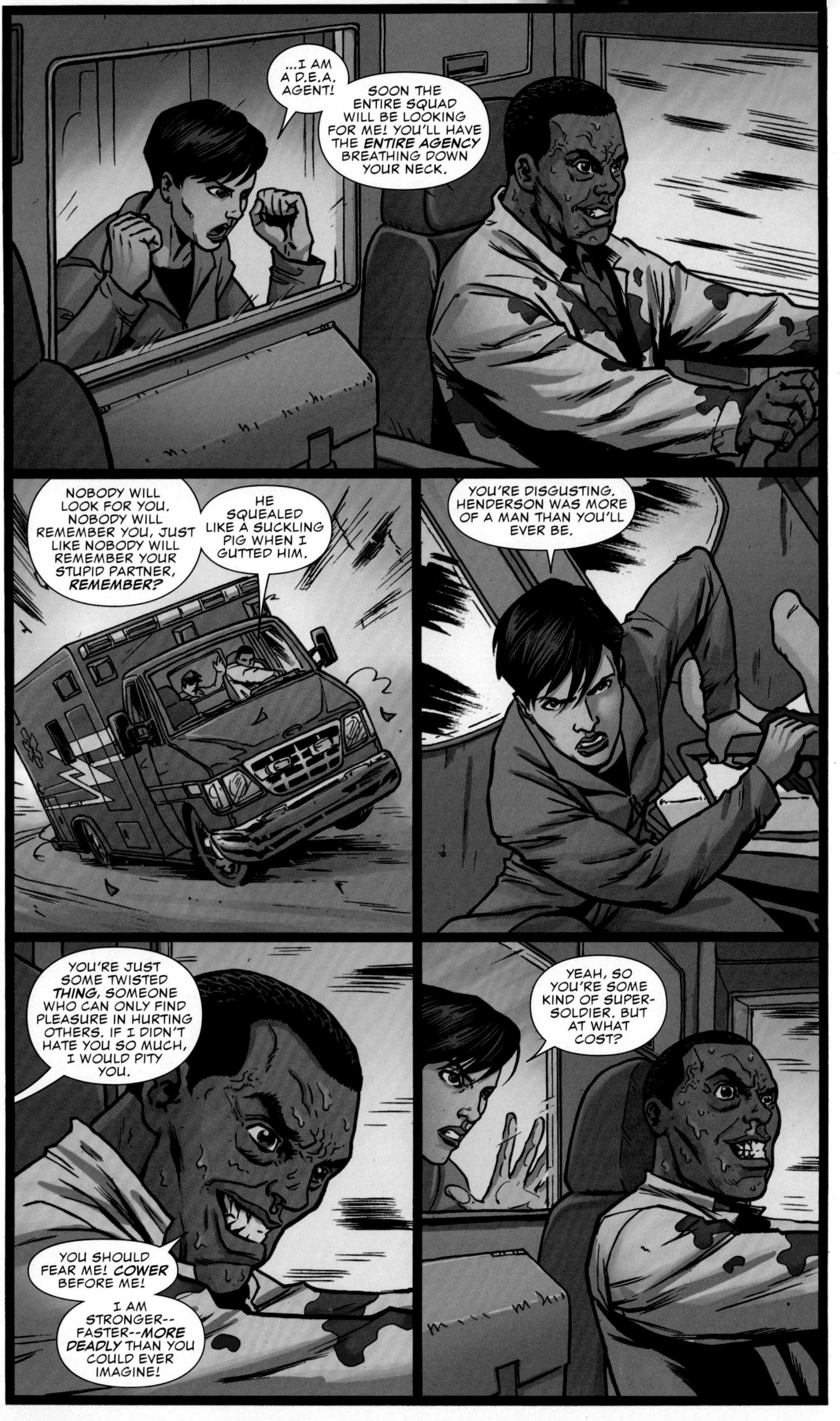
...I AM A D.E.A. AGENT!
SOON THE ENTIRE SQUAD WILL BE LOOKING FOR ME! YOU'LL HAVE THE ***ENTIRE AGENCY*** BREATHING DOWN YOUR NECK.
NOBODY WILL LOOK FOR YOU. NOBODY WILL REMEMBER YOU, JUST LIKE NOBODY WILL REMEMBER YOUR STUPID PARTNER, ***REMEMBER?***
HE SQUEALED LIKE A SUCKLING PIG WHEN I GUTTED HIM.
YOU'RE DISGUSTING. HENDERSON WAS MORE OF A MAN THAN YOU'LL EVER BE.
YOU'RE JUST SOME TWISTED ***THING,*** SOMEONE WHO CAN ONLY FIND PLEASURE IN HURTING OTHERS. IF I DIDN'T HATE YOU SO MUCH, I WOULD PITY YOU.
YOU SHOULD FEAR ME! ***COWER*** BEFORE ME!
I AM STRONGER--FASTER--***MORE DEADLY*** THAN YOU COULD EVER IMAGINE!
YEAH, SO YOU'RE SOME KIND OF SUPER-SOLDIER. BUT AT WHAT COST?

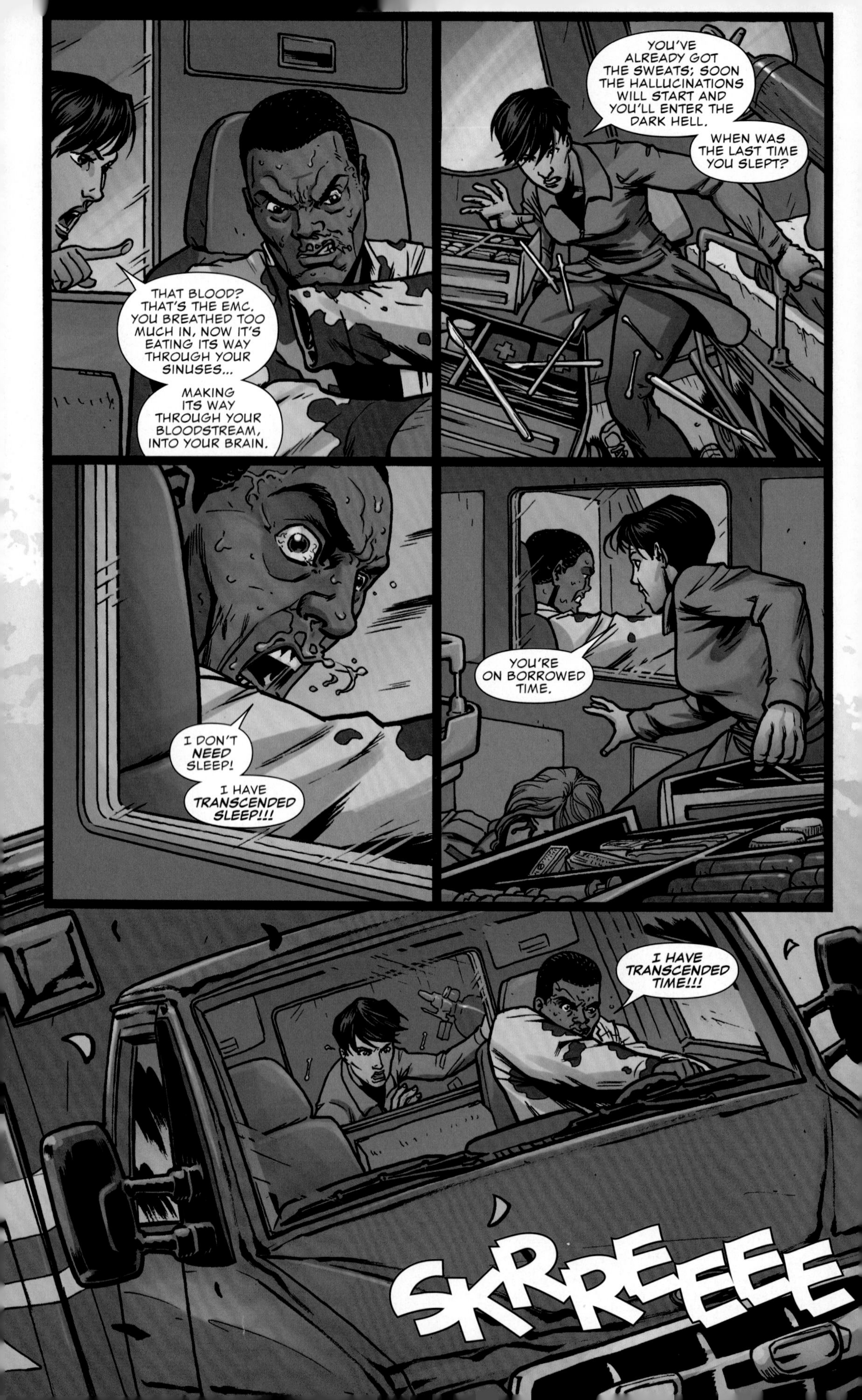
THAT BLOOD? THAT'S THE EMC. YOU BREATHED TOO MUCH IN, NOW IT'S EATING ITS WAY THROUGH YOUR SINUSES...
MAKING ITS WAY THROUGH YOUR BLOODSTREAM, INTO YOUR BRAIN.
YOU'VE ALREADY GOT THE SWEATS; SOON THE HALLUCINATIONS WILL START AND YOU'LL ENTER THE DARK HELL.
WHEN WAS THE LAST TIME YOU SLEPT?
I DON'T NEED SLEEP!
I HAVE TRANSCENDED SLEEP!!!
YOU'RE ON BORROWED TIME.
I HAVE TRANSCENDED TIME!!!
SKRREEEE

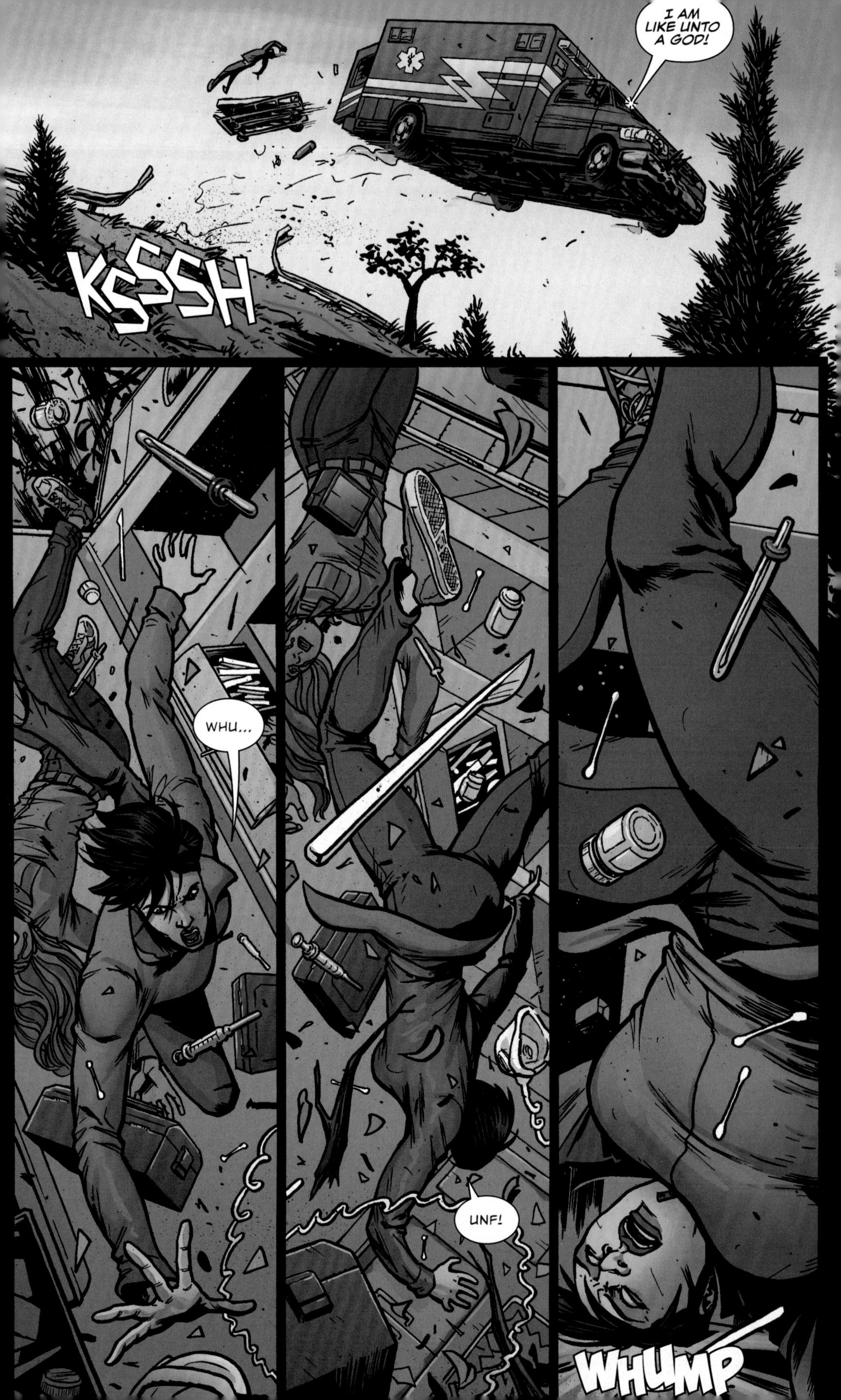
I AM LIKE UNTO A GOD!
KSSSH
WHU...
UNF!
WHUMP

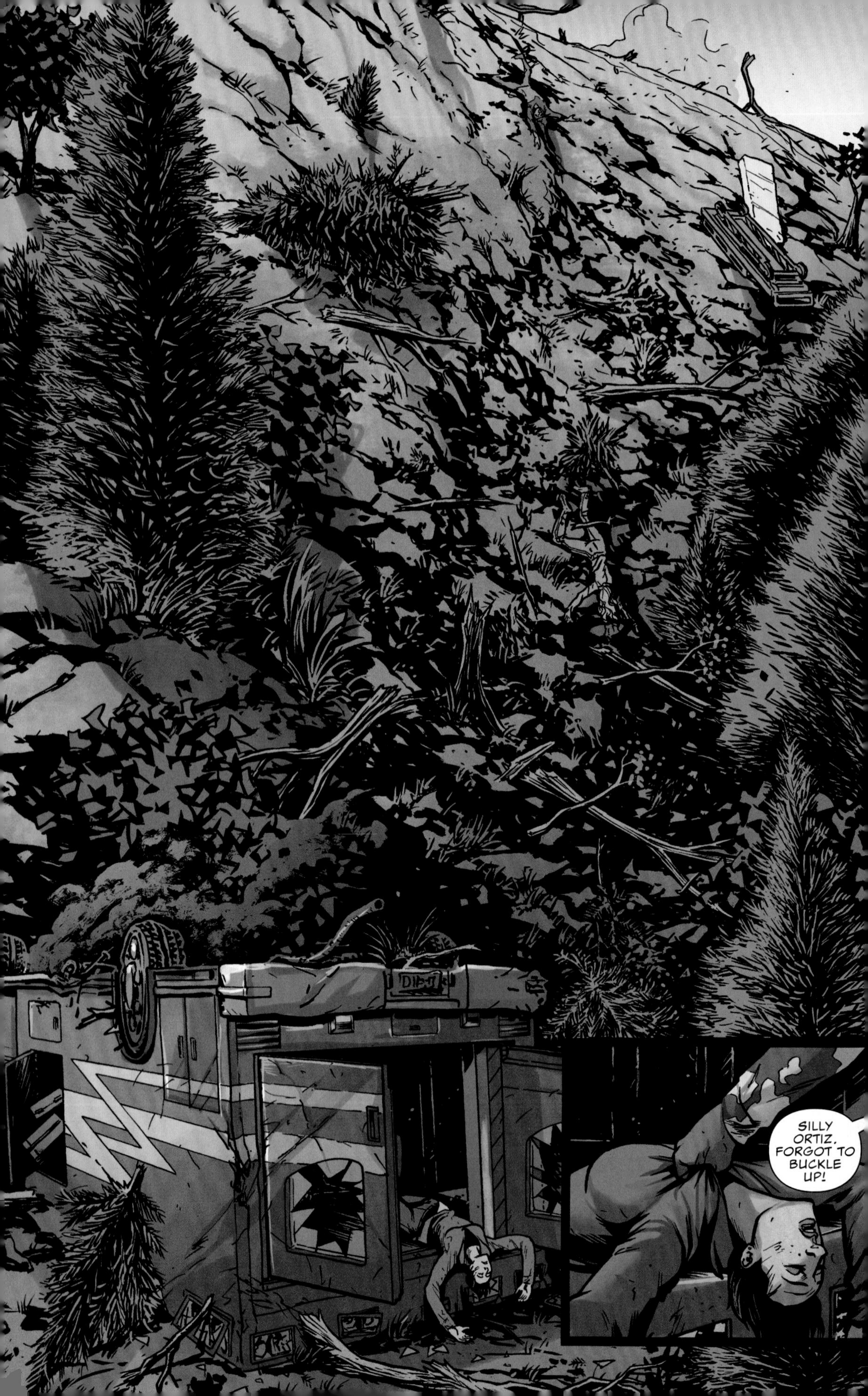
SILLY ORTIZ. FORGOT TO BUCKLE UP!

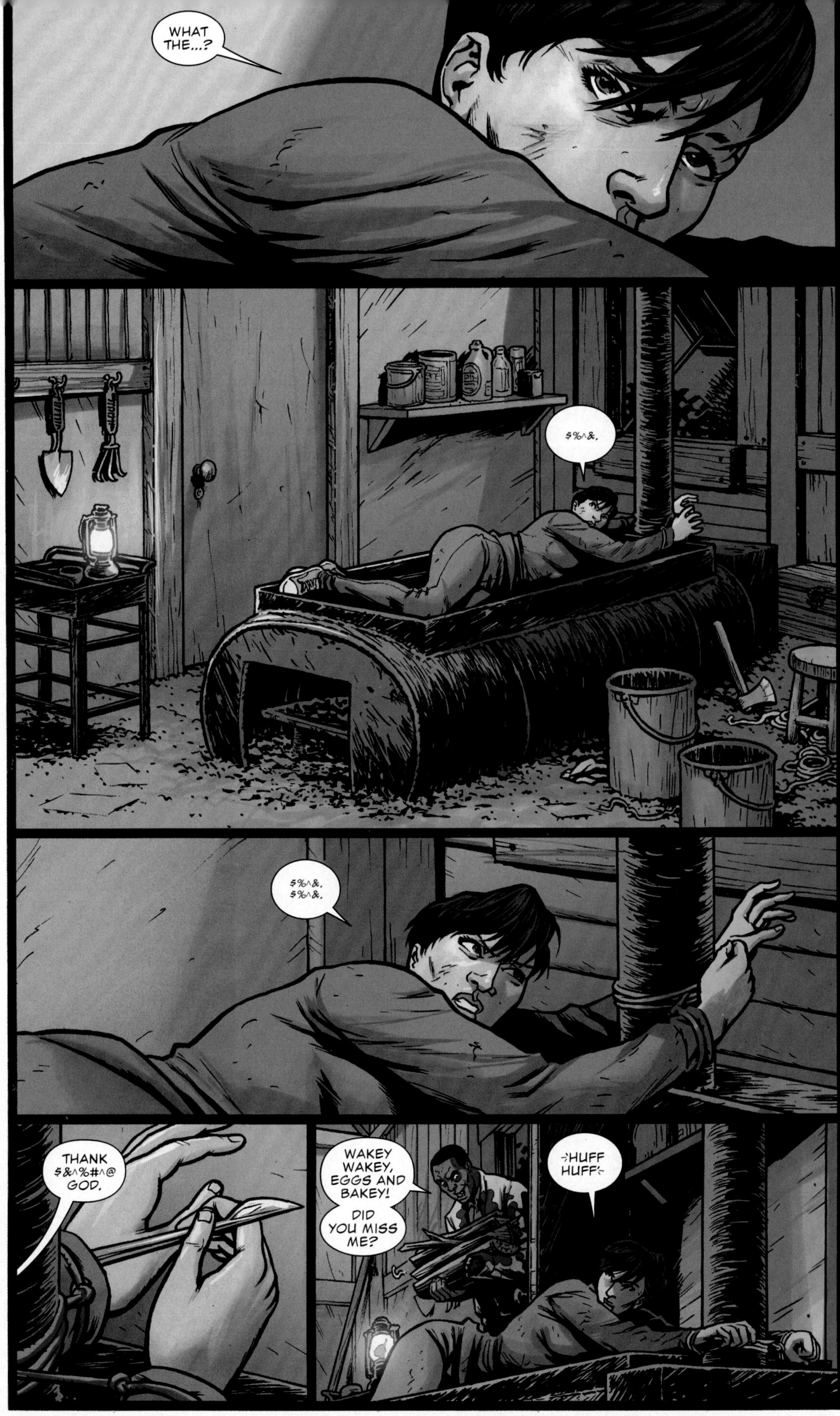
WHAT THE...?
$%^&.
$%^&. $%^&.
THANK $&^%#^@ GOD.
WAKEY WAKEY, EGGS AND BAKEY!
DID YOU MISS ME?
HUFF HUFF

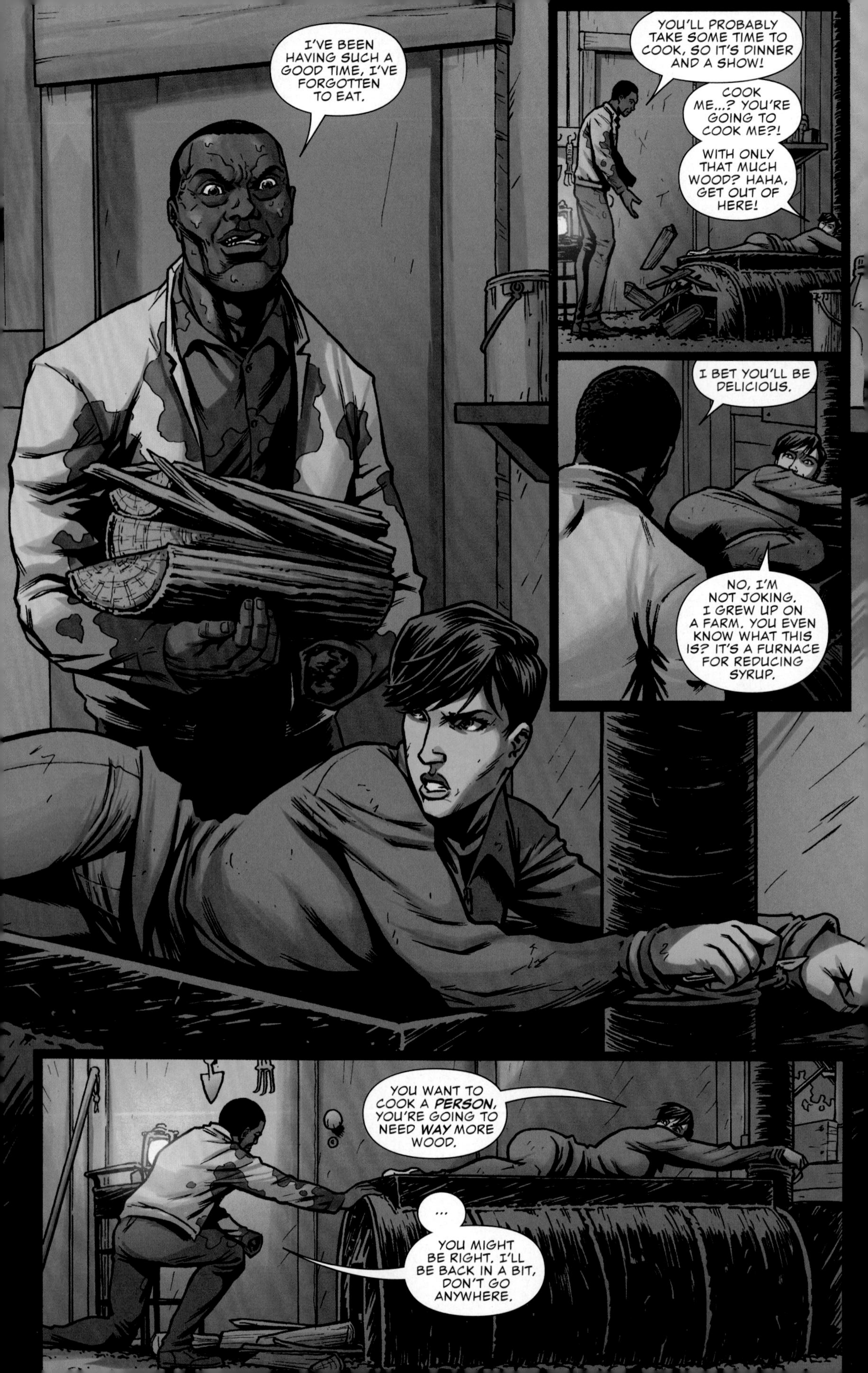
I'VE BEEN HAVING SUCH A GOOD TIME, I'VE FORGOTTEN TO EAT.
YOU'LL PROBABLY TAKE SOME TIME TO COOK, SO IT'S DINNER AND A SHOW!
COOK ME...? YOU'RE GOING TO COOK ME?!
WITH ONLY THAT MUCH WOOD? HAHA, GET OUT OF HERE!
I BET YOU'LL BE DELICIOUS.
NO, I'M NOT JOKING. I GREW UP ON A FARM. YOU EVEN KNOW WHAT THIS IS? IT'S A FURNACE FOR REDUCING SYRUP.
YOU WANT TO COOK A *PERSON*, YOU'RE GOING TO NEED *WAY* MORE WOOD.
...
YOU MIGHT BE RIGHT. I'LL BE BACK IN A BIT, DON'T GO ANYWHERE.

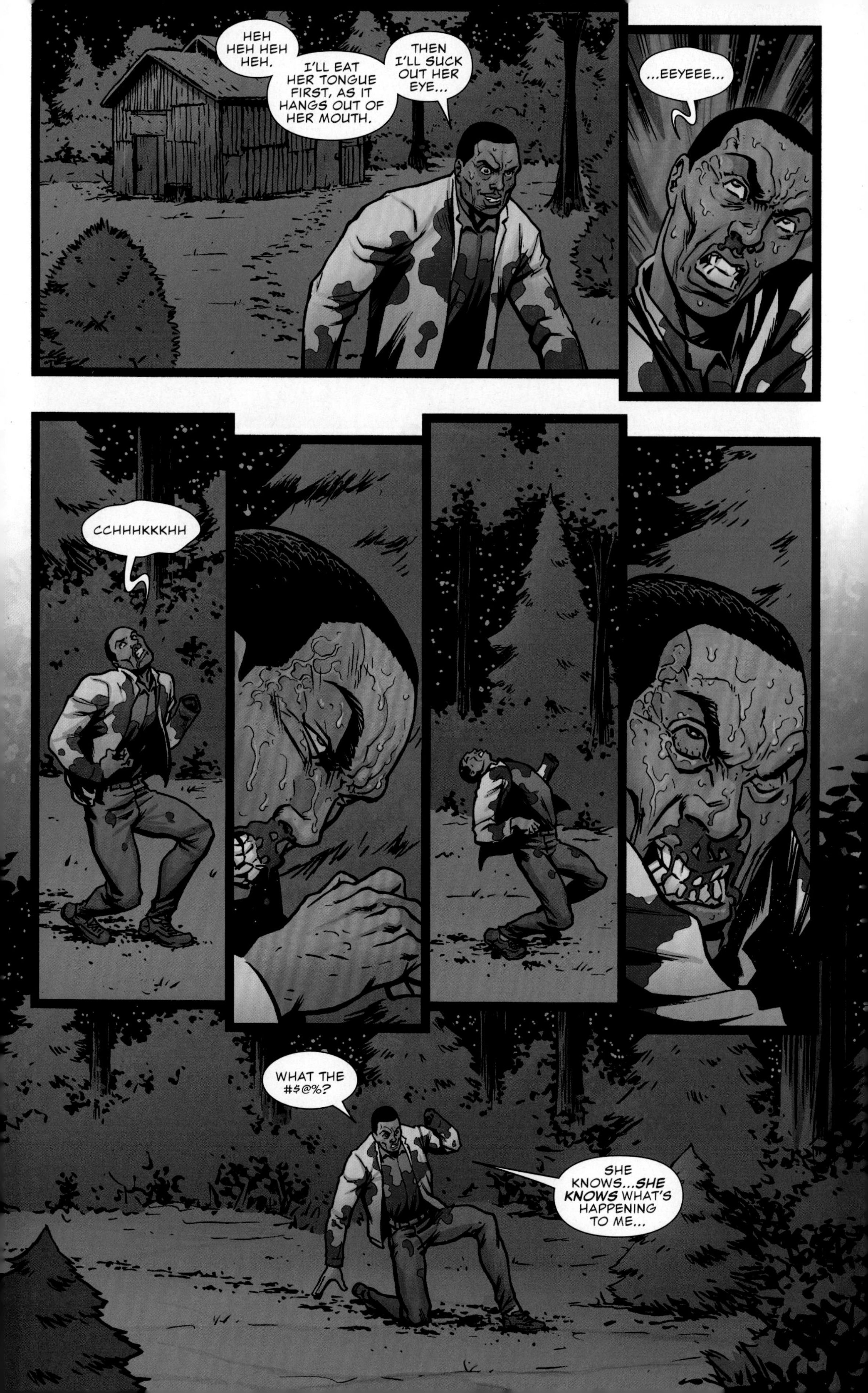
HEH HEH HEH HEH.
I'LL EAT HER TONGUE FIRST, AS IT HANGS OUT OF HER MOUTH.
THEN I'LL SUCK OUT HER EYE...
...EEYEEE...
CCHHHKKKHH
WHAT THE #$@%?
SHE KNOWS...*SHE KNOWS* WHAT'S HAPPENING TO ME...

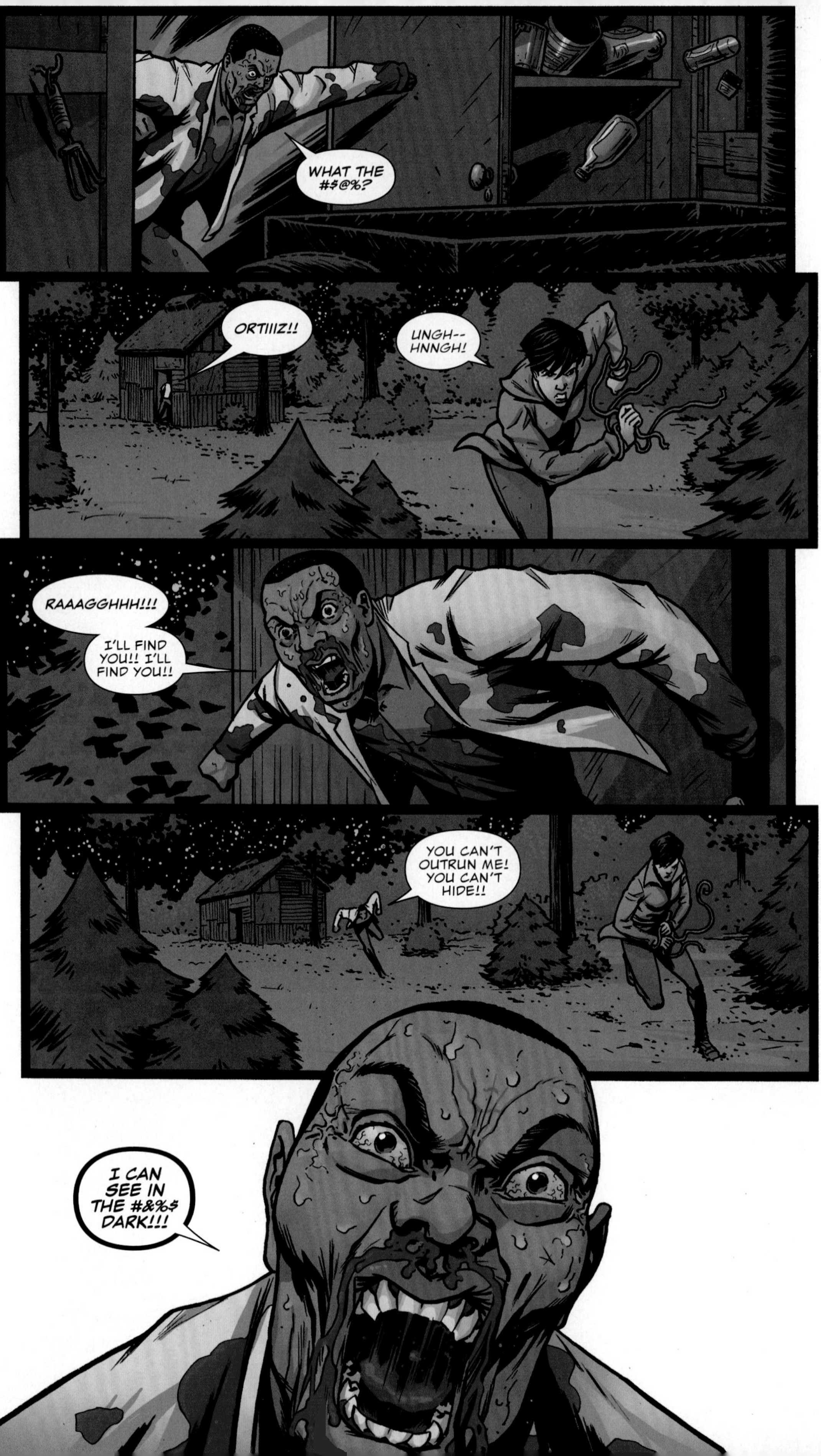
WHAT THE #$@%?
ORTIIIZ!!
UNGH-- HNNGH!
RAAAGGHHH!!!
I'LL FIND YOU!! I'LL FIND YOU!!
YOU CAN'T OUTRUN ME! YOU CAN'T HIDE!!
I CAN SEE IN THE #&%$ DARK!!!

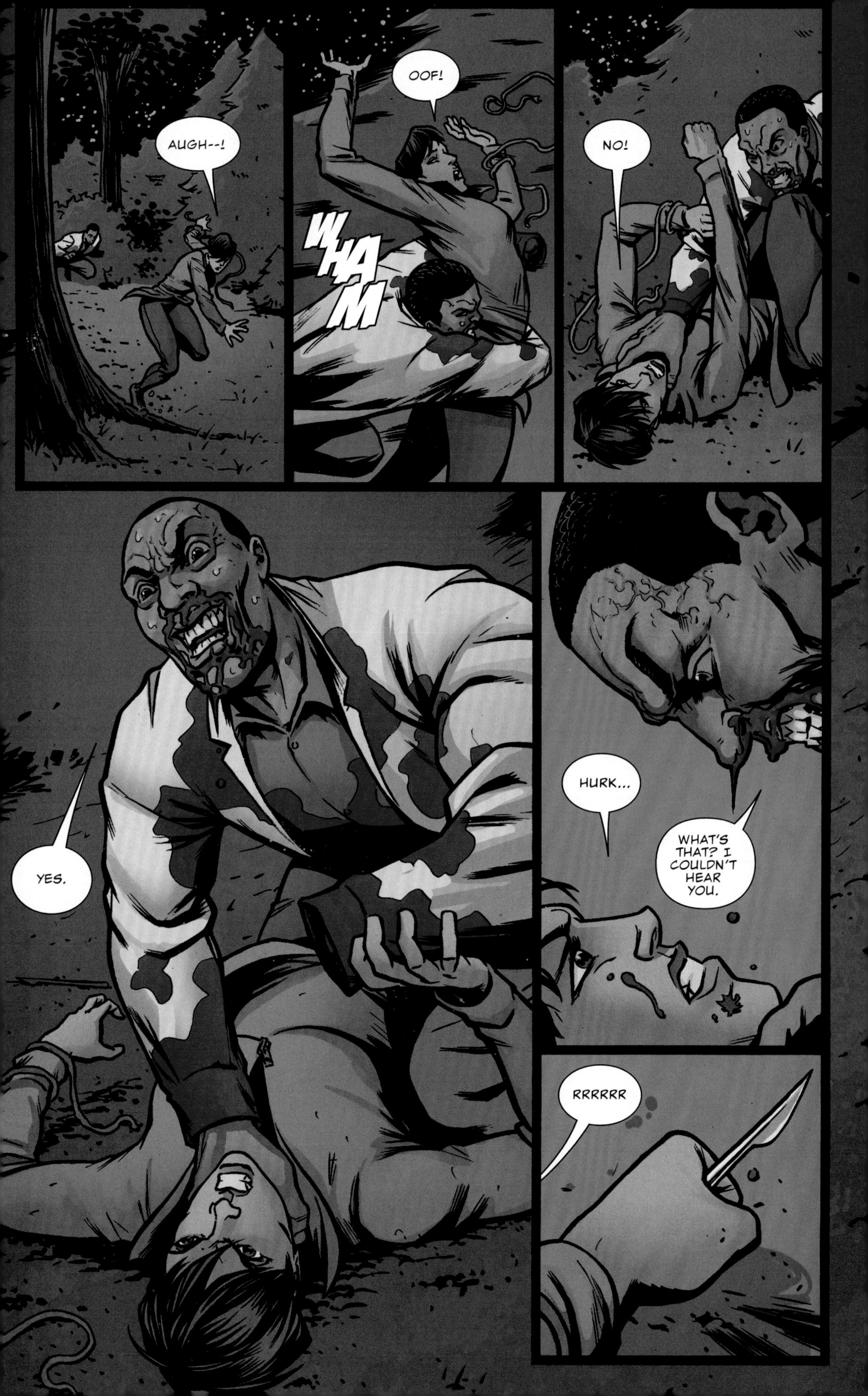
AUGH--!
OOF!
WHAM
NO!
YES.
HURK...
WHAT'S THAT? I COULDN'T HEAR YOU.
RRRRRR

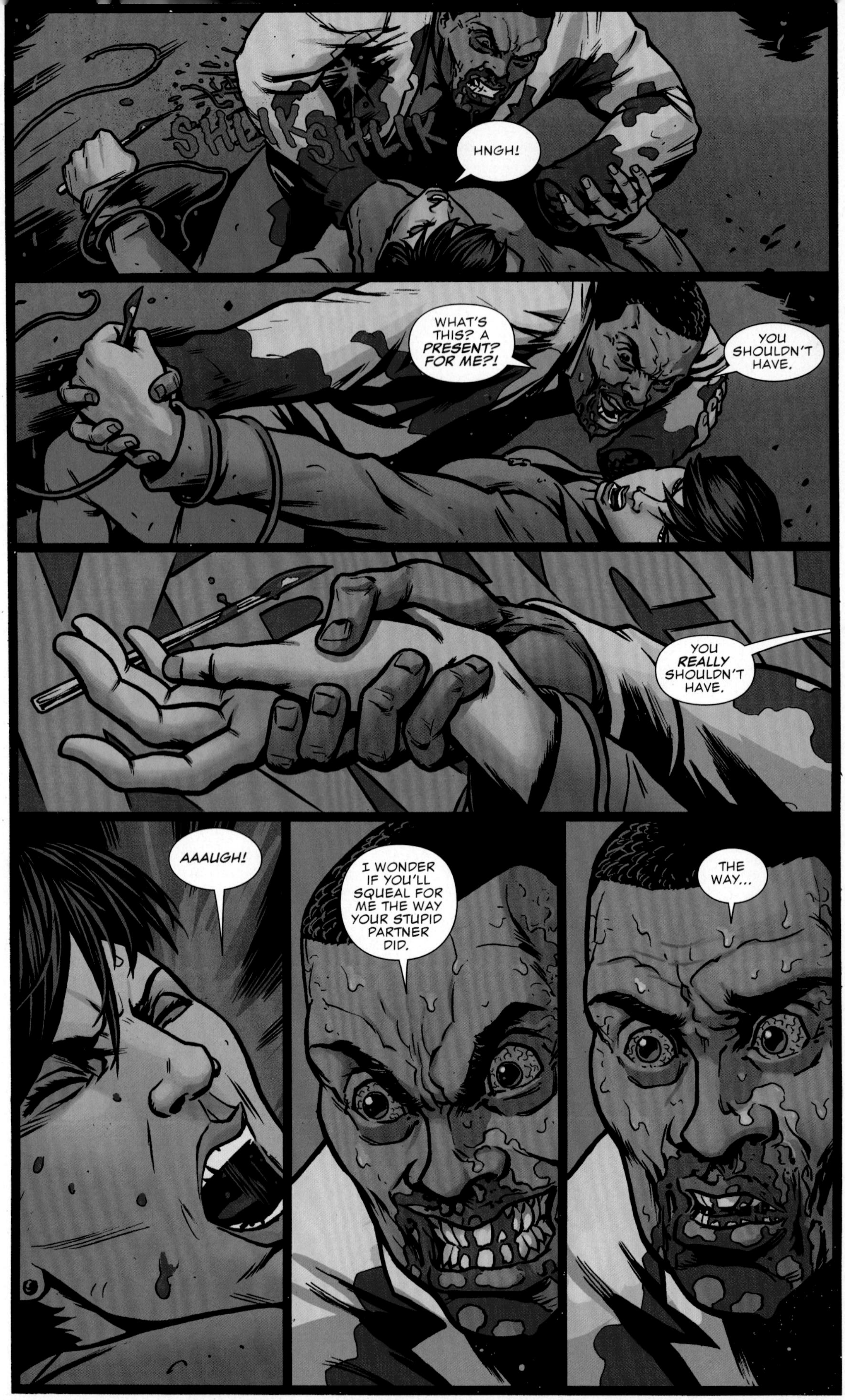
SHLIK SHLIK
HNGH!
WHAT'S THIS? A PRESENT? FOR ME?!
YOU SHOULDN'T HAVE.
YOU REALLY SHOULDN'T HAVE.
AAAUGH!
I WONDER IF YOU'LL SQUEAL FOR ME THE WAY YOUR STUPID PARTNER DID.
THE WAY...

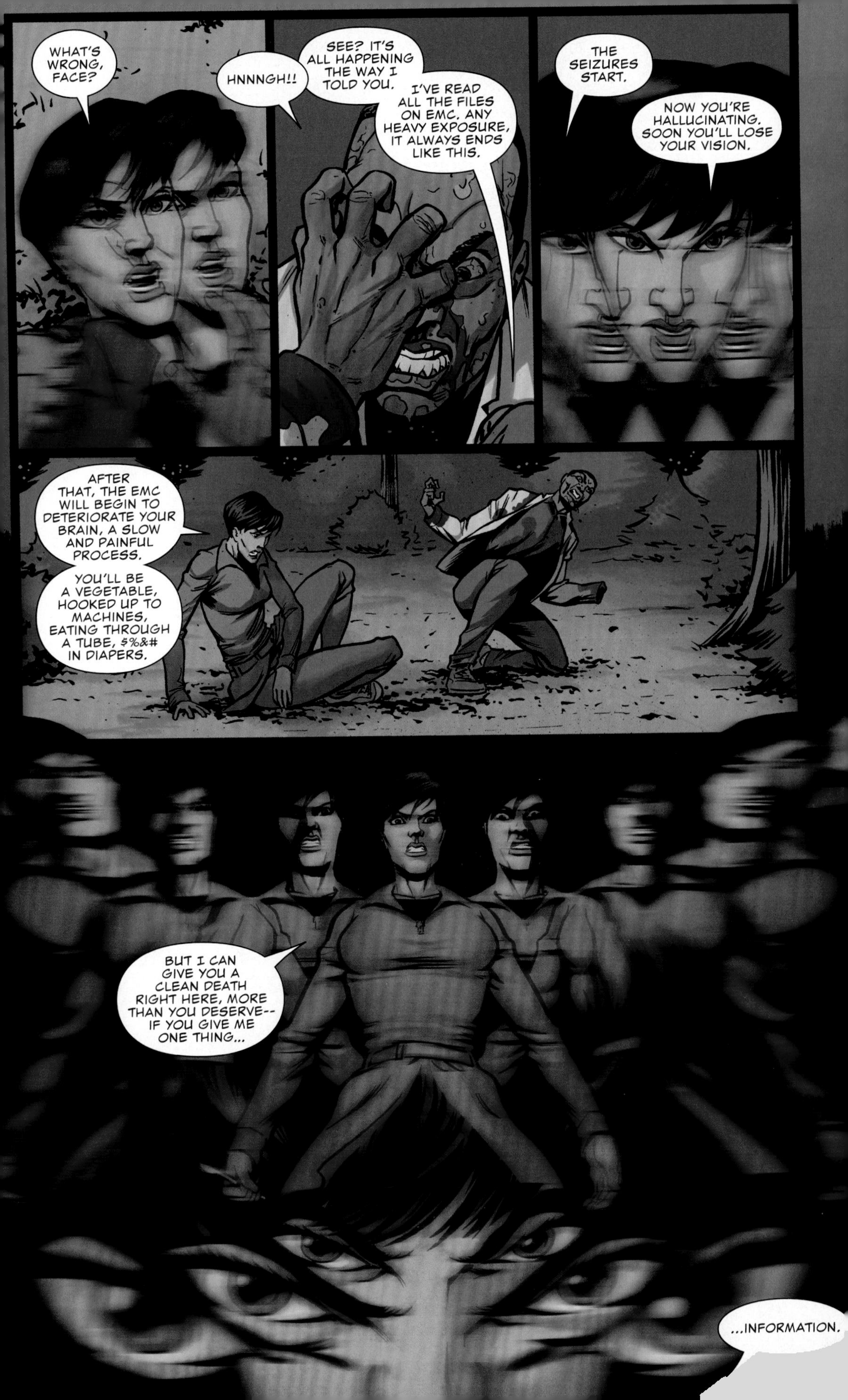
WHAT'S WRONG, FACE?
HNNNGH!!
SEE? IT'S ALL HAPPENING THE WAY I TOLD YOU.
I'VE READ ALL THE FILES ON EMC. ANY HEAVY EXPOSURE, IT ALWAYS ENDS LIKE THIS.
THE SEIZURES START.
NOW YOU'RE HALLUCINATING. SOON YOU'LL LOSE YOUR VISION.
AFTER THAT, THE EMC WILL BEGIN TO DETERIORATE YOUR BRAIN, A SLOW AND PAINFUL PROCESS.
YOU'LL BE A VEGETABLE, HOOKED UP TO MACHINES, EATING THROUGH A TUBE, $%&# IN DIAPERS.
BUT I CAN GIVE YOU A CLEAN DEATH RIGHT HERE, MORE THAN YOU DESERVE--IF YOU GIVE ME ONE THING...
...INFORMATION.

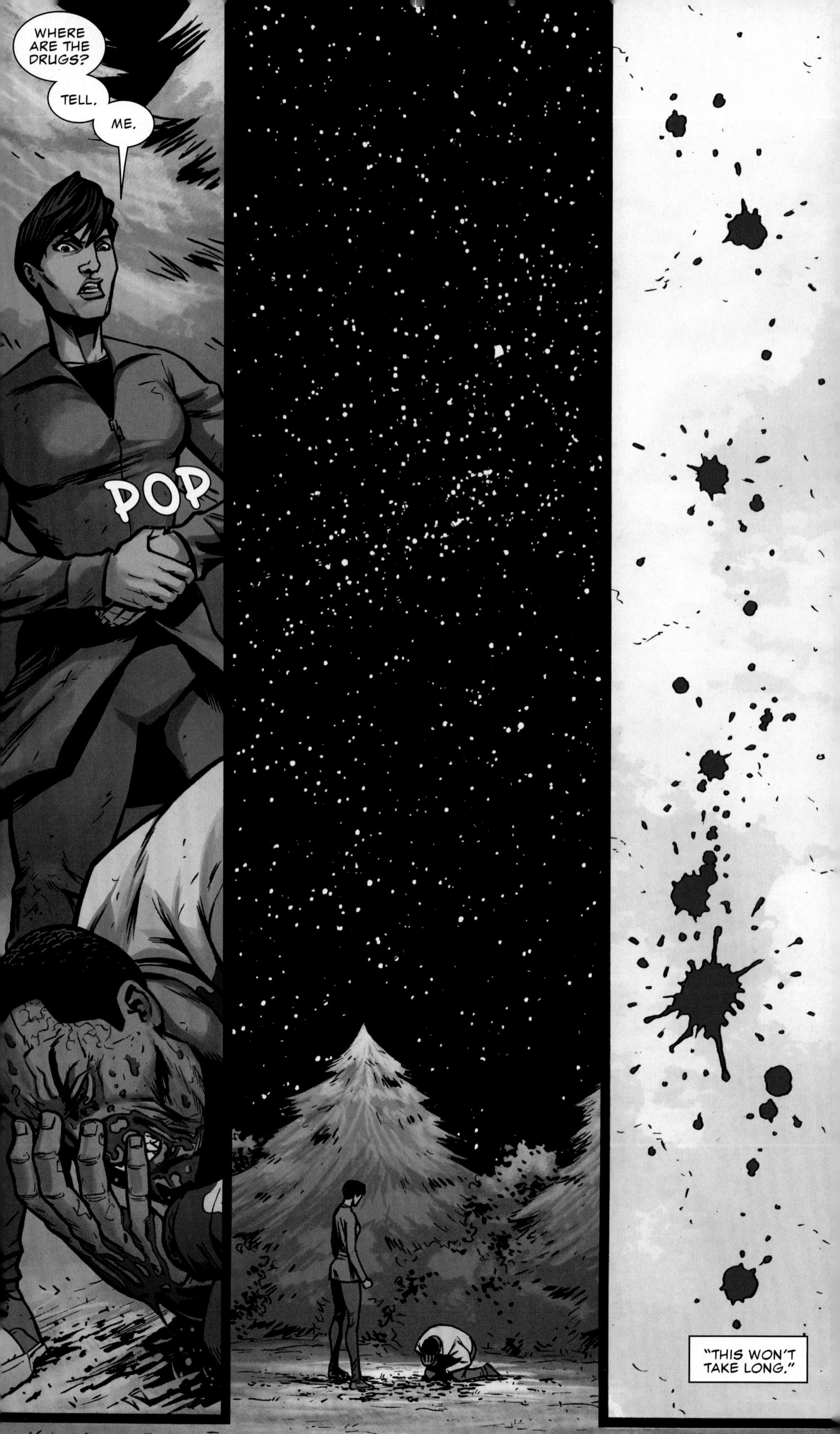
WHERE ARE THE DRUGS?
TELL.
ME.
POP
"THIS WON'T TAKE LONG."

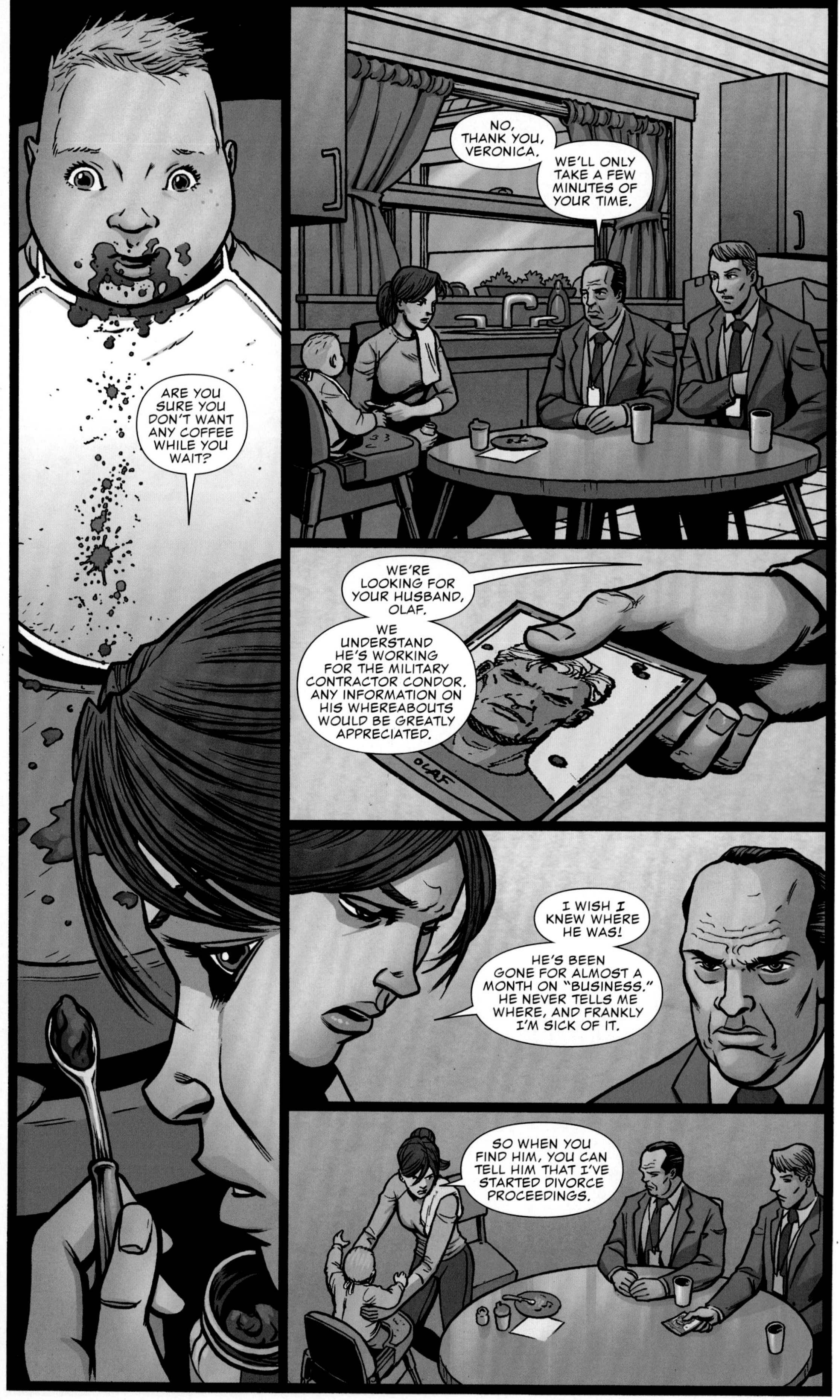
NO, THANK YOU, VERONICA.
WE'LL ONLY TAKE A FEW MINUTES OF YOUR TIME.
ARE YOU SURE YOU DON'T WANT ANY COFFEE WHILE YOU WAIT?
WE'RE LOOKING FOR YOUR HUSBAND, OLAF.
WE UNDERSTAND HE'S WORKING FOR THE MILITARY CONTRACTOR CONDOR. ANY INFORMATION ON HIS WHEREABOUTS WOULD BE GREATLY APPRECIATED.
OLAF
I WISH I KNEW WHERE HE WAS!
HE'S BEEN GONE FOR ALMOST A MONTH ON "BUSINESS." HE NEVER TELLS ME WHERE, AND FRANKLY I'M SICK OF IT.
SO WHEN YOU FIND HIM, YOU CAN TELL HIM THAT I'VE STARTED DIVORCE PROCEEDINGS.

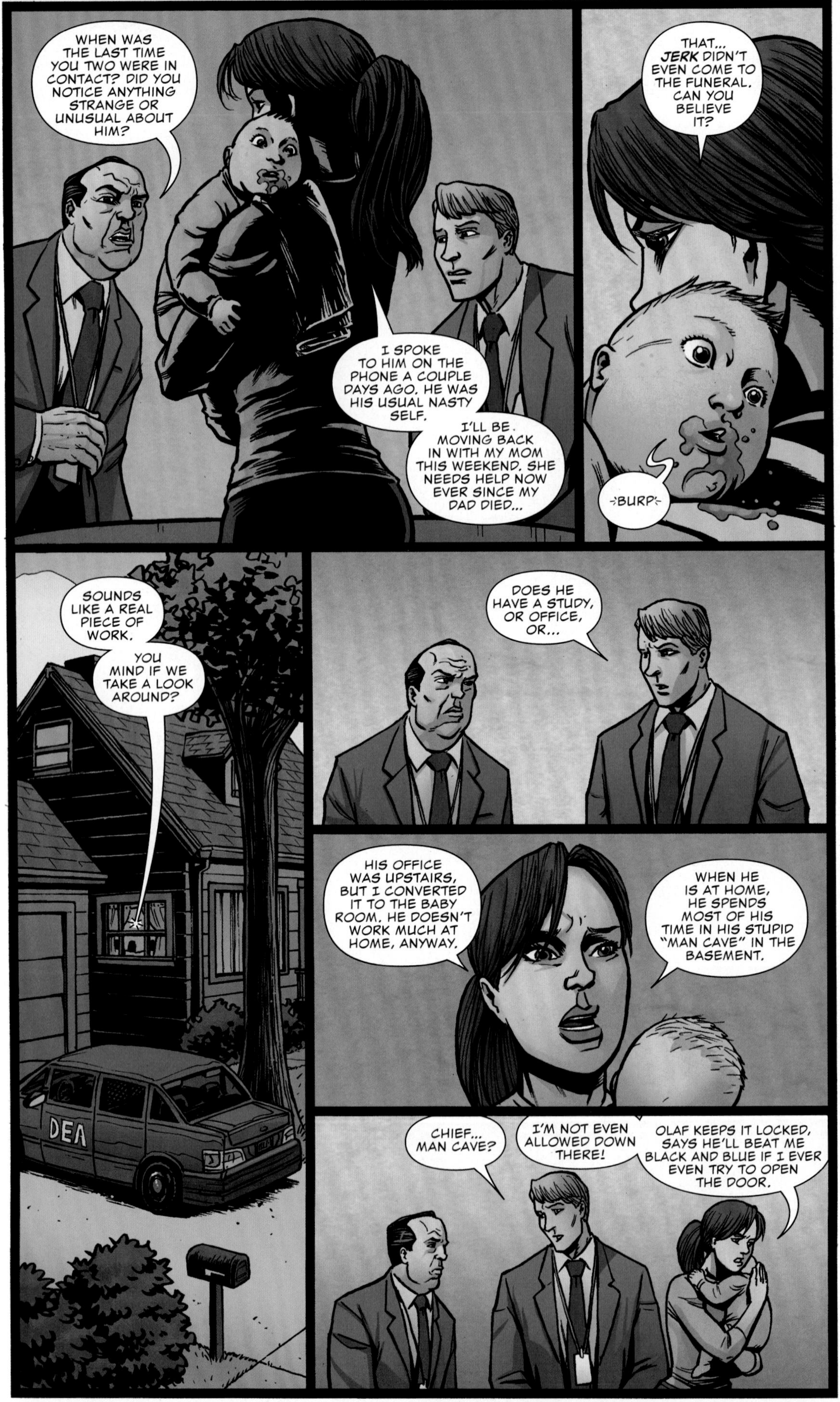
WHEN WAS THE LAST TIME YOU TWO WERE IN CONTACT? DID YOU NOTICE ANYTHING STRANGE OR UNUSUAL ABOUT HIM?
I SPOKE TO HIM ON THE PHONE A COUPLE DAYS AGO. HE WAS HIS USUAL NASTY SELF.
I'LL BE MOVING BACK IN WITH MY MOM THIS WEEKEND. SHE NEEDS HELP NOW EVER SINCE MY DAD DIED...
THAT... JERK DIDN'T EVEN COME TO THE FUNERAL. CAN YOU BELIEVE IT?
BURP
SOUNDS LIKE A REAL PIECE OF WORK.
YOU MIND IF WE TAKE A LOOK AROUND?
DEA
DOES HE HAVE A STUDY, OR OFFICE, OR...
HIS OFFICE WAS UPSTAIRS, BUT I CONVERTED IT TO THE BABY ROOM. HE DOESN'T WORK MUCH AT HOME, ANYWAY.
WHEN HE IS AT HOME, HE SPENDS MOST OF HIS TIME IN HIS STUPID "MAN CAVE" IN THE BASEMENT.
CHIEF... MAN CAVE?
I'M NOT EVEN ALLOWED DOWN THERE!
OLAF KEEPS IT LOCKED, SAYS HE'LL BEAT ME BLACK AND BLUE IF I EVER EVEN TRY TO OPEN THE DOOR.

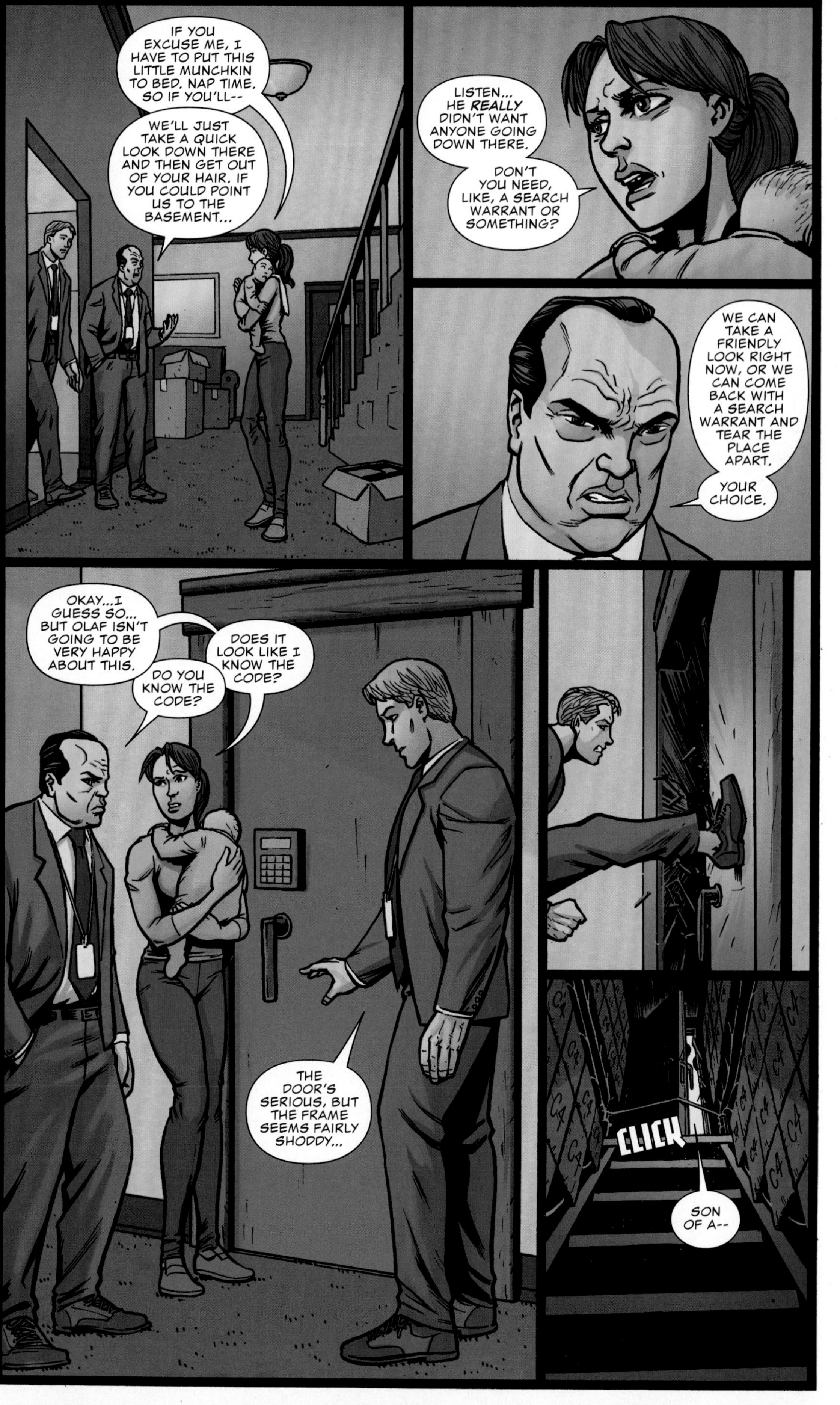
IF YOU EXCUSE ME, I HAVE TO PUT THIS LITTLE MUNCHKIN TO BED. NAP TIME. SO IF YOU'LL--
WE'LL JUST TAKE A QUICK LOOK DOWN THERE AND THEN GET OUT OF YOUR HAIR. IF YOU COULD POINT US TO THE BASEMENT...
LISTEN... HE REALLY DIDN'T WANT ANYONE GOING DOWN THERE.
DON'T YOU NEED, LIKE, A SEARCH WARRANT OR SOMETHING?
WE CAN TAKE A FRIENDLY LOOK RIGHT NOW, OR WE CAN COME BACK WITH A SEARCH WARRANT AND TEAR THE PLACE APART.
YOUR CHOICE.
OKAY...I GUESS SO... BUT OLAF ISN'T GOING TO BE VERY HAPPY ABOUT THIS.
DO YOU KNOW THE CODE?
DOES IT LOOK LIKE I KNOW THE CODE?
THE DOOR'S SERIOUS, BUT THE FRAME SEEMS FAIRLY SHODDY...
CLICK
SON OF A--

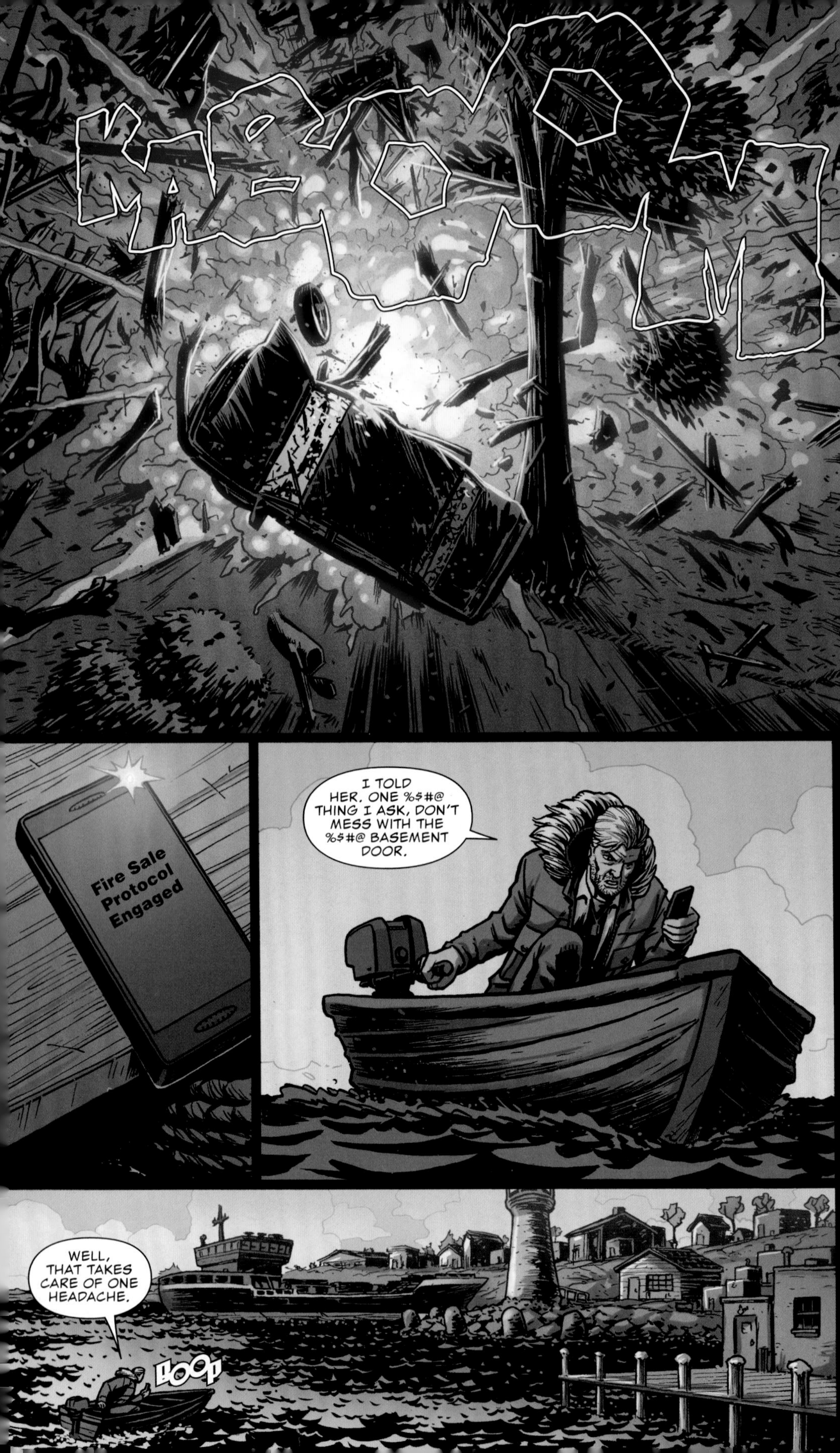
KABOOM
Fire Sale Protocol Engaged
I TOLD HER. ONE %$#@ THING I ASK, DON'T MESS WITH THE %$#@ BASEMENT DOOR.
WELL, THAT TAKES CARE OF ONE HEADACHE.
BOOP

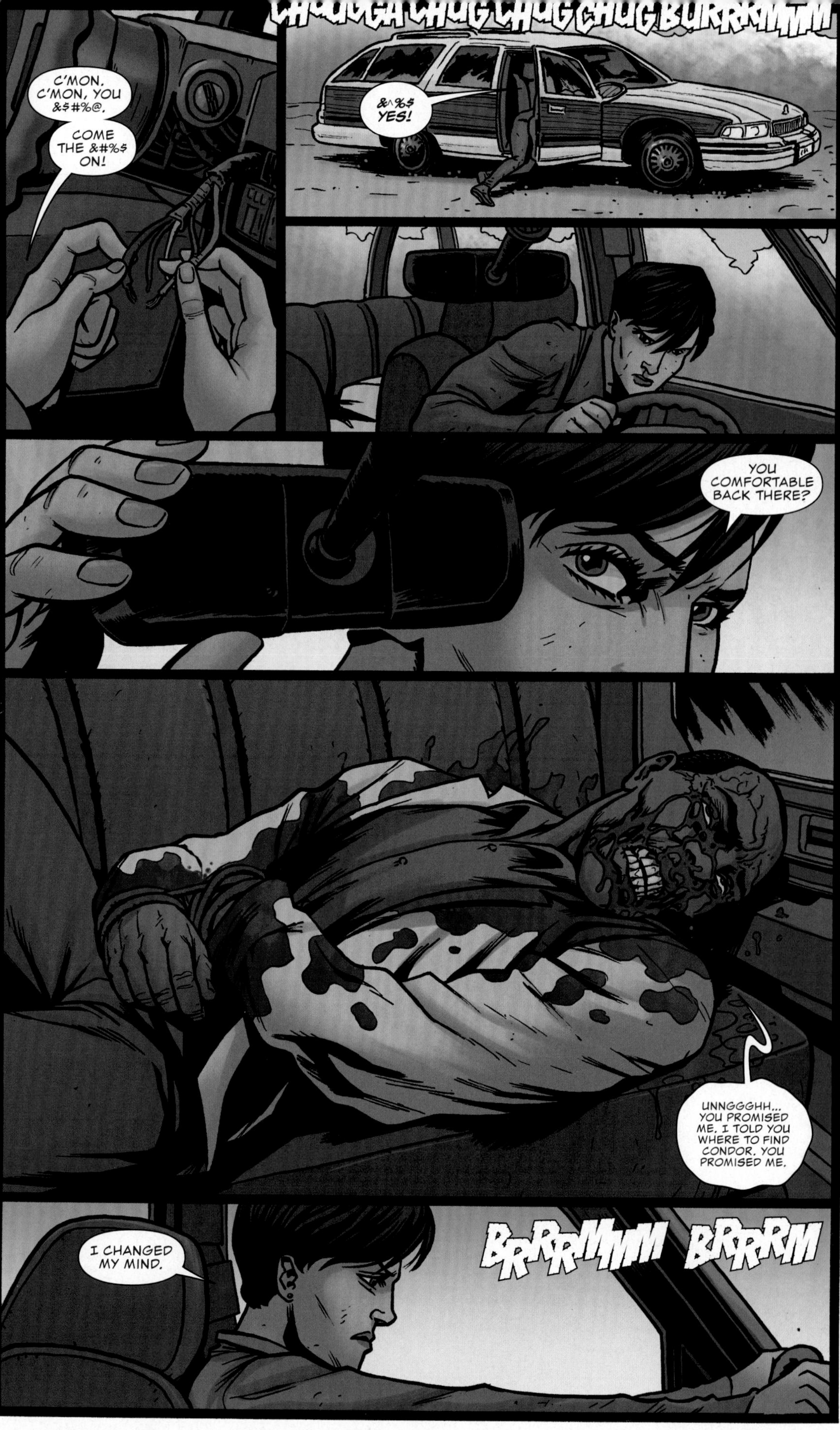
CHUGGA CHUG CHUG CHUG BURRRMMM
C'MON. C'MON, YOU &$#%@.
COME THE &#%$ ON!
&^%$ YES!
YOU COMFORTABLE BACK THERE?
UNNGGGHH... YOU PROMISED ME. I TOLD YOU WHERE TO FIND CONDOR. YOU PROMISED ME.
I CHANGED MY MIND.
BRRRMMM BRRRM

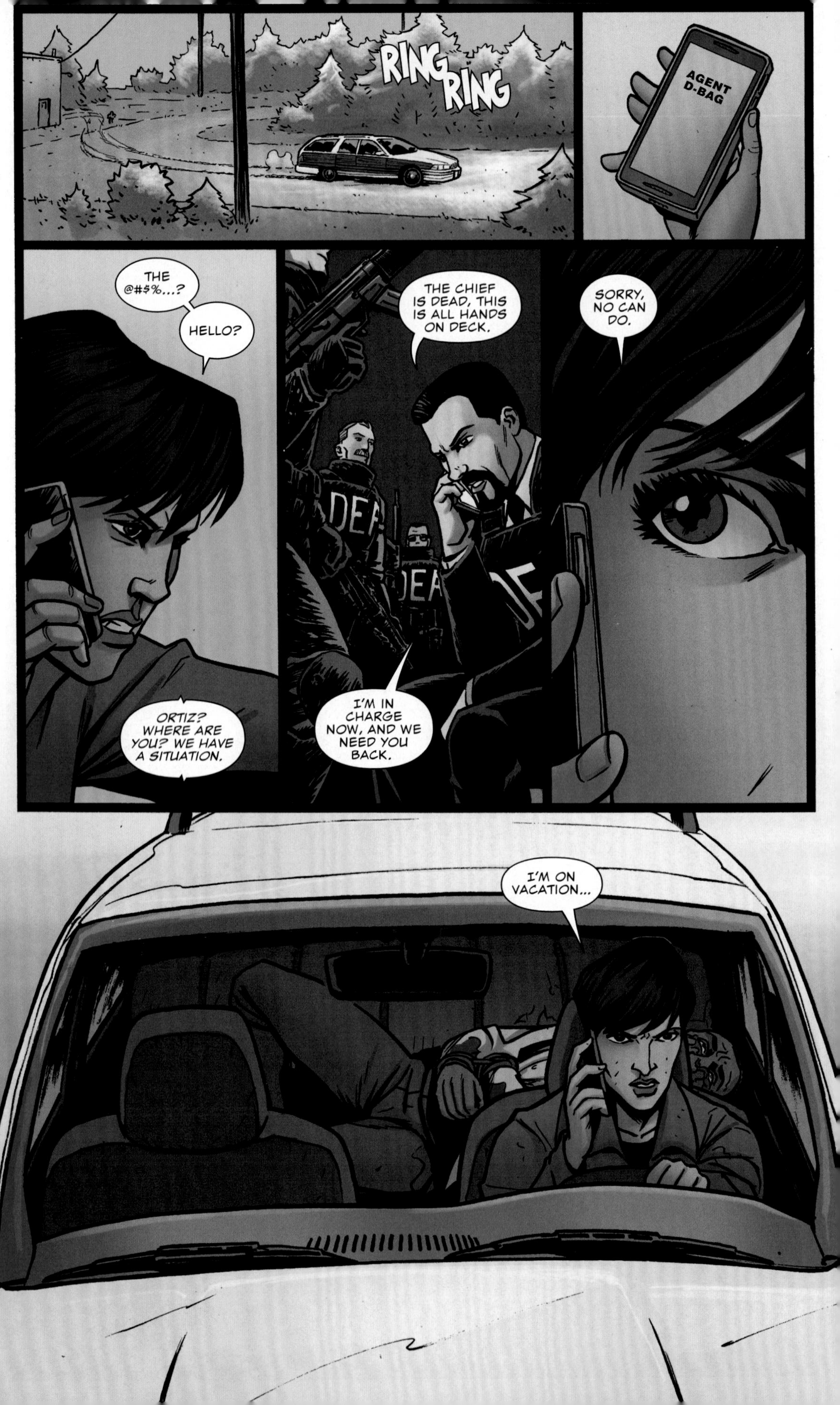
RING RING
AGENT D-BAG
THE @#$%...?
HELLO?
ORTIZ? WHERE ARE YOU? WE HAVE A SITUATION.
THE CHIEF IS DEAD, THIS IS ALL HANDS ON DECK.
I'M IN CHARGE NOW, AND WE NEED YOU BACK.
DEA
DEA
SORRY, NO CAN DO.
I'M ON VACATION...

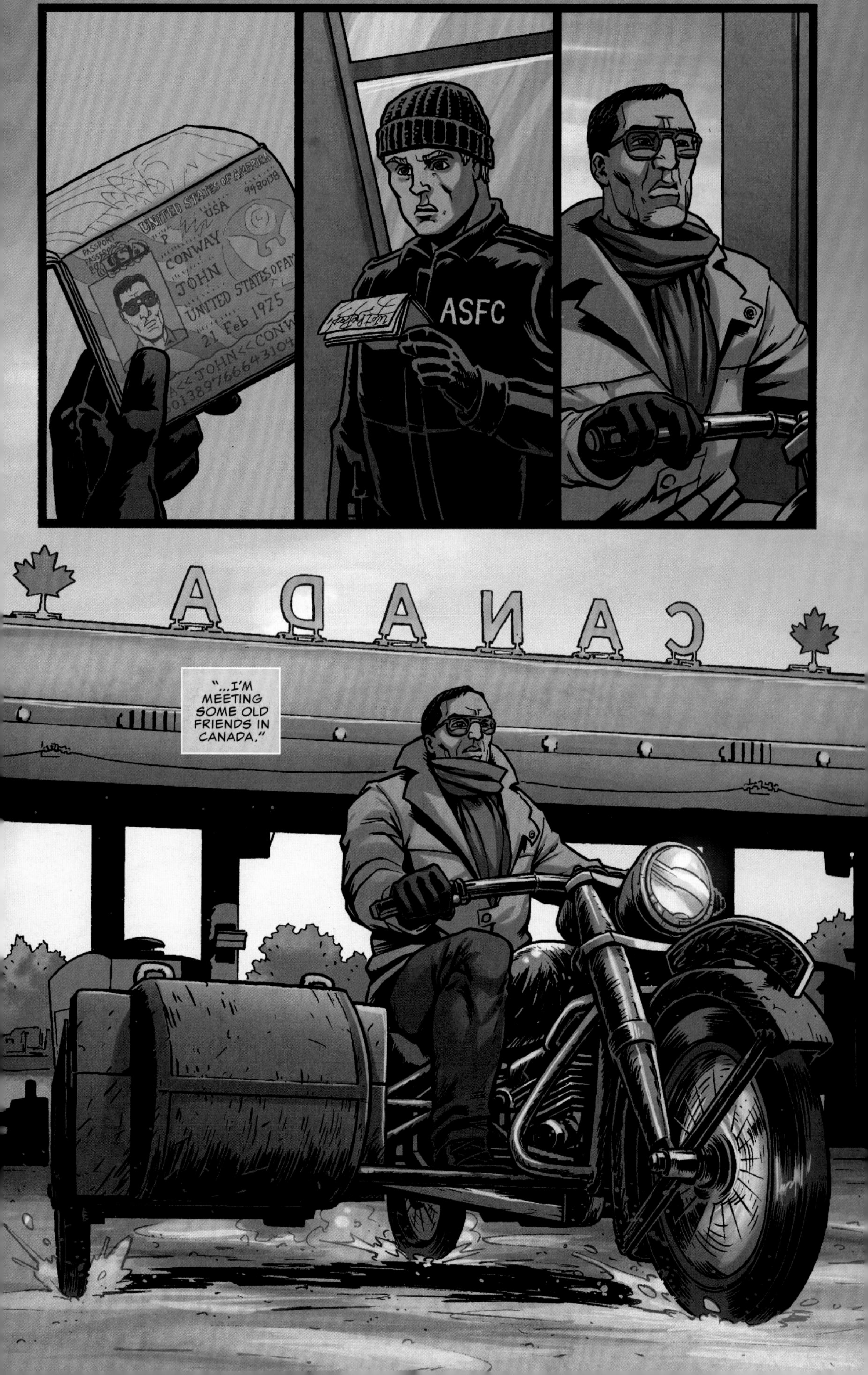
UNITED STATES OF AMERICA
USA
9480138
P
CONWAY
JOHN
UNITED STATES OF AM
21 Feb 1975
ASFC
"...I'M MEETING SOME OLD FRIENDS IN CANADA."

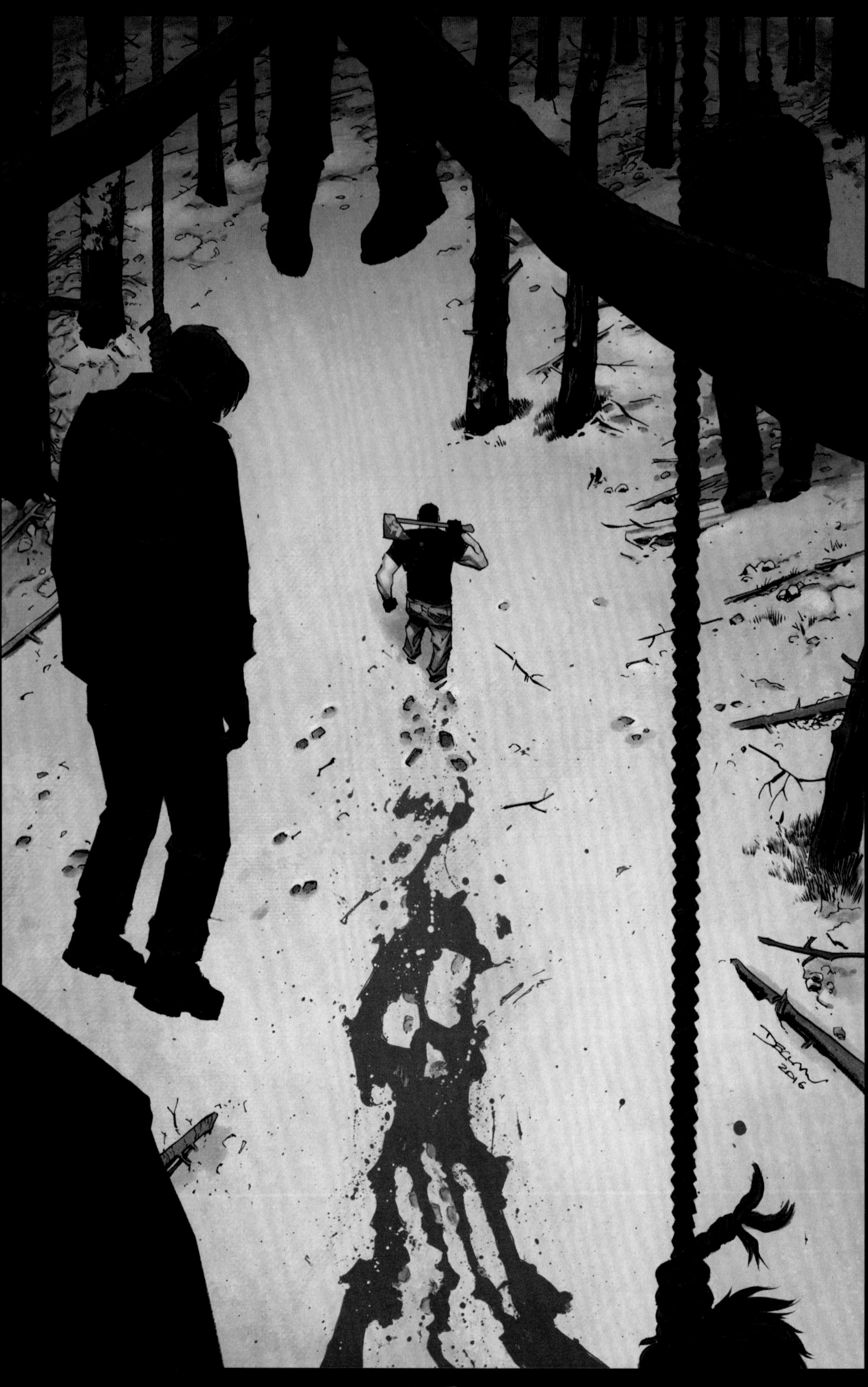

10

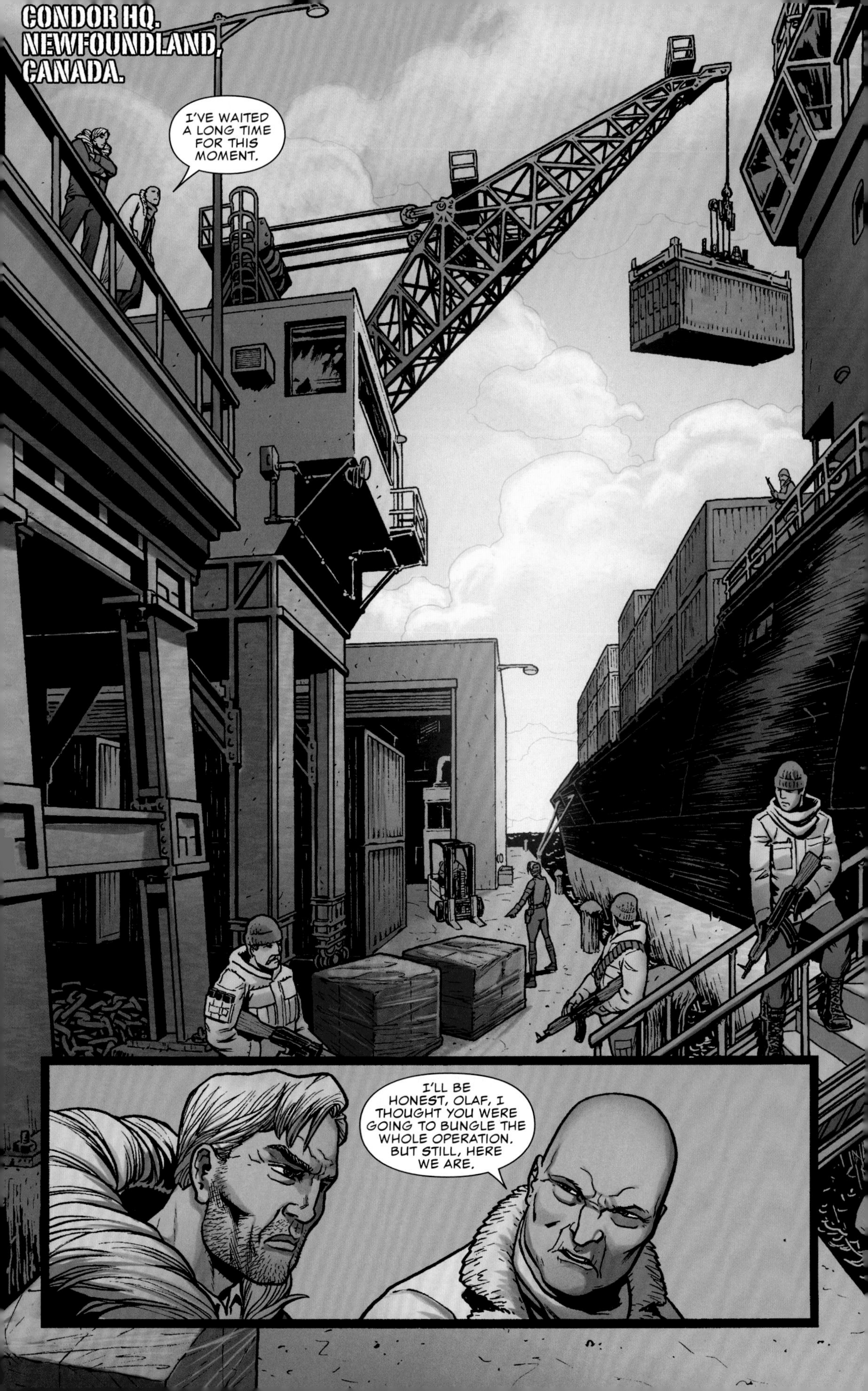
CONDOR HQ. NEWFOUNDLAND, CANADA.
I'VE WAITED A LONG TIME FOR THIS MOMENT.
I'LL BE HONEST, OLAF, I THOUGHT YOU WERE GOING TO BUNGLE THE WHOLE OPERATION. BUT STILL, HERE WE ARE.

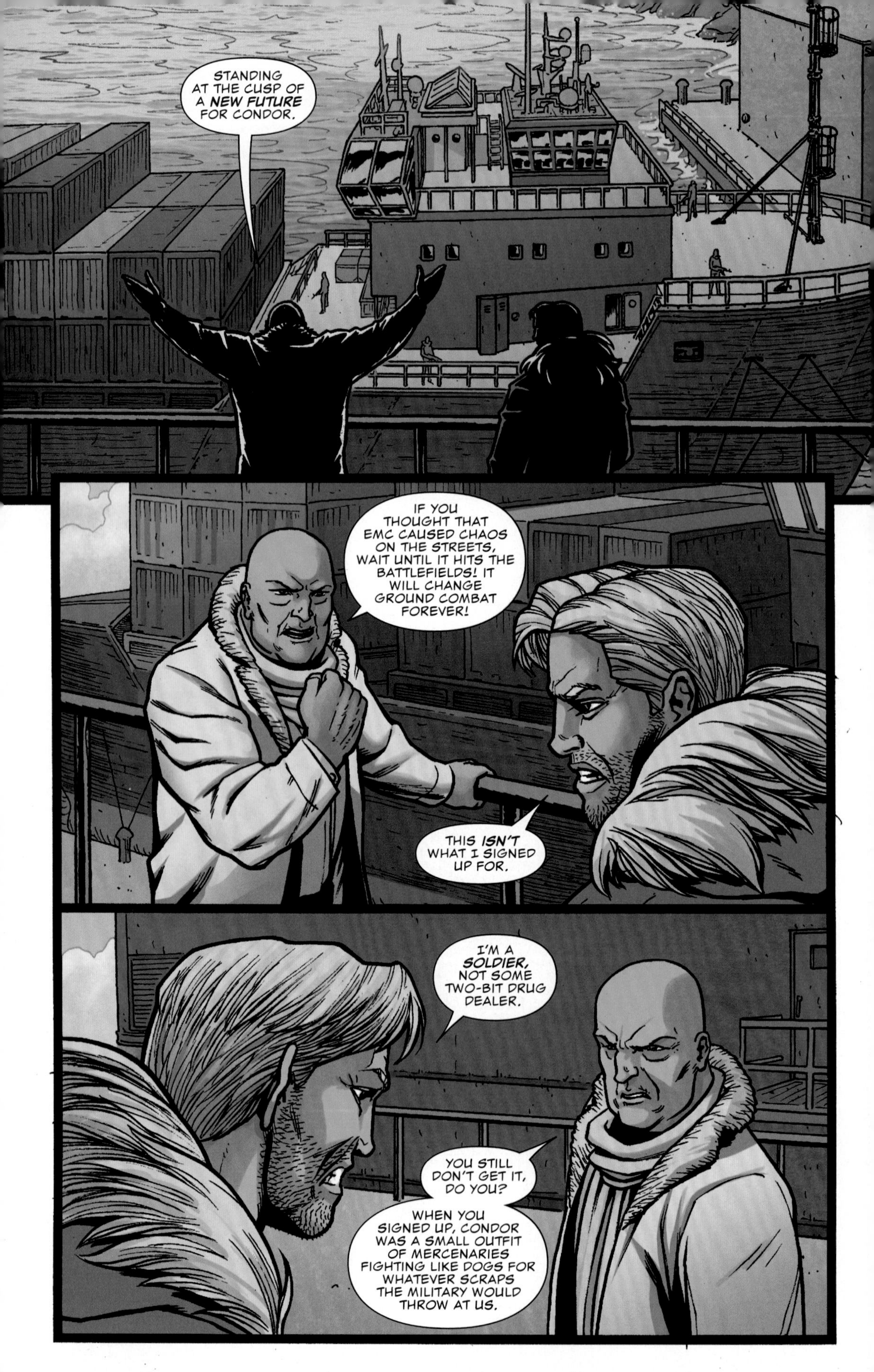
STANDING AT THE CUSP OF A NEW FUTURE FOR CONDOR.
IF YOU THOUGHT THAT EMC CAUSED CHAOS ON THE STREETS, WAIT UNTIL IT HITS THE BATTLEFIELDS! IT WILL CHANGE GROUND COMBAT FOREVER!
THIS ISN'T WHAT I SIGNED UP FOR.
I'M A SOLDIER, NOT SOME TWO-BIT DRUG DEALER.
YOU STILL DON'T GET IT, DO YOU?
WHEN YOU SIGNED UP, CONDOR WAS A SMALL OUTFIT OF MERCENARIES FIGHTING LIKE DOGS FOR WHATEVER SCRAPS THE MILITARY WOULD THROW AT US.

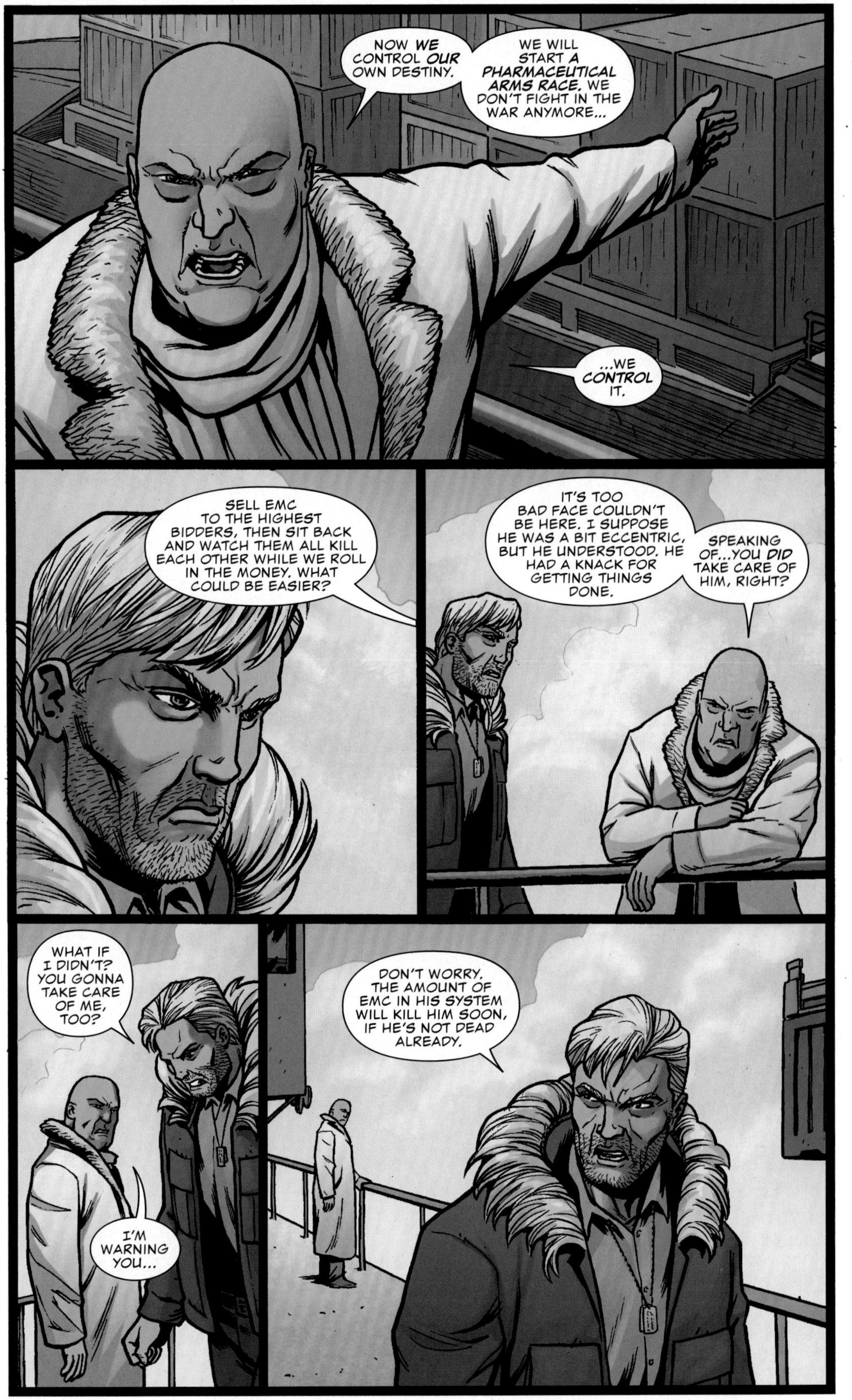
NOW WE CONTROL OUR OWN DESTINY.
WE WILL START A PHARMACEUTICAL ARMS RACE. WE DON'T FIGHT IN THE WAR ANYMORE...
...WE CONTROL IT.
SELL EMC TO THE HIGHEST BIDDERS, THEN SIT BACK AND WATCH THEM ALL KILL EACH OTHER WHILE WE ROLL IN THE MONEY. WHAT COULD BE EASIER?
IT'S TOO BAD FACE COULDN'T BE HERE. I SUPPOSE HE WAS A BIT ECCENTRIC, BUT HE UNDERSTOOD. HE HAD A KNACK FOR GETTING THINGS DONE.
SPEAKING OF...YOU DID TAKE CARE OF HIM, RIGHT?
WHAT IF I DIDN'T? YOU GONNA TAKE CARE OF ME, TOO?
I'M WARNING YOU...
DON'T WORRY. THE AMOUNT OF EMC IN HIS SYSTEM WILL KILL HIM SOON, IF HE'S NOT DEAD ALREADY.

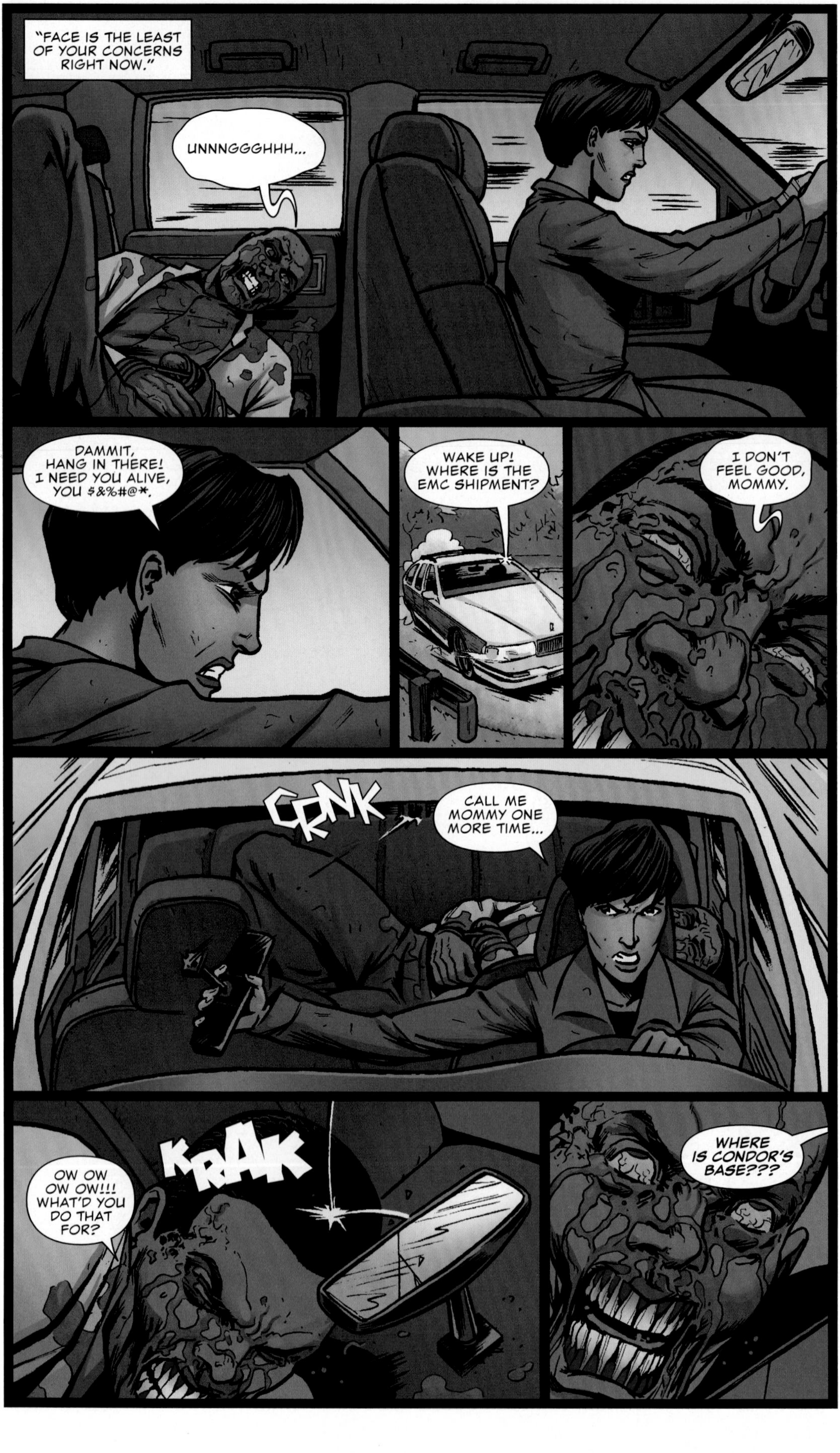

"FACE IS THE LEAST OF YOUR CONCERNS RIGHT NOW."
UNNNGGGHHH...
DAMMIT, HANG IN THERE! I NEED YOU ALIVE, YOU $&%#@*.
WAKE UP! WHERE IS THE EMC SHIPMENT?
I DON'T FEEL GOOD, MOMMY.
CRNK
CALL ME MOMMY ONE MORE TIME...
KRAK
OW OW OW OW!!! WHAT'D YOU DO THAT FOR?
WHERE IS CONDOR'S BASE???

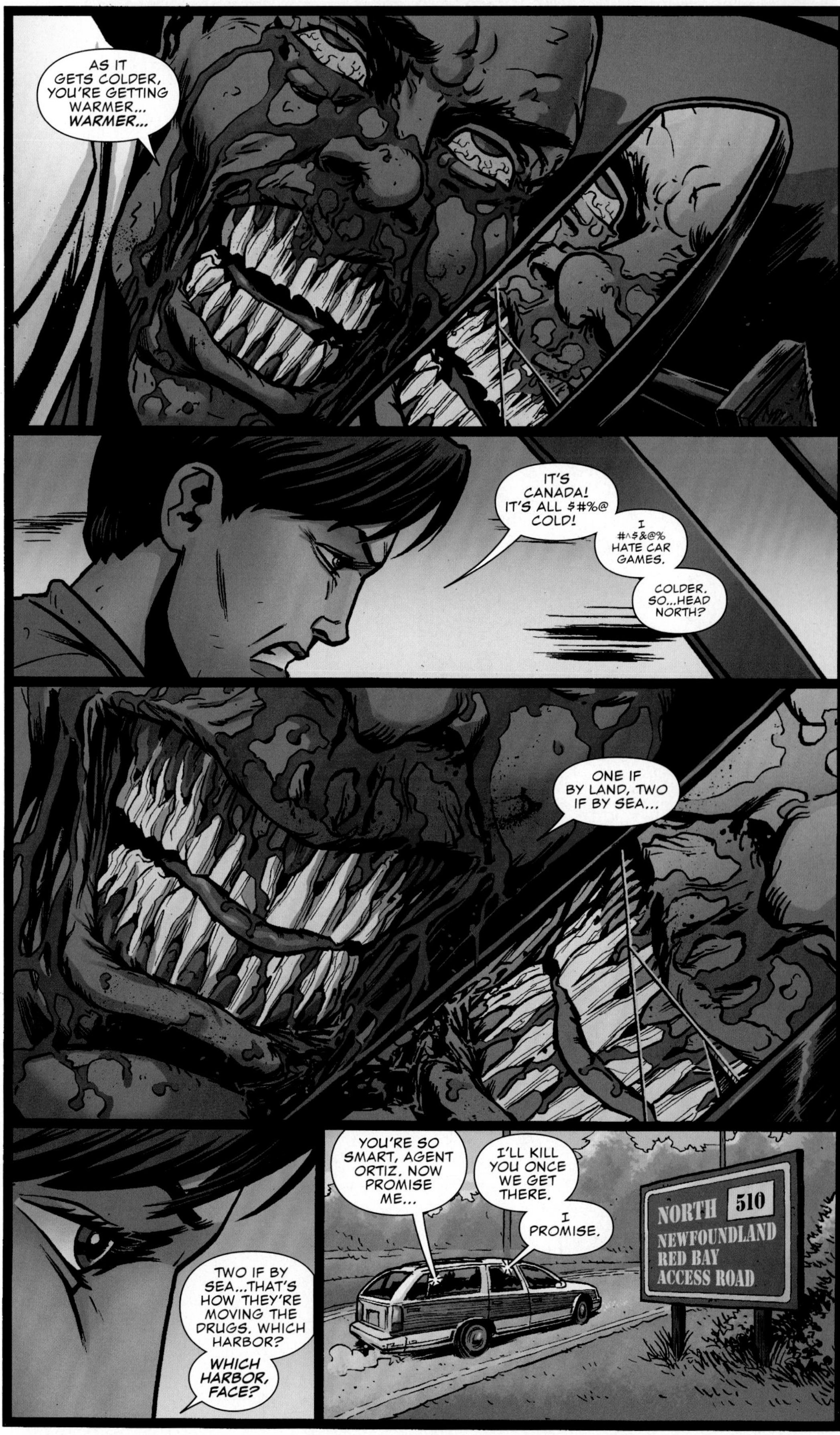
AS IT GETS COLDER, YOU'RE GETTING WARMER... WARMER...
IT'S CANADA! IT'S ALL $#%@ COLD!
I #^$&@% HATE CAR GAMES.
COLDER. SO...HEAD NORTH?
ONE IF BY LAND, TWO IF BY SEA...
TWO IF BY SEA...THAT'S HOW THEY'RE MOVING THE DRUGS. WHICH HARBOR?
WHICH HARBOR, FACE?
YOU'RE SO SMART, AGENT ORTIZ. NOW PROMISE ME...
I'LL KILL YOU ONCE WE GET THERE.
I PROMISE.
NORTH 510
NEWFOUNDLAND
RED BAY
ACCESS ROAD

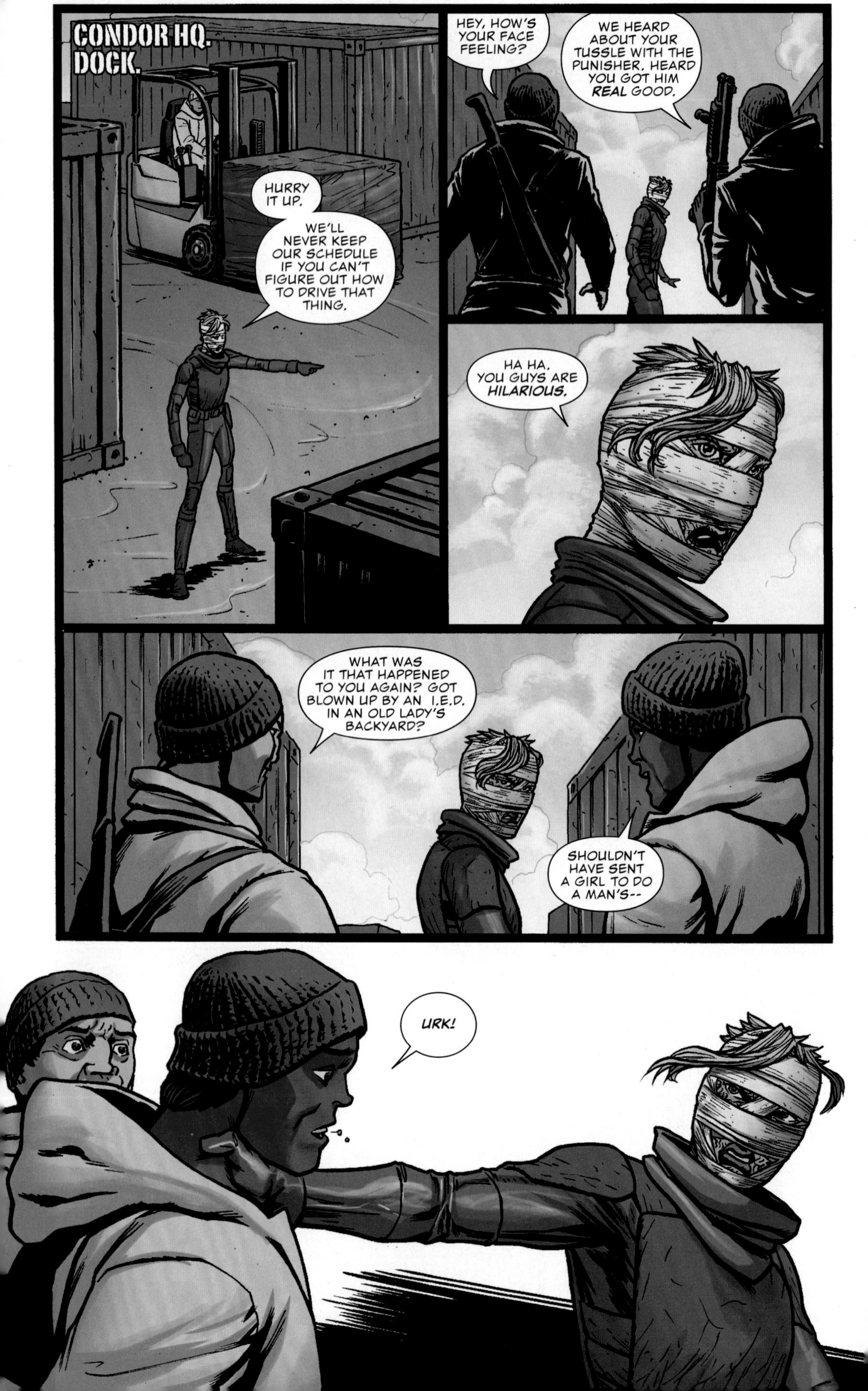
CONDOR HQ. DOCK.
HURRY IT UP.
WE'LL NEVER KEEP OUR SCHEDULE IF YOU CAN'T FIGURE OUT HOW TO DRIVE THAT THING.
HEY, HOW'S YOUR FACE FEELING?
WE HEARD ABOUT YOUR TUSSLE WITH THE PUNISHER. HEARD YOU GOT HIM REAL GOOD.
HA HA. YOU GUYS ARE HILARIOUS.
WHAT WAS IT THAT HAPPENED TO YOU AGAIN? GOT BLOWN UP BY AN I.E.D. IN AN OLD LADY'S BACKYARD?
SHOULDN'T HAVE SENT A GIRL TO DO A MAN'S--
URK!

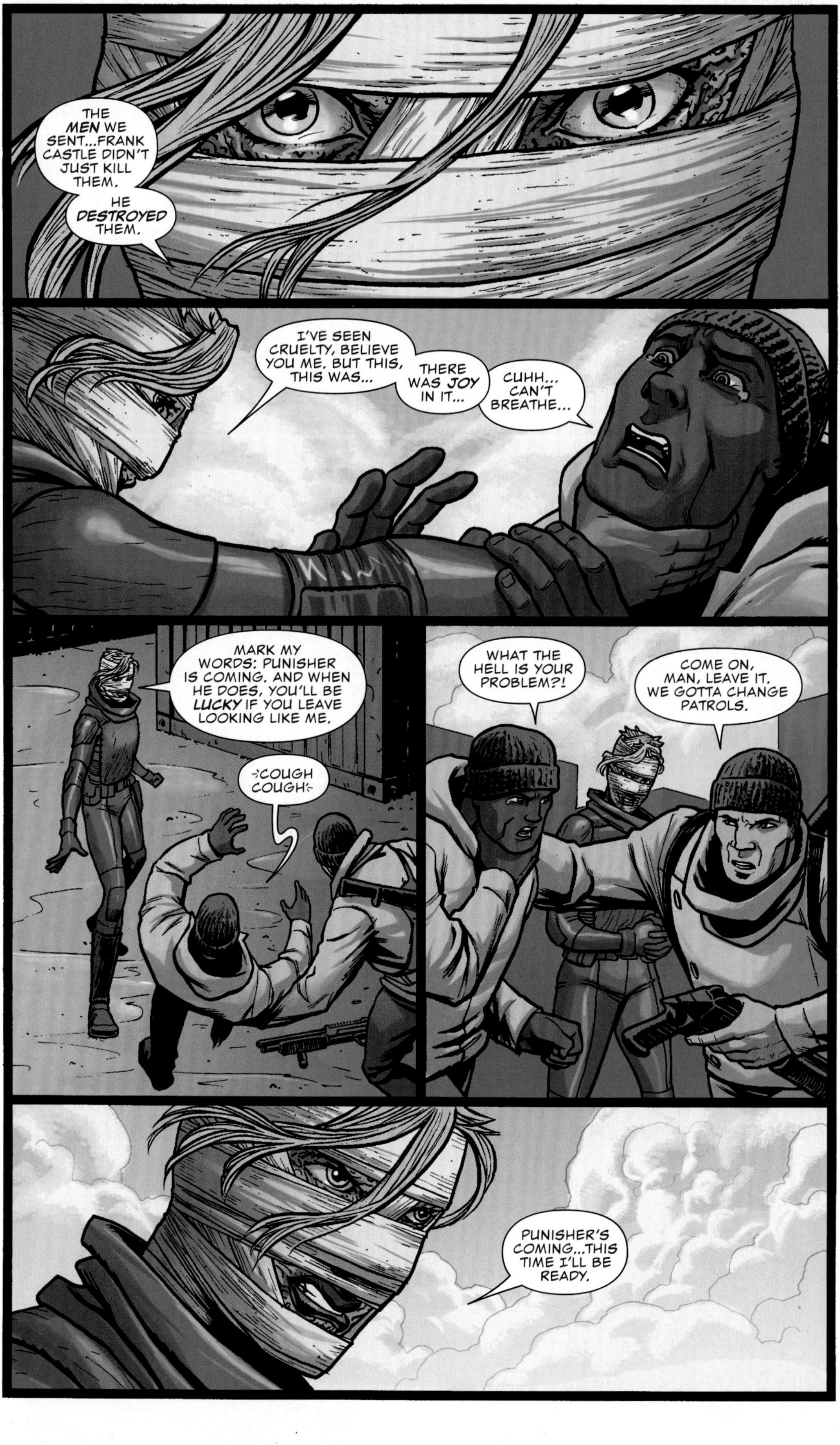
THE MEN WE SENT...FRANK CASTLE DIDN'T JUST KILL THEM.
HE DESTROYED THEM.
I'VE SEEN CRUELTY, BELIEVE YOU ME. BUT THIS, THIS WAS...
THERE WAS JOY IN IT...
CUHH... CAN'T BREATHE...
MARK MY WORDS: PUNISHER IS COMING. AND WHEN HE DOES, YOU'LL BE LUCKY IF YOU LEAVE LOOKING LIKE ME.
COUGH COUGH
WHAT THE HELL IS YOUR PROBLEM?!
COME ON, MAN, LEAVE IT. WE GOTTA CHANGE PATROLS.
PUNISHER'S COMING...THIS TIME I'LL BE READY.

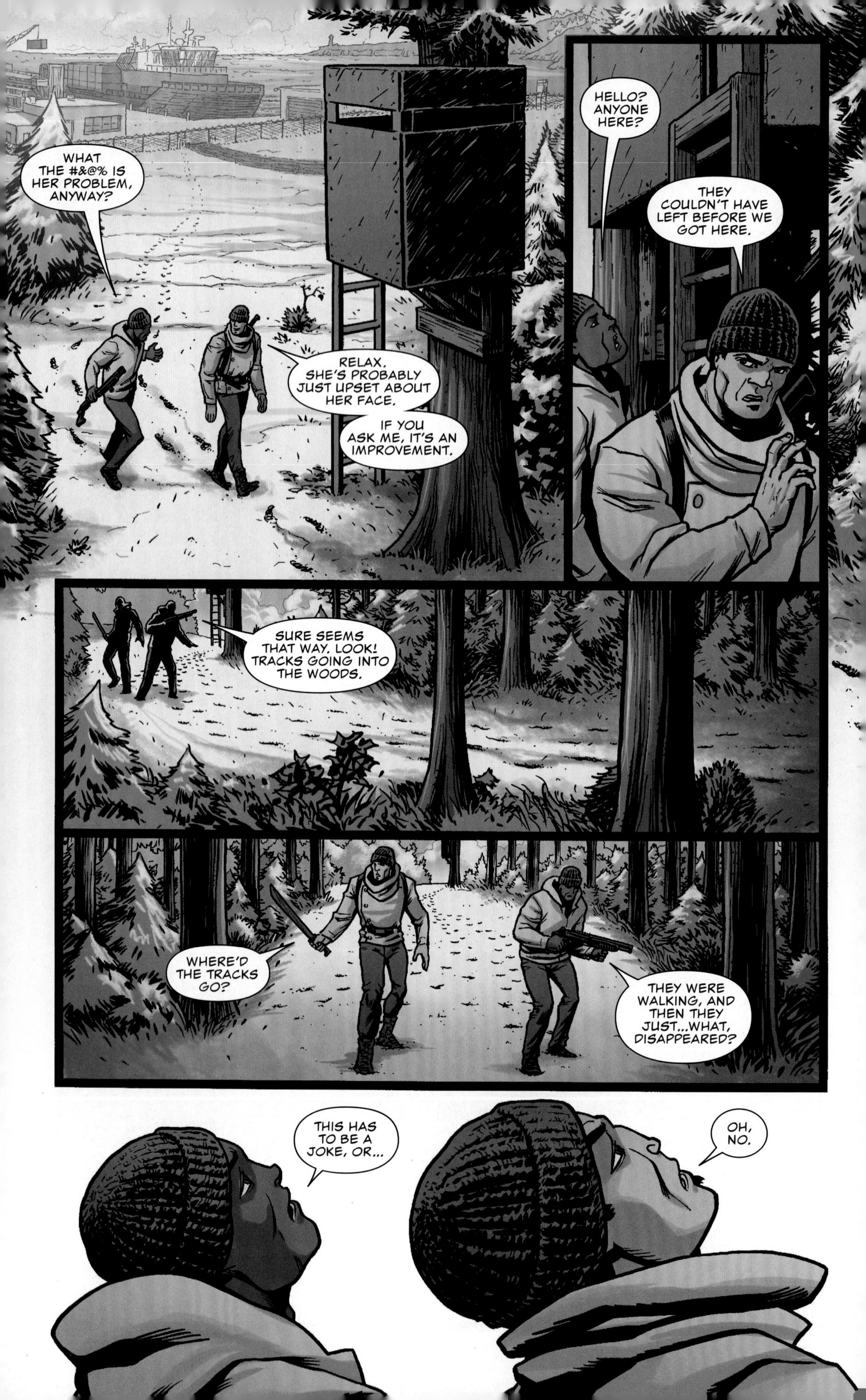
WHAT THE #&@% IS HER PROBLEM, ANYWAY?
RELAX. SHE'S PROBABLY JUST UPSET ABOUT HER FACE.
IF YOU ASK ME, IT'S AN IMPROVEMENT.
HELLO? ANYONE HERE?
THEY COULDN'T HAVE LEFT BEFORE WE GOT HERE.
SURE SEEMS THAT WAY. LOOK! TRACKS GOING INTO THE WOODS.
WHERE'D THE TRACKS GO?
THEY WERE WALKING, AND THEN THEY JUST...WHAT, DISAPPEARED?
THIS HAS TO BE A JOKE, OR...
OH, NO.

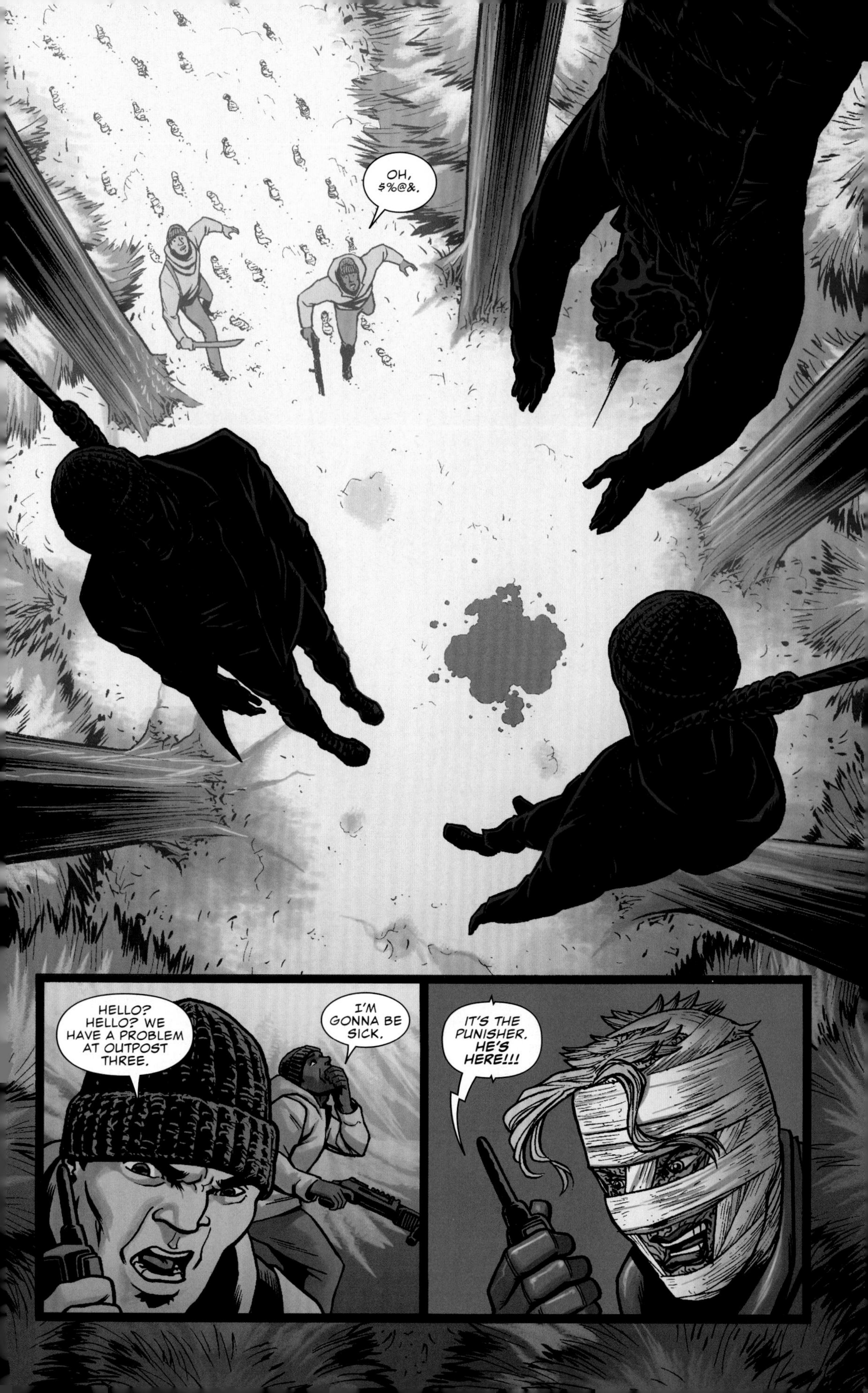
OH, $%@&.
HELLO? HELLO? WE HAVE A PROBLEM AT OUTPOST THREE.
I'M GONNA BE SICK.
IT'S THE PUNISHER. HE'S HERE!!!

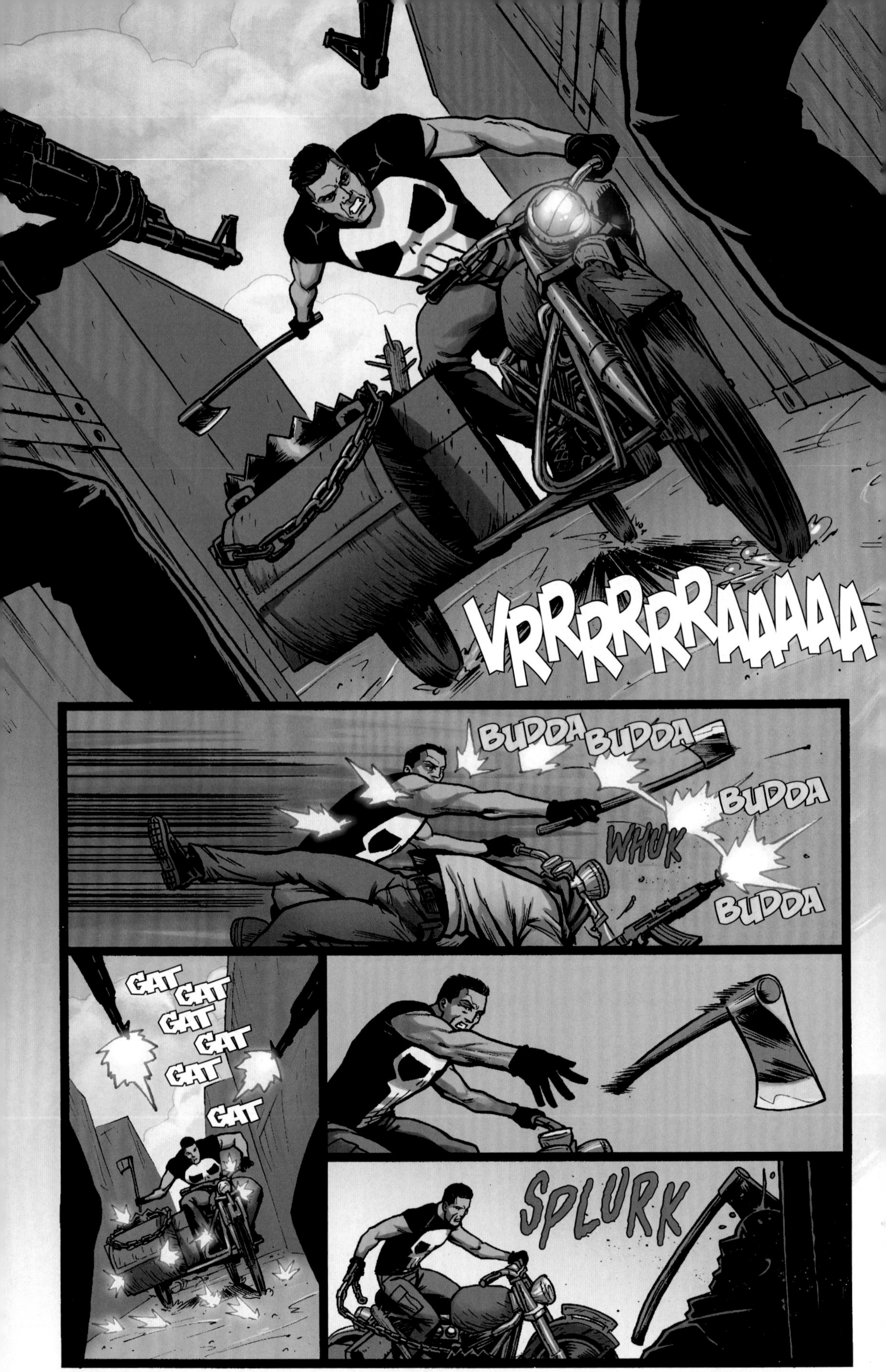
VRRRRRRAAAAAA
BUDDA BUDDA
BUDDA
WHUK
BUDDA
GAT GAT GAT GAT GAT GAT
SPLURK

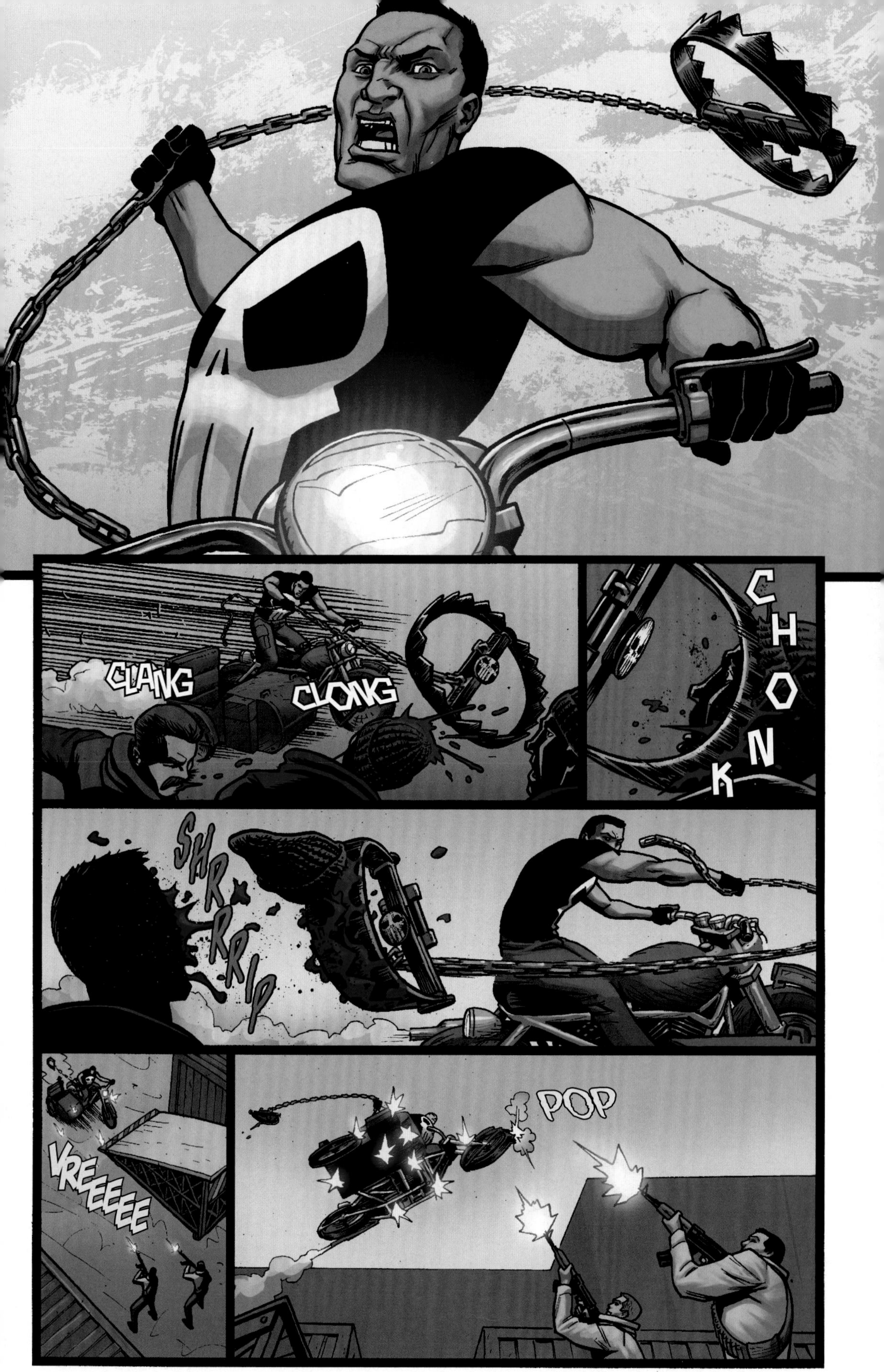
CLANG
CLONG
CHONK
SHRRRIP
VREEEEEE
POP

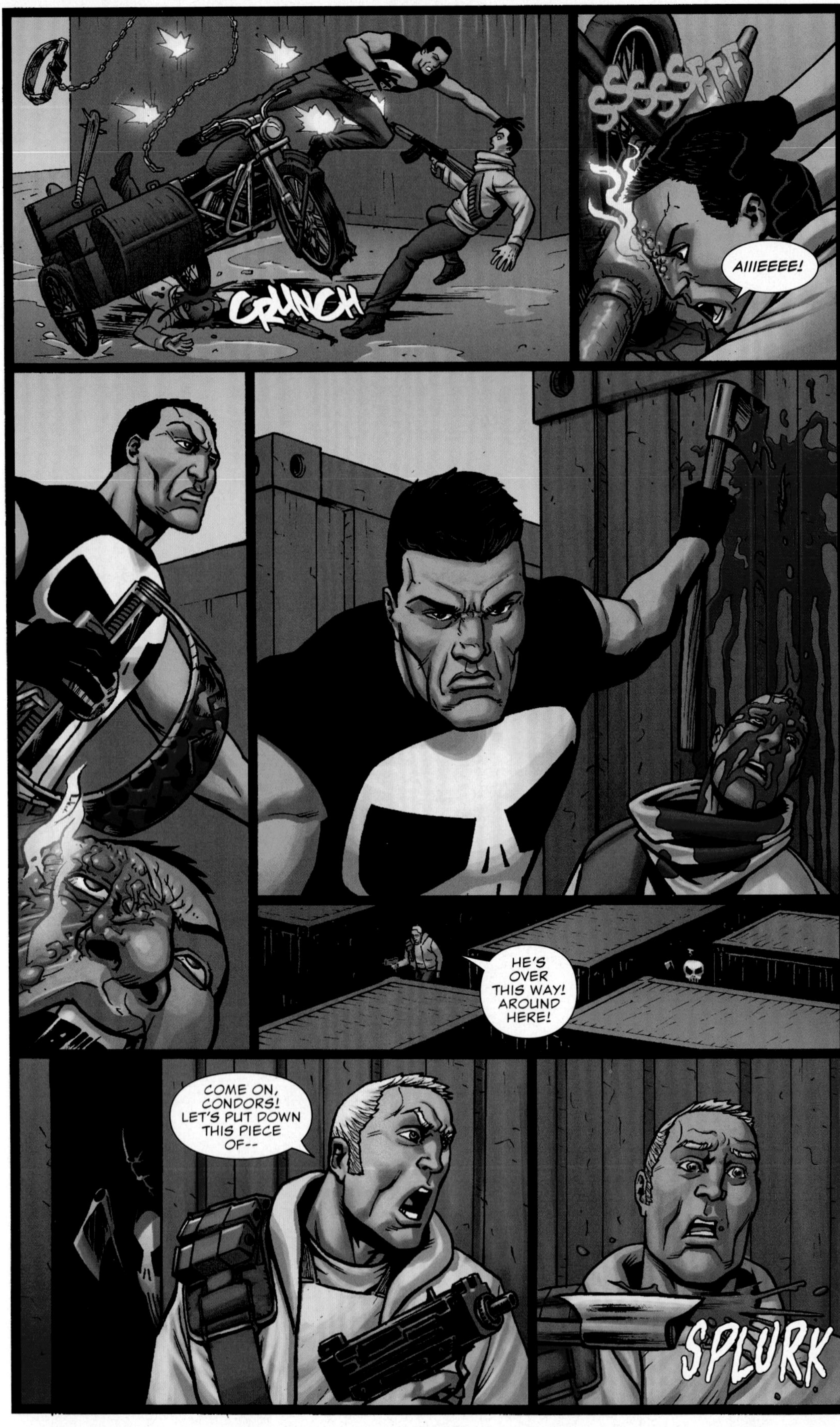
CRUNCH
SSSSSFFF
AIIIEEEE!
HE'S OVER THIS WAY! AROUND HERE!
COME ON, CONDORS! LET'S PUT DOWN THIS PIECE OF--
SPLURK

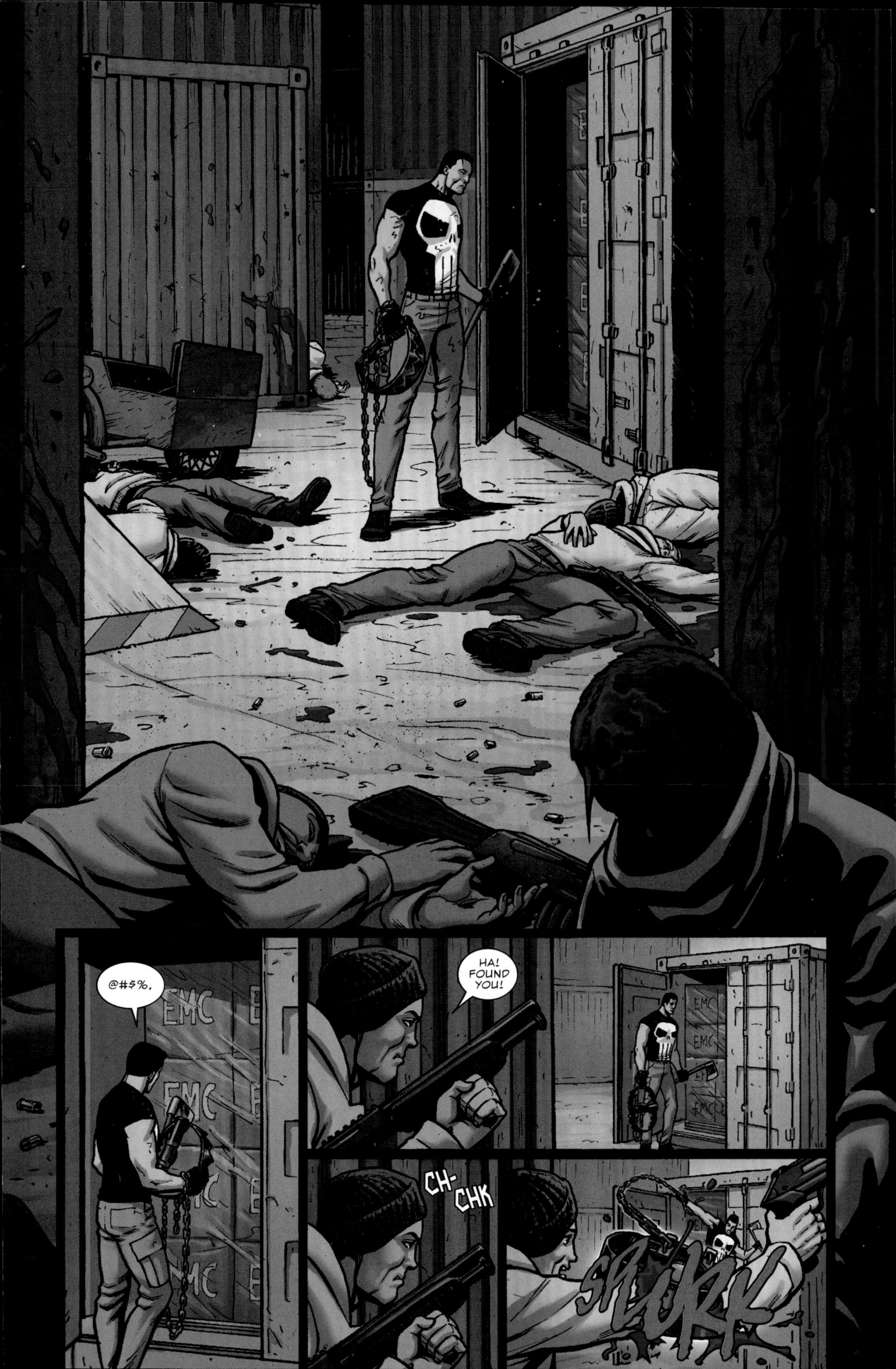
@#$%.
HA! FOUND YOU!
CH-CHK
SHUKK

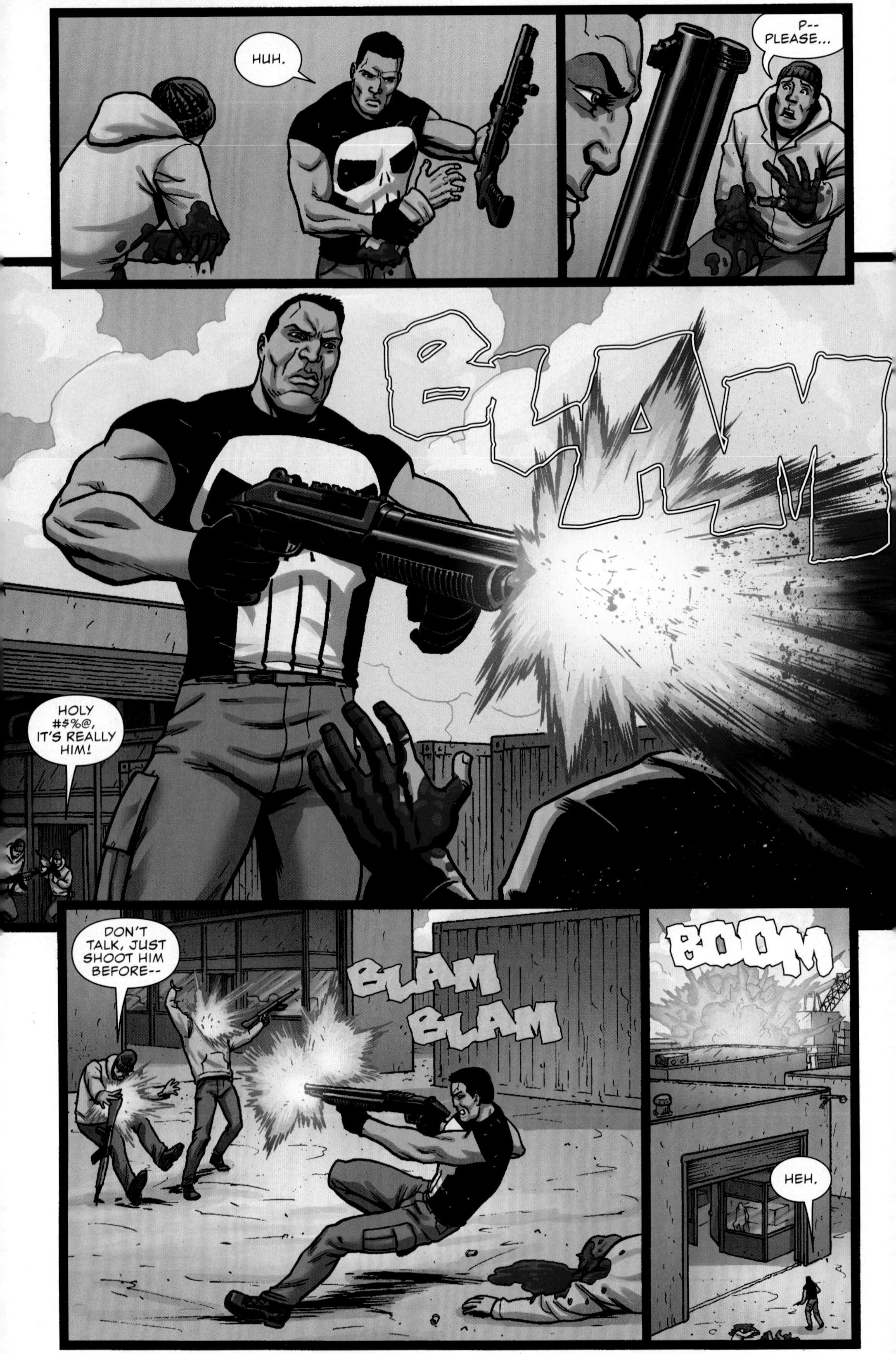
HUH.
P-- PLEASE...
BLAM
HOLY #$%@, IT'S REALLY HIM!
DON'T TALK, JUST SHOOT HIM BEFORE--
BLAM
BLAM
BOOM
HEH.

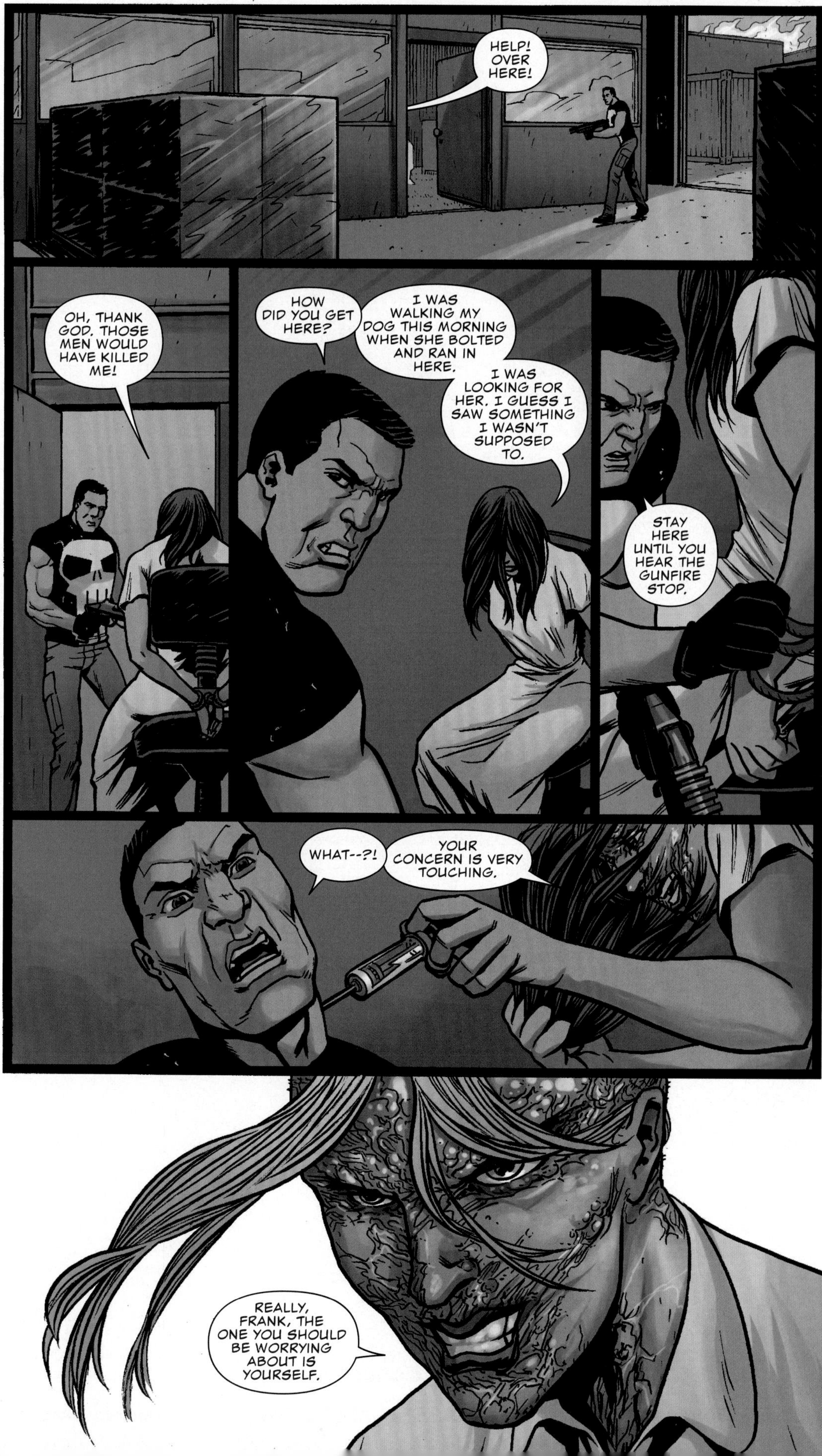
HELP! OVER HERE!
OH, THANK GOD. THOSE MEN WOULD HAVE KILLED ME!
HOW DID YOU GET HERE?
I WAS WALKING MY DOG THIS MORNING WHEN SHE BOLTED AND RAN IN HERE.
I WAS LOOKING FOR HER. I GUESS I SAW SOMETHING I WASN'T SUPPOSED TO.
STAY HERE UNTIL YOU HEAR THE GUNFIRE STOP.
WHAT--?!
YOUR CONCERN IS VERY TOUCHING.
REALLY, FRANK, THE ONE YOU SHOULD BE WORRYING ABOUT IS YOURSELF.

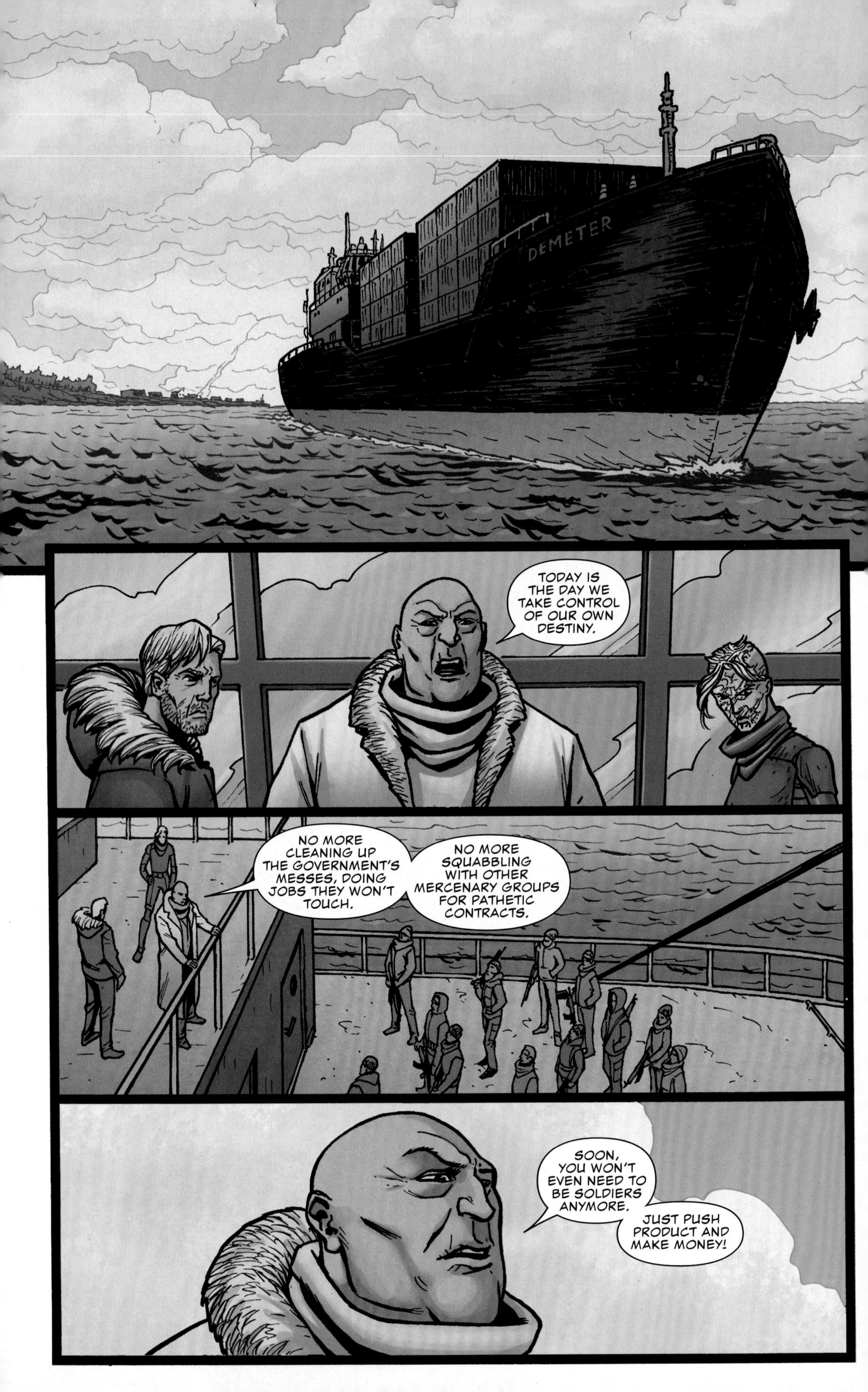
DEMETER
TODAY IS THE DAY WE TAKE CONTROL OF OUR OWN DESTINY.
NO MORE CLEANING UP THE GOVERNMENT'S MESSES, DOING JOBS THEY WON'T TOUCH.
NO MORE SQUABBLING WITH OTHER MERCENARY GROUPS FOR PATHETIC CONTRACTS.
SOON, YOU WON'T EVEN NEED TO BE SOLDIERS ANYMORE.
JUST PUSH PRODUCT AND MAKE MONEY!

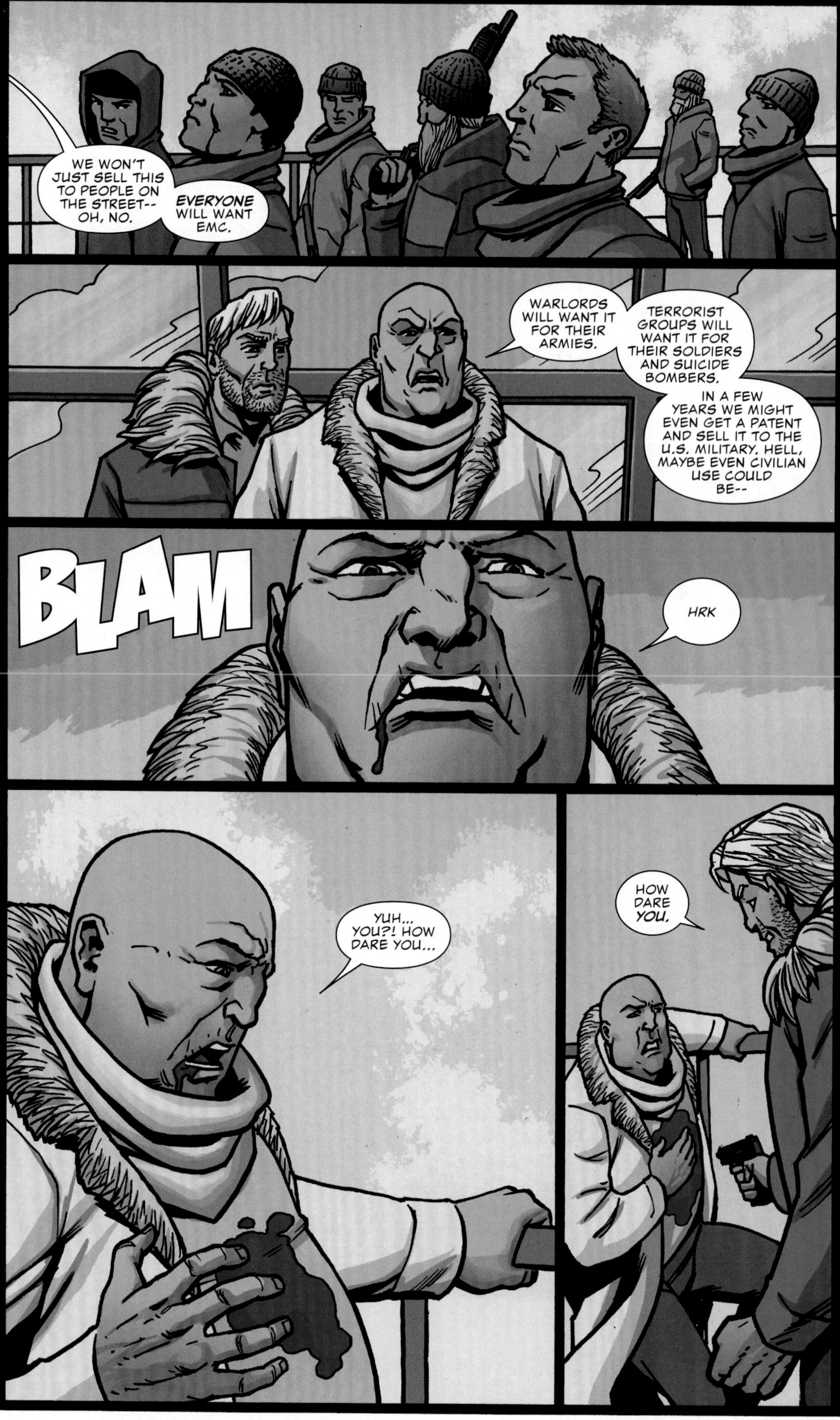
WE WON'T JUST SELL THIS TO PEOPLE ON THE STREET-- OH, NO.
EVERYONE WILL WANT EMC.
WARLORDS WILL WANT IT FOR THEIR ARMIES.
TERRORIST GROUPS WILL WANT IT FOR THEIR SOLDIERS AND SUICIDE BOMBERS.
IN A FEW YEARS WE MIGHT EVEN GET A PATENT AND SELL IT TO THE U.S. MILITARY. HELL, MAYBE EVEN CIVILIAN USE COULD BE--
BLAM
HRK
YUH... YOU?! HOW DARE YOU...
HOW DARE YOU.

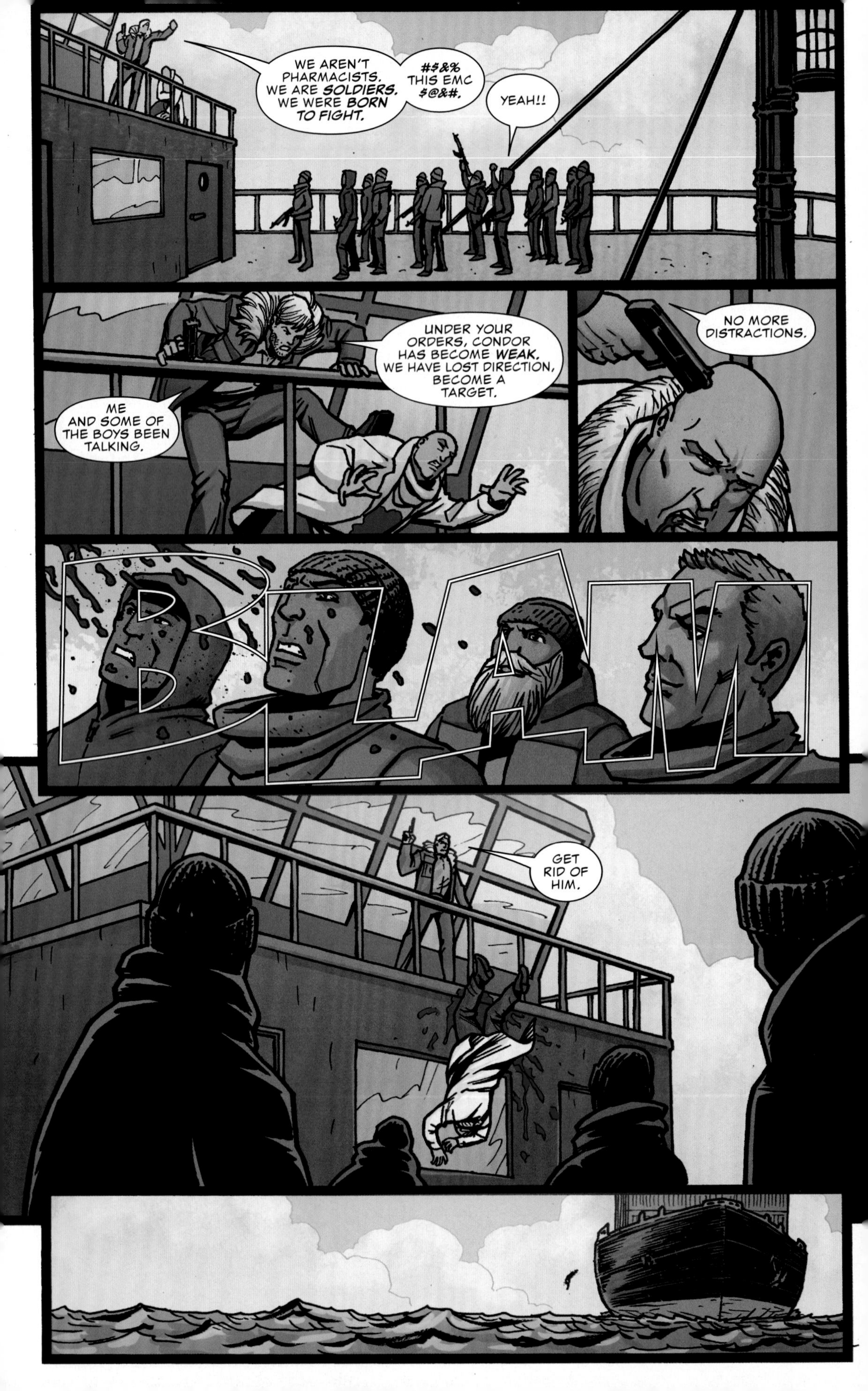
WE AREN'T PHARMACISTS. WE ARE SOLDIERS. WE WERE BORN TO FIGHT.
#$&% THIS EMC $@&#.
YEAH!!
ME AND SOME OF THE BOYS BEEN TALKING.
UNDER YOUR ORDERS, CONDOR HAS BECOME WEAK. WE HAVE LOST DIRECTION, BECOME A TARGET.
NO MORE DISTRACTIONS.
BLAM
GET RID OF HIM.

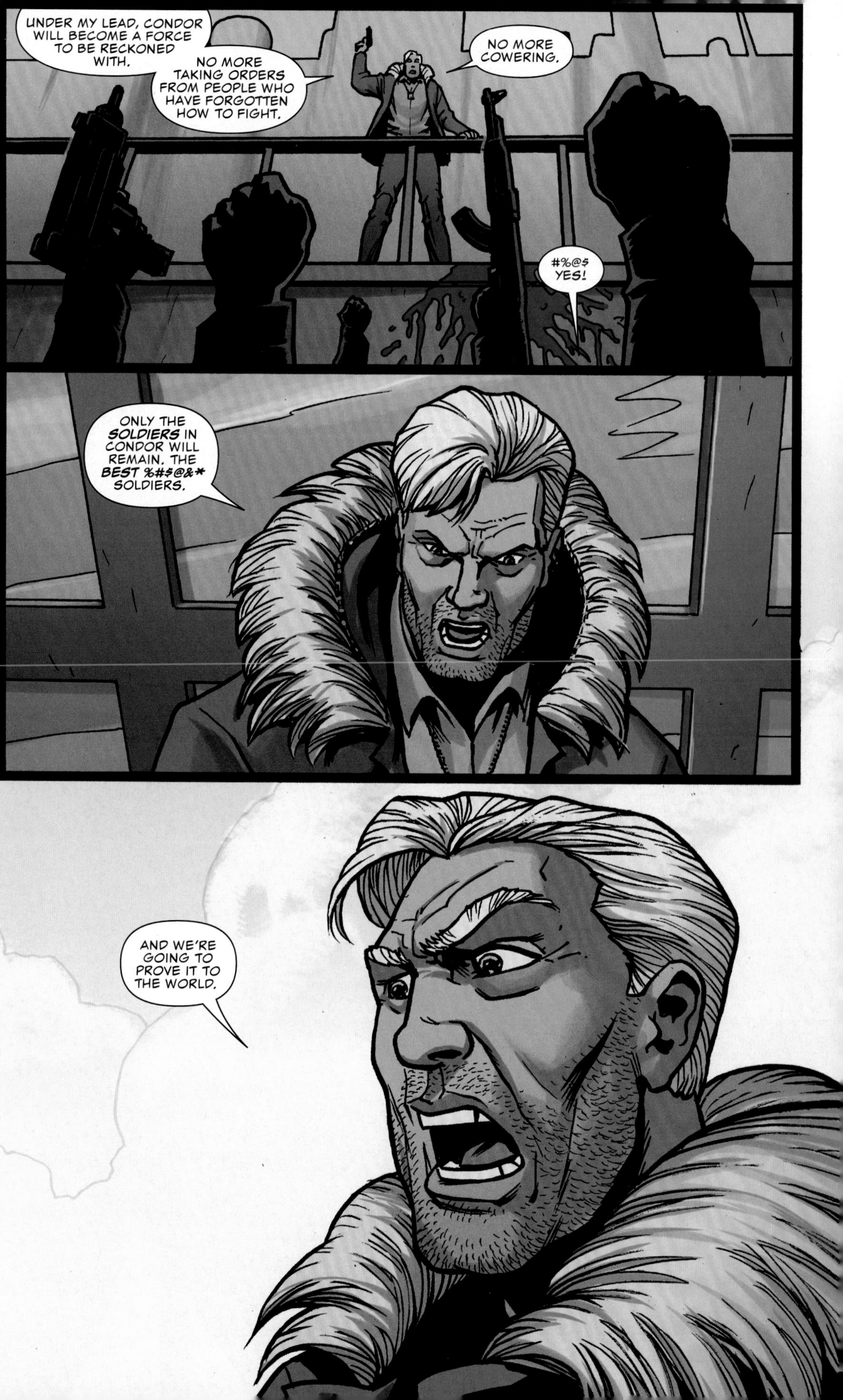
UNDER MY LEAD, CONDOR WILL BECOME A FORCE TO BE RECKONED WITH.
NO MORE TAKING ORDERS FROM PEOPLE WHO HAVE FORGOTTEN HOW TO FIGHT.
NO MORE COWERING.
#%@$ YES!
ONLY THE SOLDIERS IN CONDOR WILL REMAIN. THE BEST %#$@&* SOLDIERS.
AND WE'RE GOING TO PROVE IT TO THE WORLD.

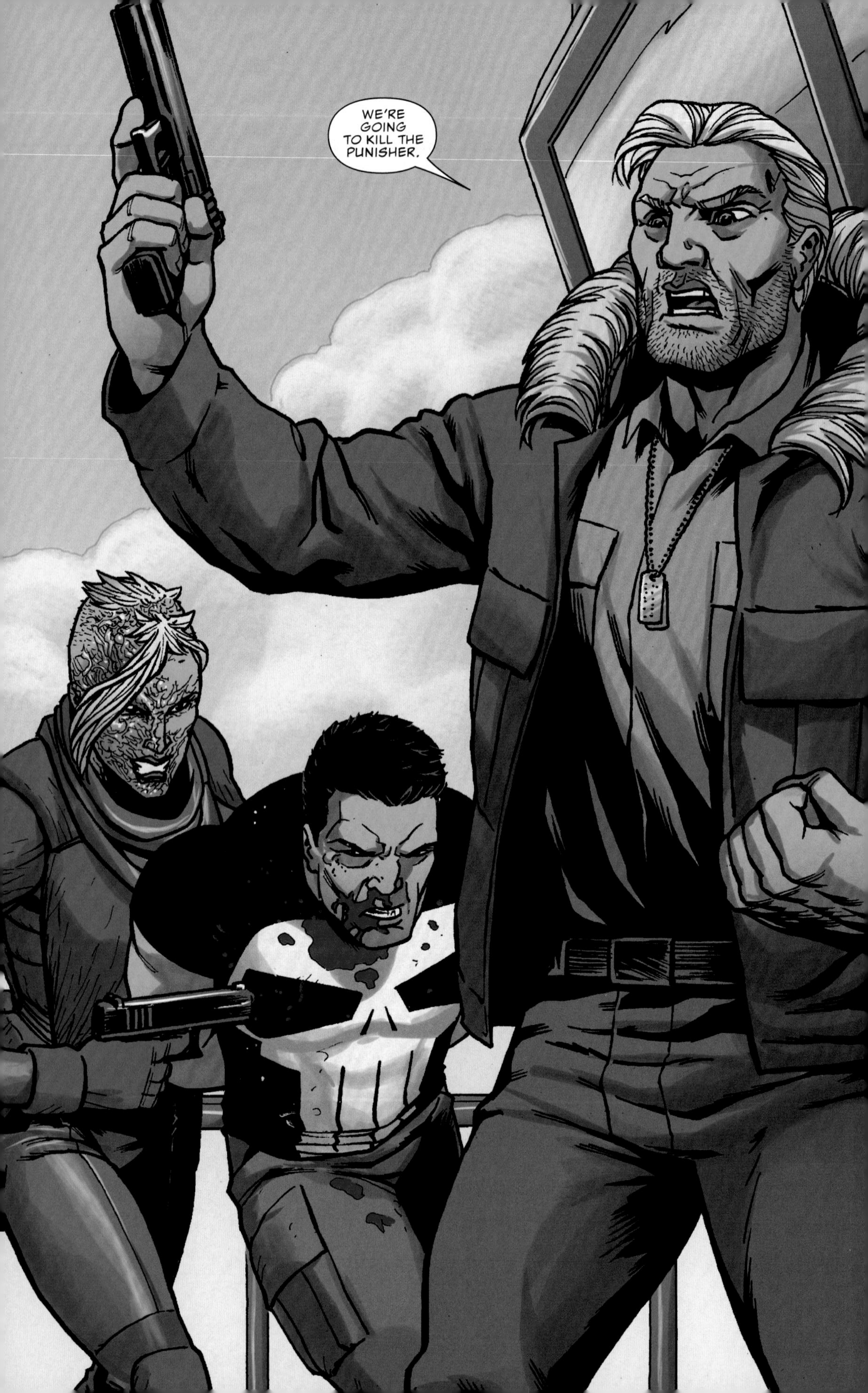
WE'RE GOING TO KILL THE PUNISHER.

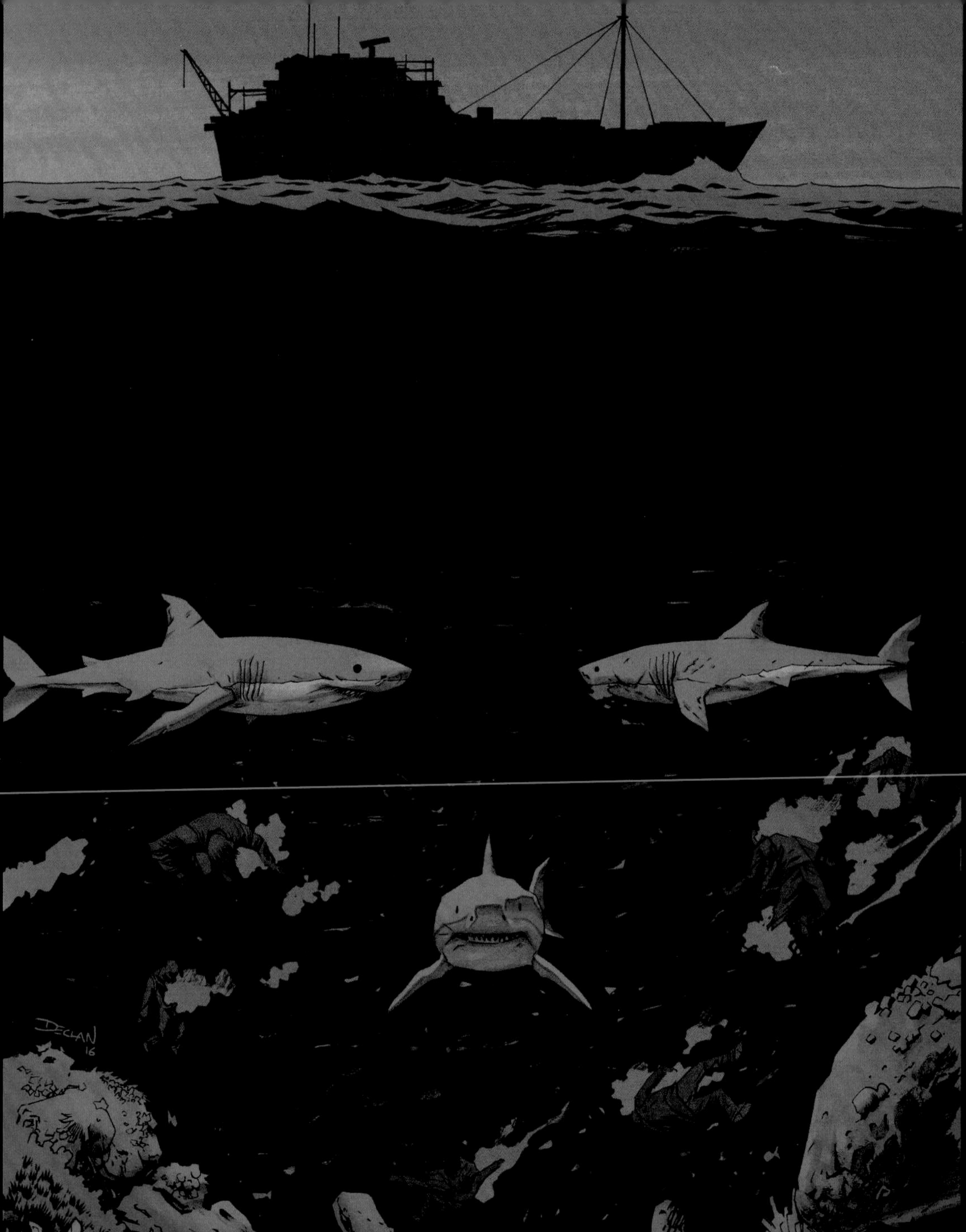
DECLAN
'16

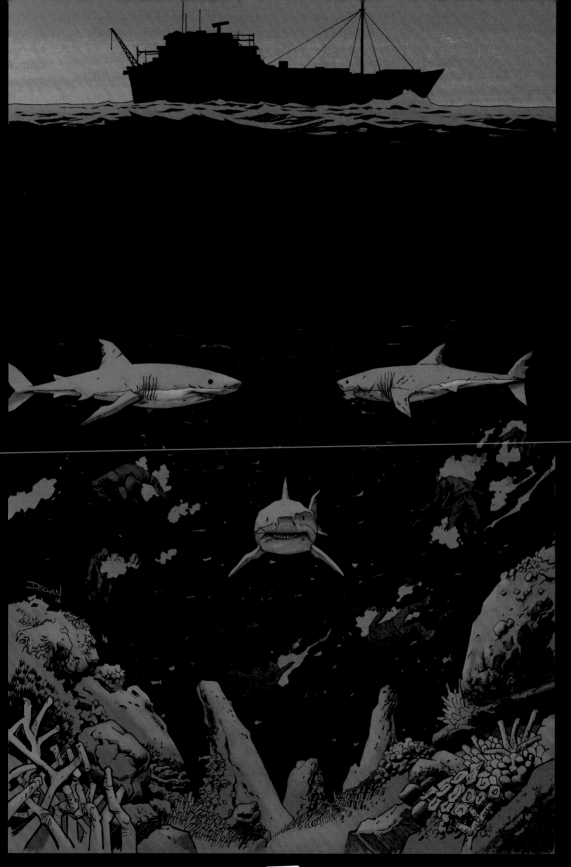

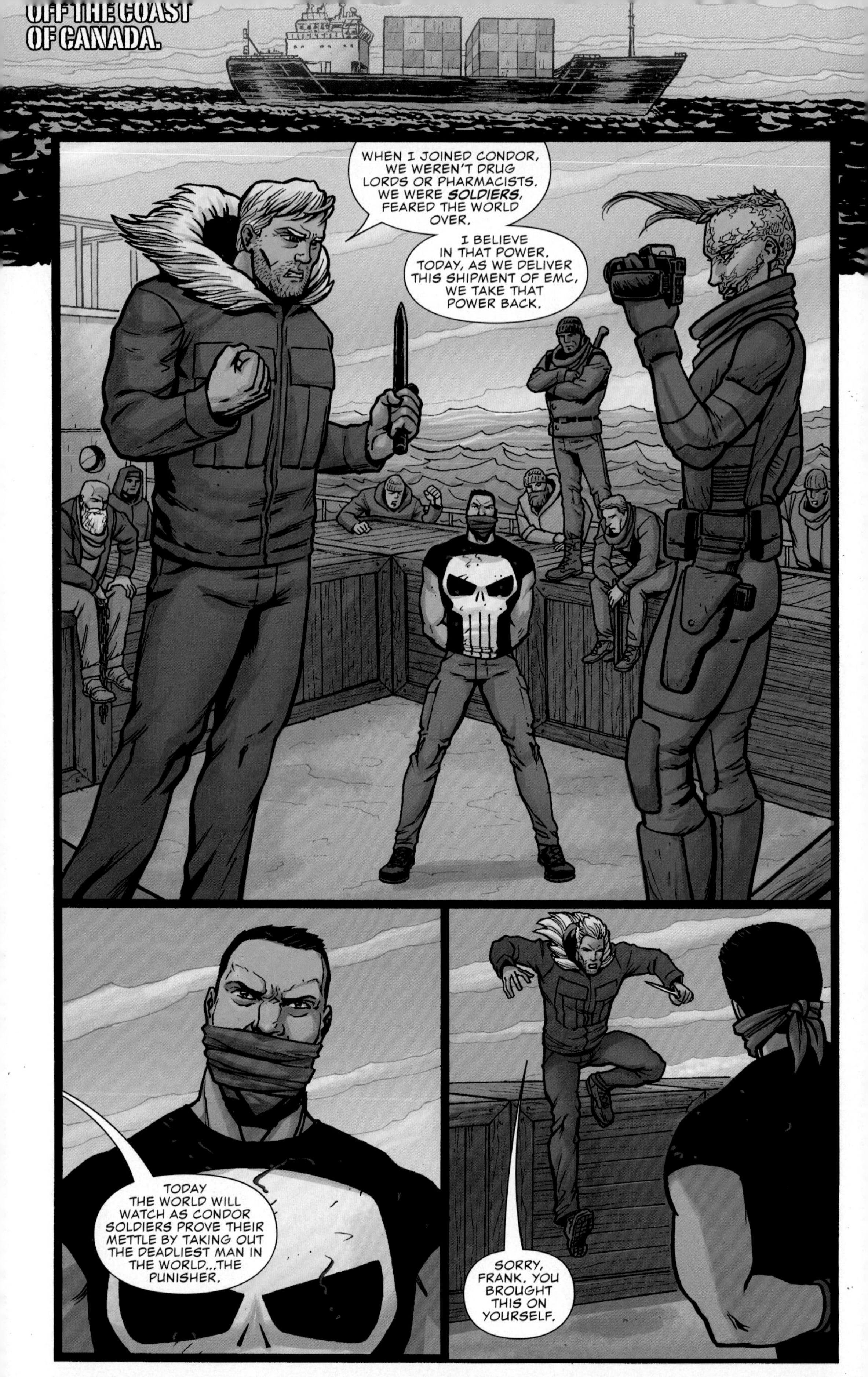
OFF THE COAST OF CANADA.
WHEN I JOINED CONDOR, WE WEREN'T DRUG LORDS OR PHARMACISTS. WE WERE SOLDIERS, FEARED THE WORLD OVER.
I BELIEVE IN THAT POWER. TODAY, AS WE DELIVER THIS SHIPMENT OF EMC, WE TAKE THAT POWER BACK.
TODAY THE WORLD WILL WATCH AS CONDOR SOLDIERS PROVE THEIR METTLE BY TAKING OUT THE DEADLIEST MAN IN THE WORLD...THE PUNISHER.
SORRY, FRANK. YOU BROUGHT THIS ON YOURSELF.

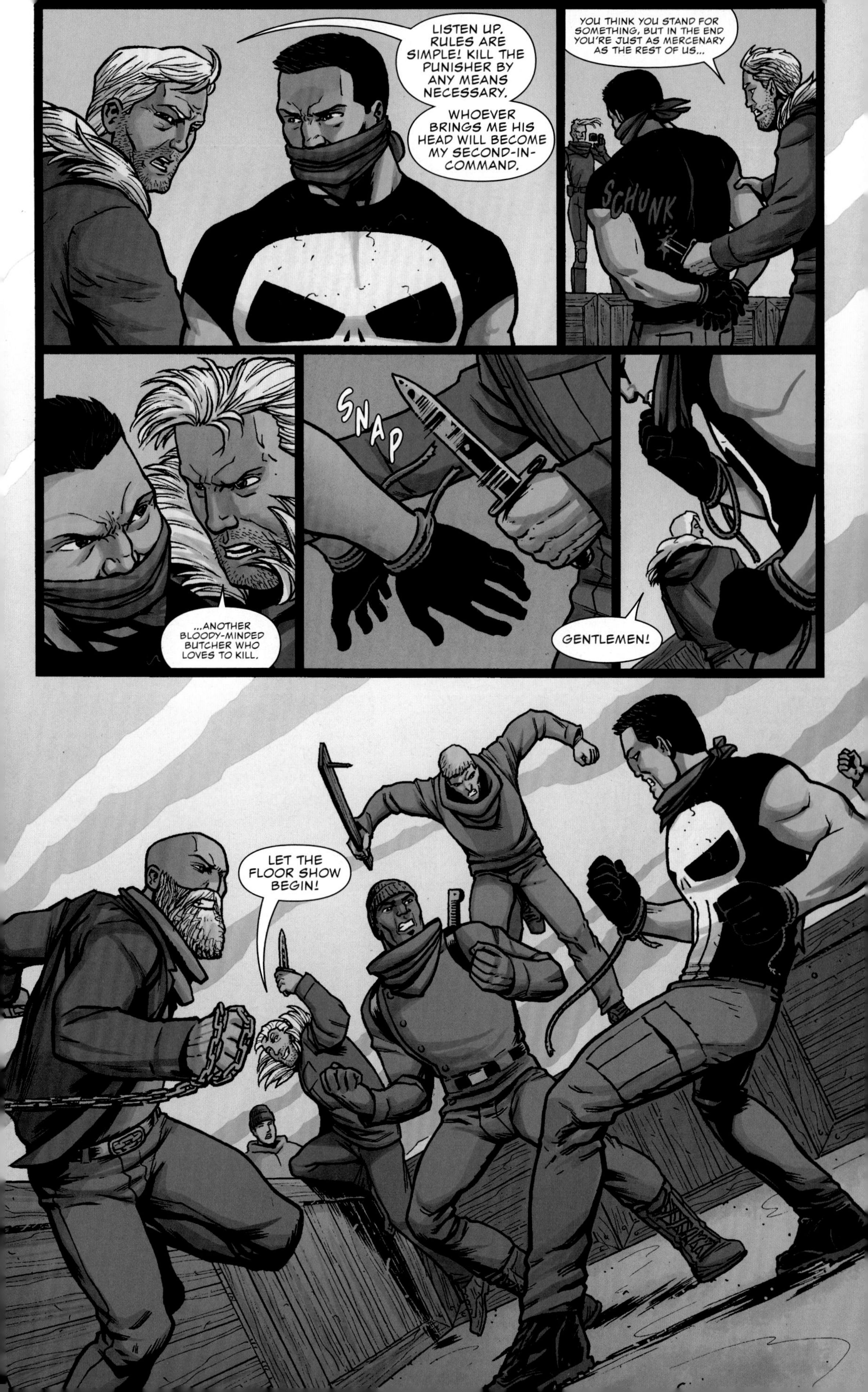
LISTEN UP. RULES ARE SIMPLE! KILL THE PUNISHER BY ANY MEANS NECESSARY.
WHOEVER BRINGS ME HIS HEAD WILL BECOME MY SECOND-IN-COMMAND.
YOU THINK YOU STAND FOR SOMETHING, BUT IN THE END YOU'RE JUST AS MERCENARY AS THE REST OF US...
SCHUNK
...ANOTHER BLOODY-MINDED BUTCHER WHO LOVES TO KILL.
SNAP
GENTLEMEN!
LET THE FLOOR SHOW BEGIN!

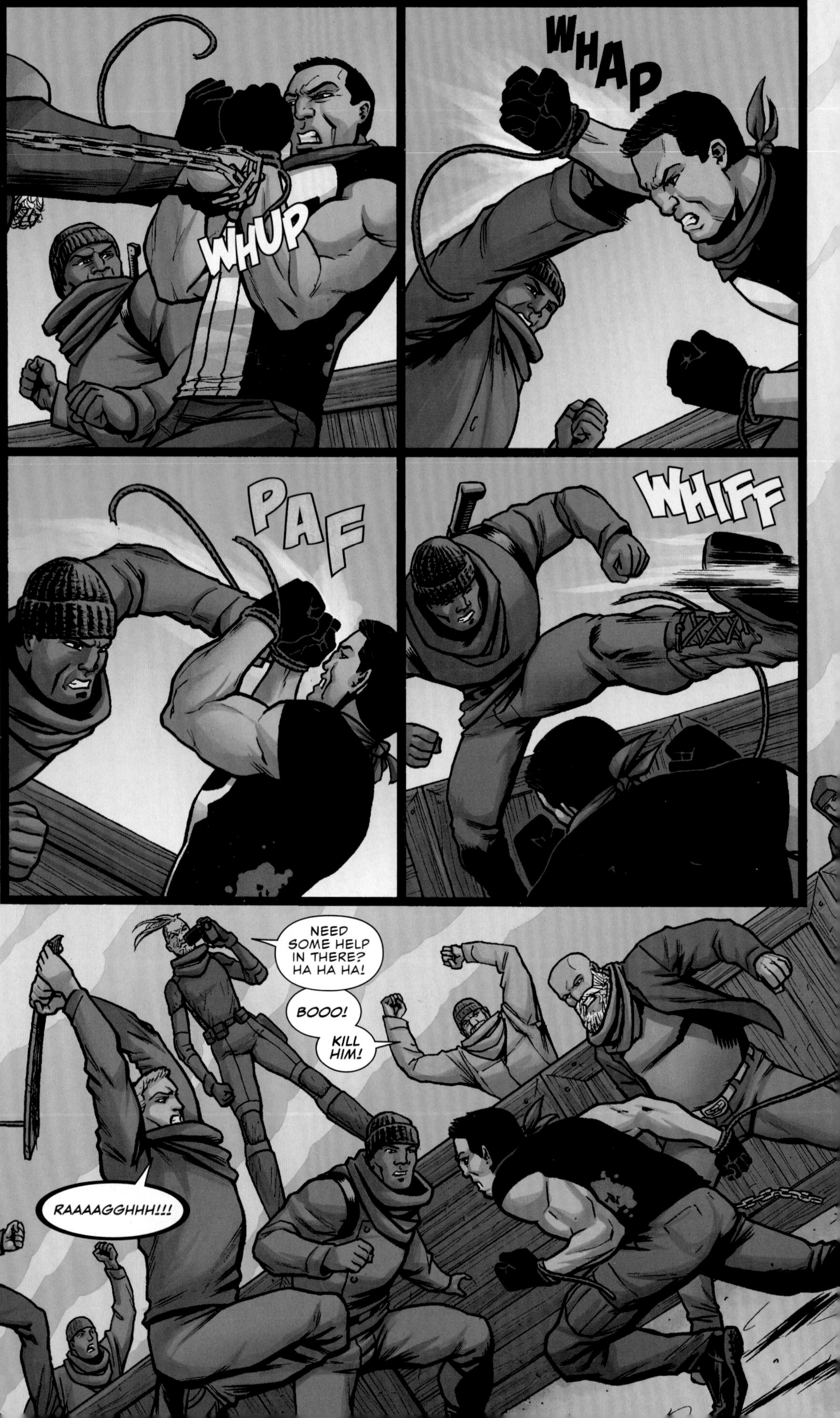
WHUP
WHAP
PAF
WHIFF
NEED SOME HELP IN THERE? HA HA HA!
BOOO!
KILL HIM!
RAAAAGGHHH!!!

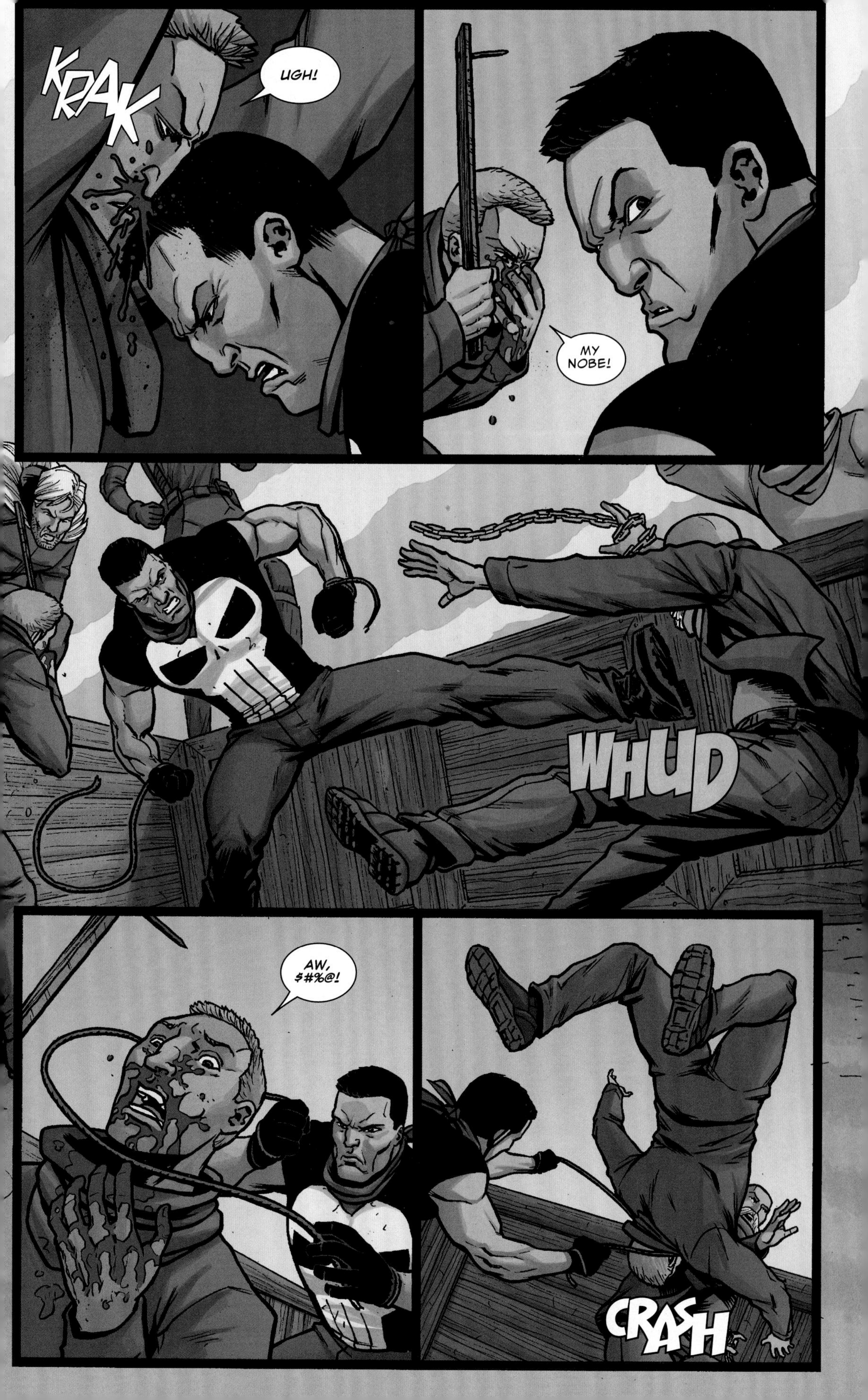
KRAK
UGH!
MY NOBE!
WHUD
AW, $#%@!
CRASH

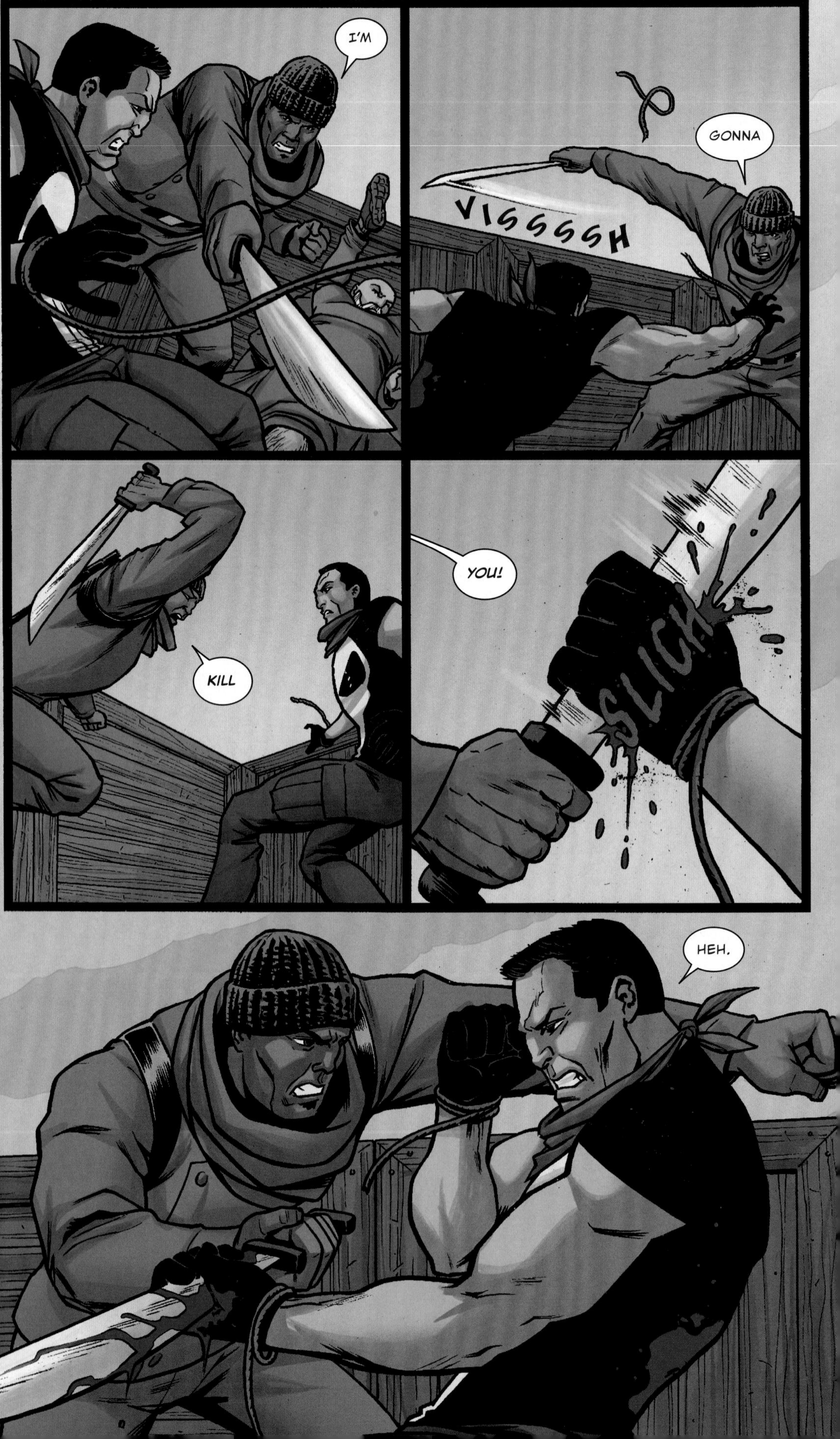
I'M
GONNA
VISSSSSH
KILL
YOU!
SLICK
HEH.

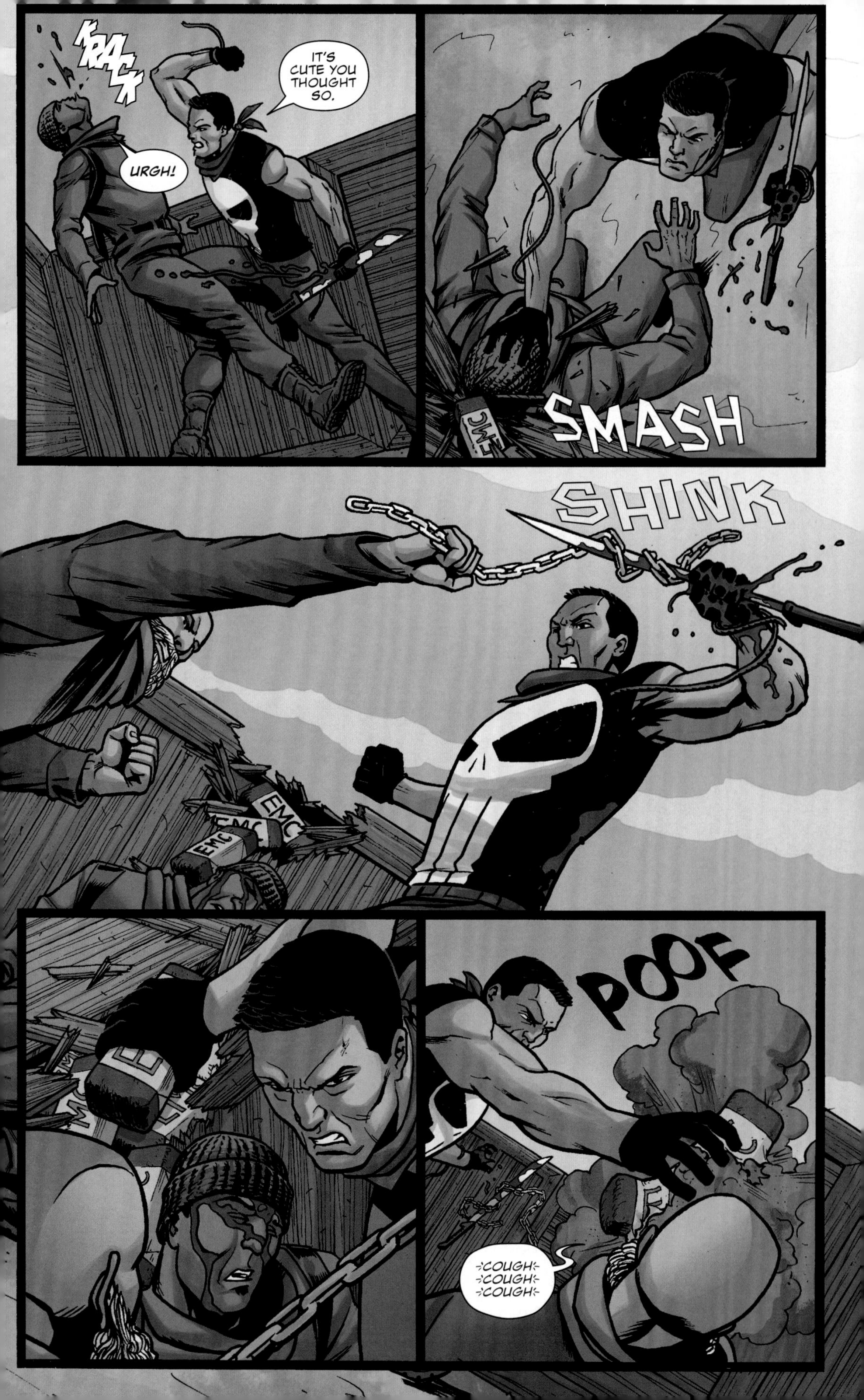
KRACK
IT'S CUTE YOU THOUGHT SO.
URGH!
SMASH
EMC
SHINK
EMC
EMC
EMC
POOF
COUGH COUGH COUGH

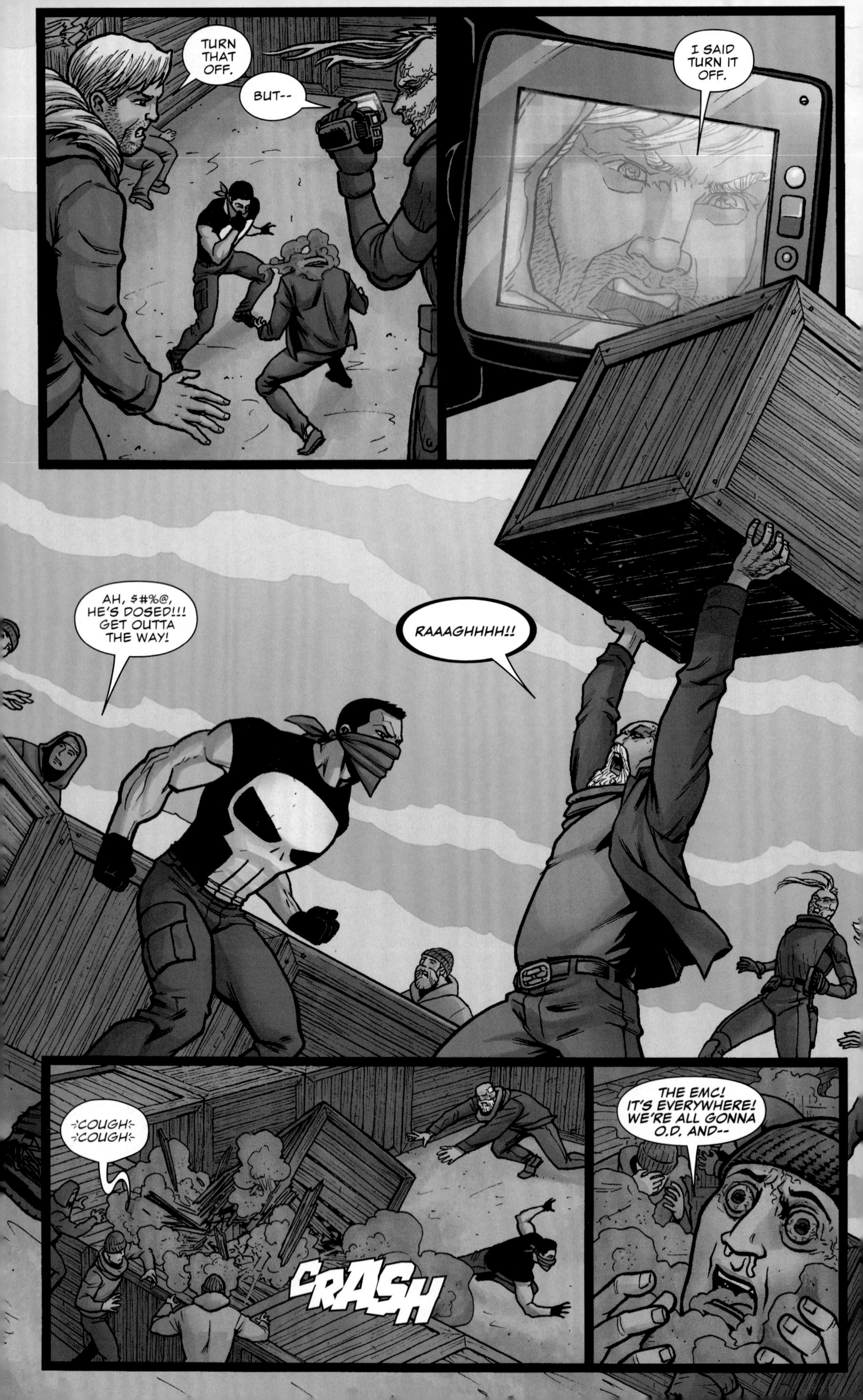
TURN THAT OFF.
BUT--
I SAID TURN IT OFF.
AH, $#%@, HE'S DOSED!!! GET OUTTA THE WAY!
RAAAGHHHH!!
COUGH COUGH
CRASH
THE EMC! IT'S EVERYWHERE! WE'RE ALL GONNA O.D. AND--

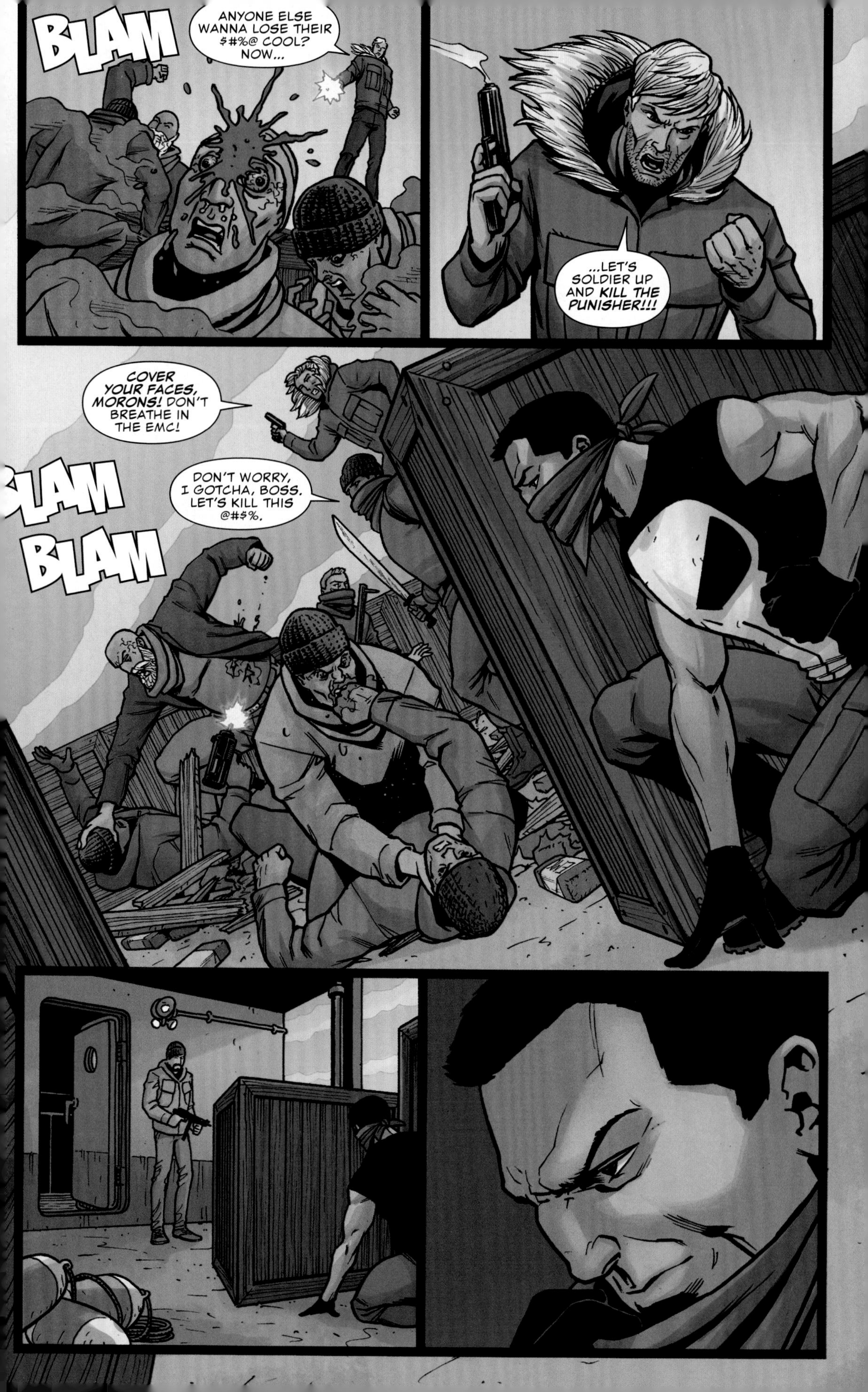
BLAM
ANYONE ELSE WANNA LOSE THEIR $#%@ COOL? NOW...
...LET'S SOLDIER UP AND KILL THE PUNISHER!!!
COVER YOUR FACES, MORONS! DON'T BREATHE IN THE EMC!
BLAM
DON'T WORRY, I GOTCHA, BOSS. LET'S KILL THIS @#$%.
BLAM

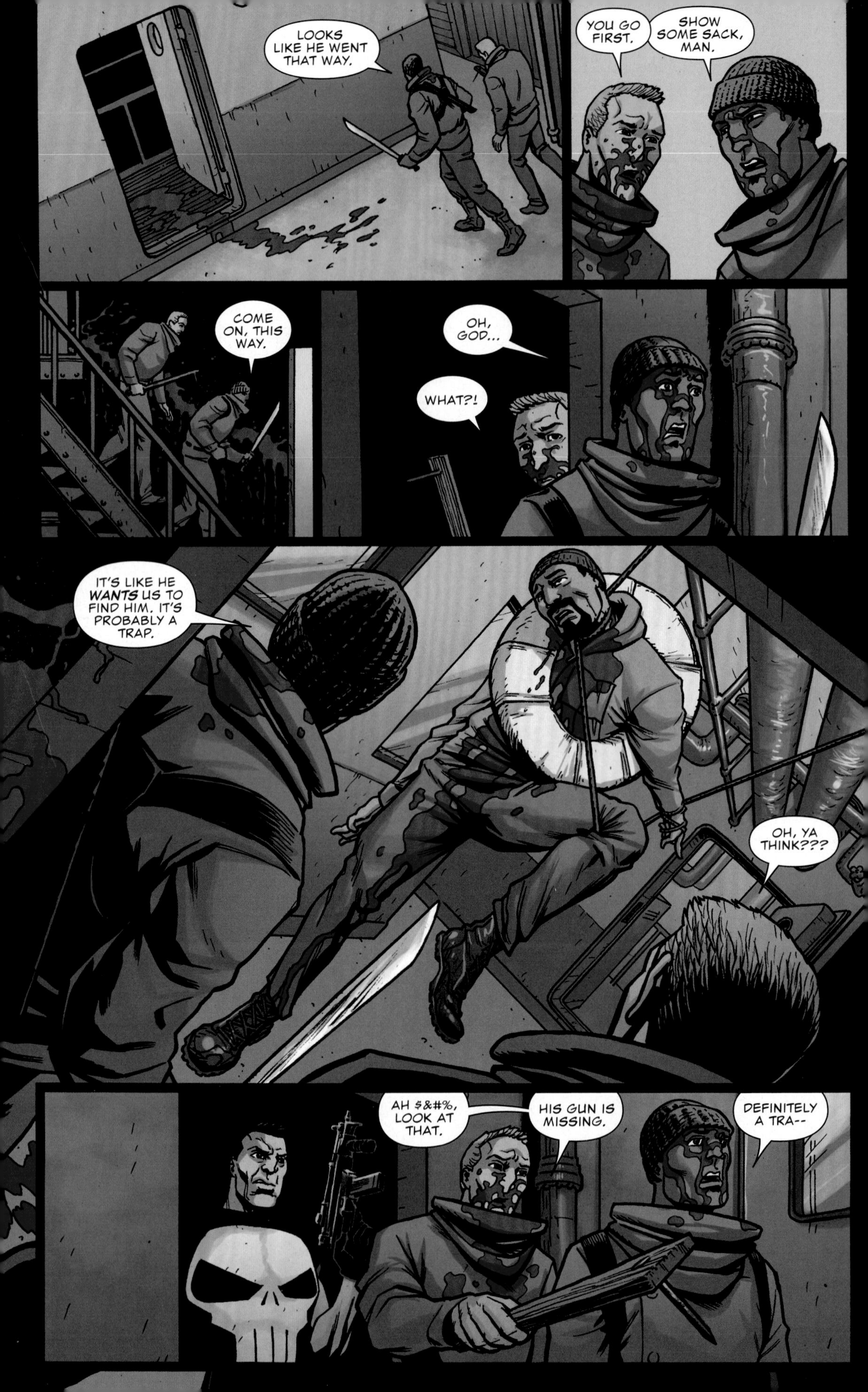
LOOKS LIKE HE WENT THAT WAY.
YOU GO FIRST.
SHOW SOME SACK, MAN.
COME ON, THIS WAY.
OH, GOD...
WHAT?!
IT'S LIKE HE *WANTS* US TO FIND HIM. IT'S PROBABLY A TRAP.
OH, YA THINK???
AH $&#%, LOOK AT THAT.
HIS GUN IS MISSING.
DEFINITELY A TRA--

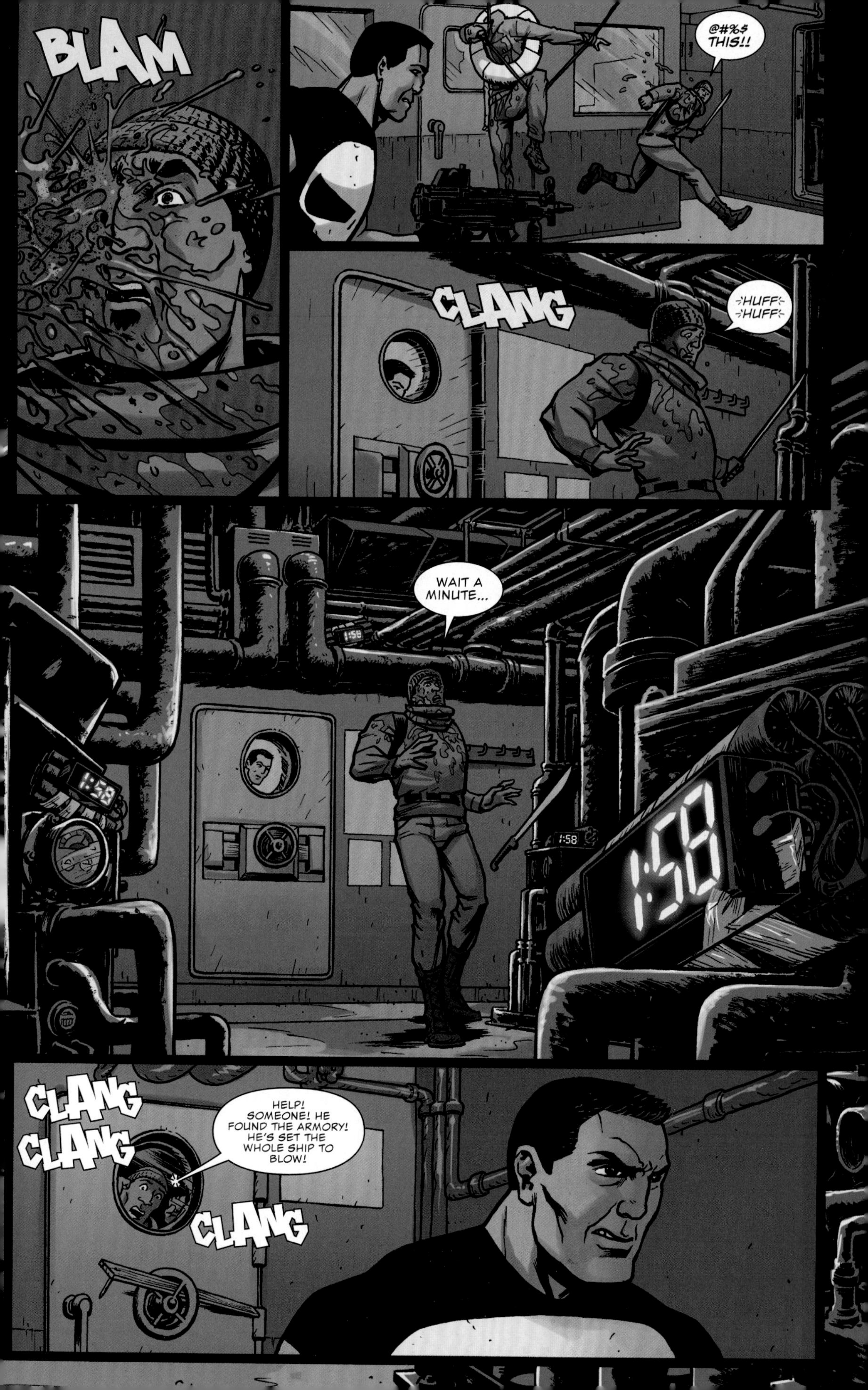
BLAM
@#%$ THIS!!
CLANG
HUFF HUFF
WAIT A MINUTE...
1:58
CLANG
CLANG
HELP! SOMEONE! HE FOUND THE ARMORY! HE'S SET THE WHOLE SHIP TO BLOW!
CLANG

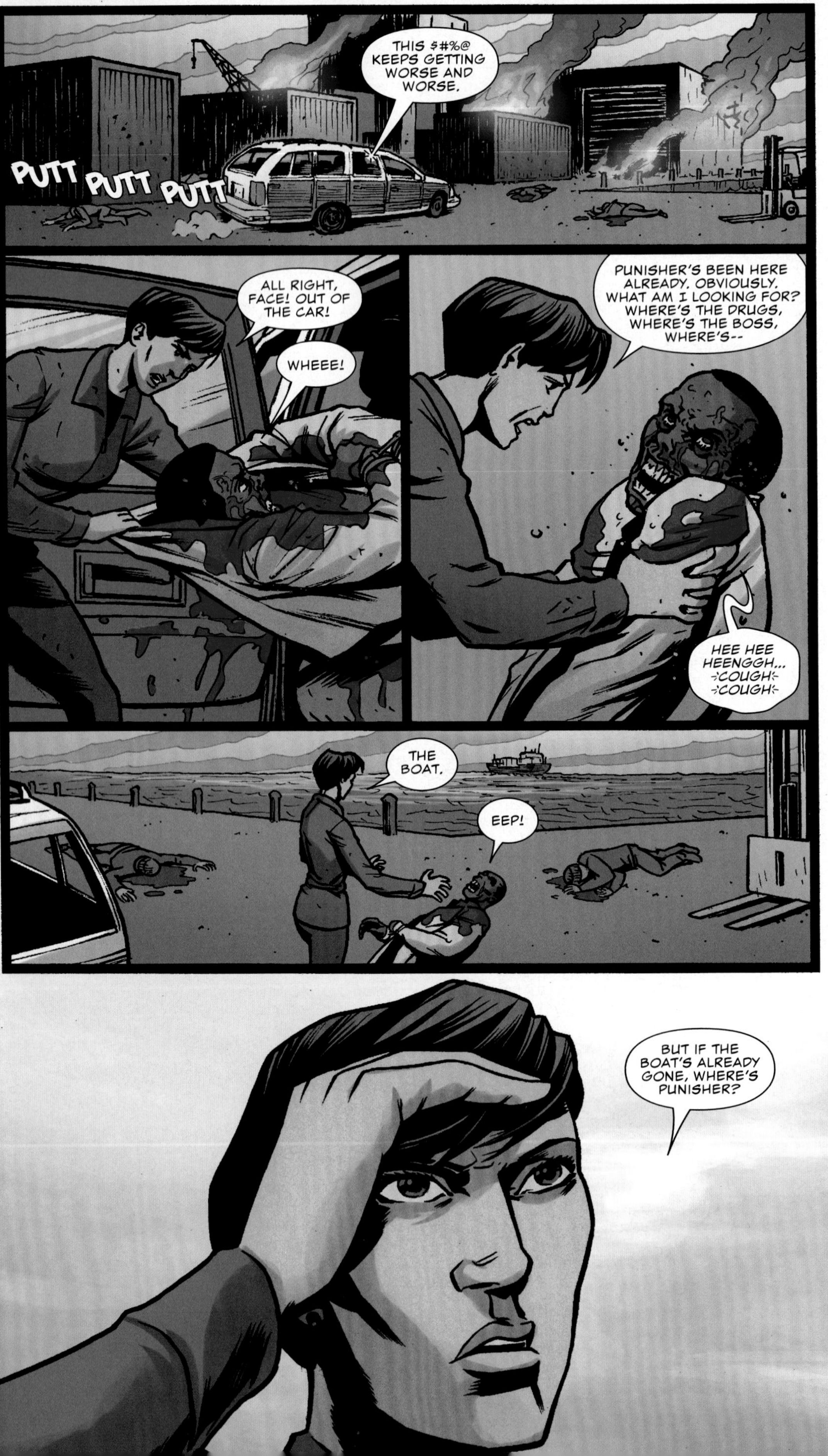

THIS $#%@ KEEPS GETTING WORSE AND WORSE.
PUTT PUTT PUTT
ALL RIGHT, FACE! OUT OF THE CAR!
WHEEE!
PUNISHER'S BEEN HERE ALREADY, OBVIOUSLY. WHAT AM I LOOKING FOR? WHERE'S THE DRUGS, WHERE'S THE BOSS, WHERE'S--
HEE HEE HEENGGH... *COUGH* *COUGH*
THE BOAT.
EEP!
BUT IF THE BOAT'S ALREADY GONE, WHERE'S PUNISHER?

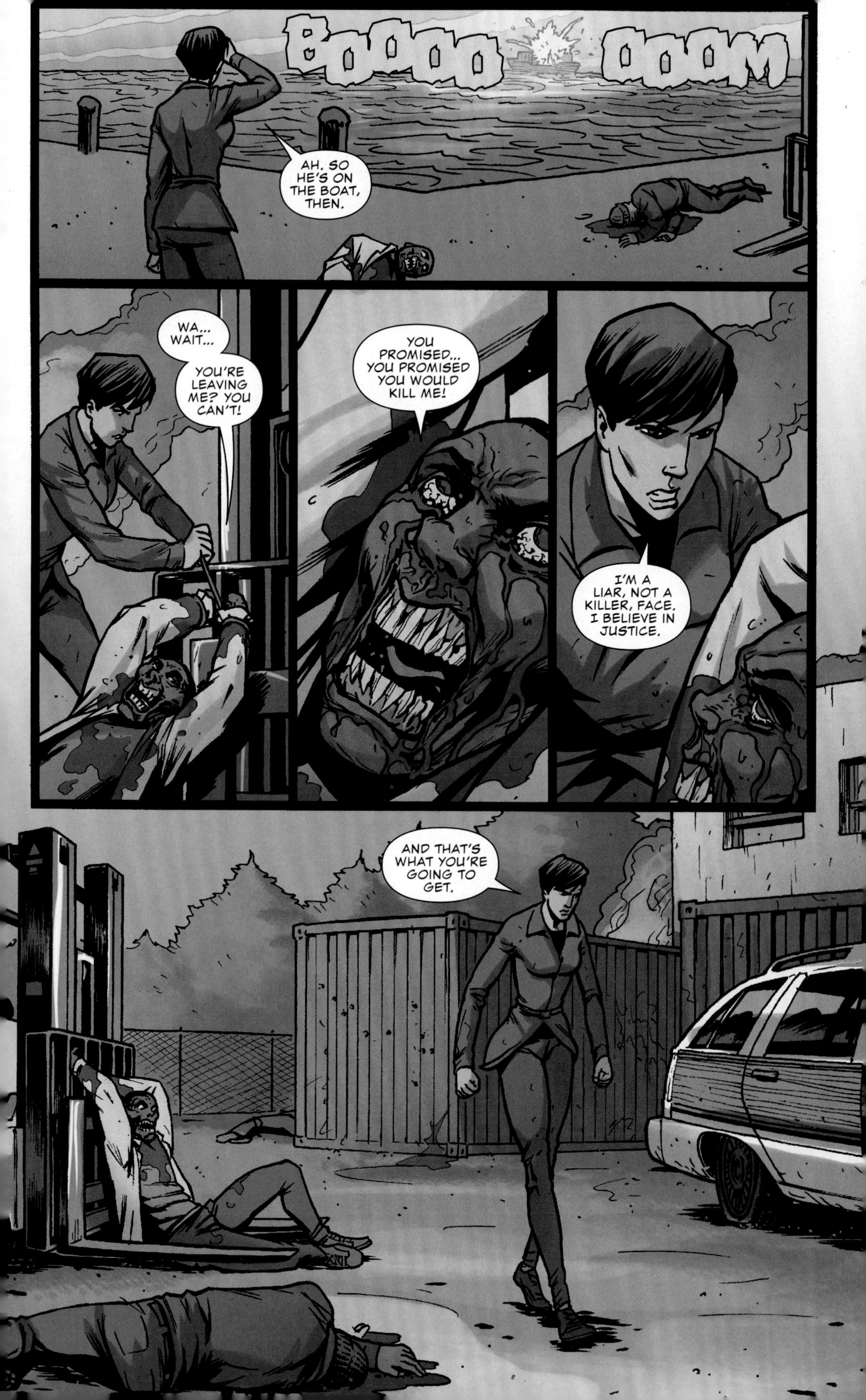
BOOOO OOOM
AH. SO HE'S ON THE BOAT, THEN.
WA... WAIT...
YOU'RE LEAVING ME? YOU CAN'T!
YOU PROMISED... YOU PROMISED YOU WOULD KILL ME!
I'M A LIAR, NOT A KILLER, FACE. I BELIEVE IN JUSTICE.
AND THAT'S WHAT YOU'RE GOING TO GET.

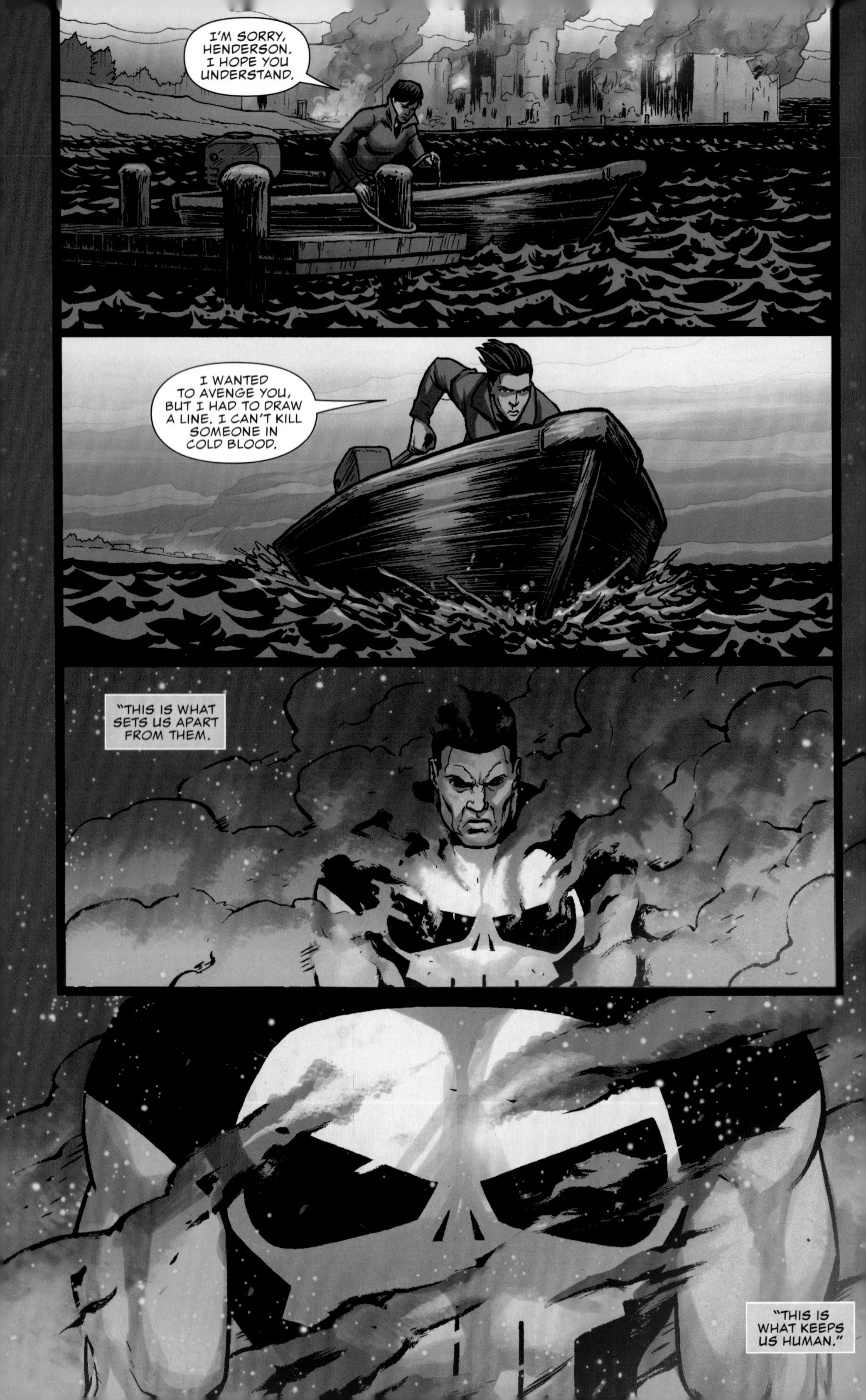
I'M SORRY, HENDERSON. I HOPE YOU UNDERSTAND.
I WANTED TO AVENGE YOU, BUT I HAD TO DRAW A LINE. I CAN'T KILL SOMEONE IN COLD BLOOD.
"THIS IS WHAT SETS US APART FROM THEM.
"THIS IS WHAT KEEPS US HUMAN."

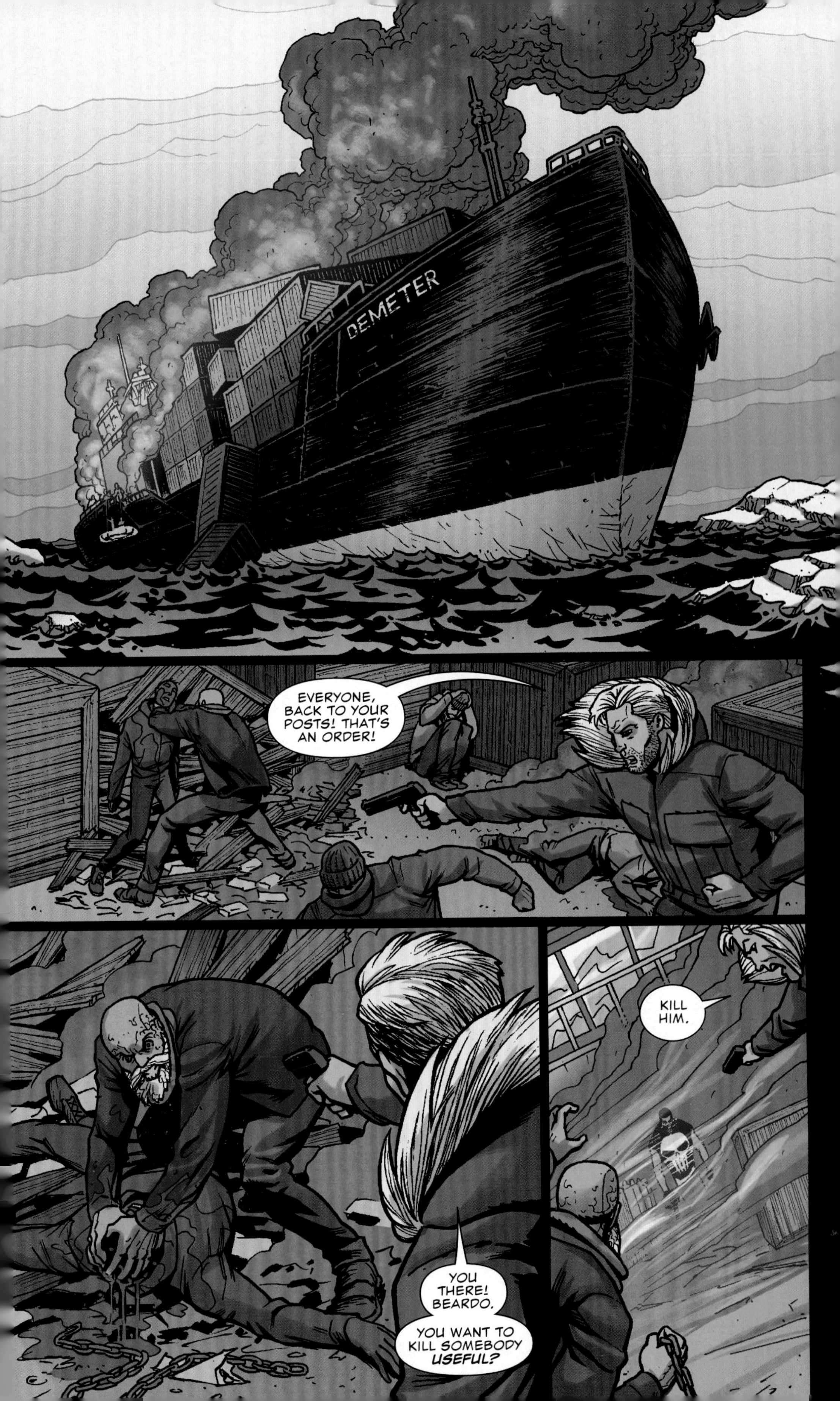
DEMETER
EVERYONE, BACK TO YOUR POSTS! THAT'S AN ORDER!
KILL HIM.
YOU THERE! BEARDO.
YOU WANT TO KILL SOMEBODY *USEFUL?*

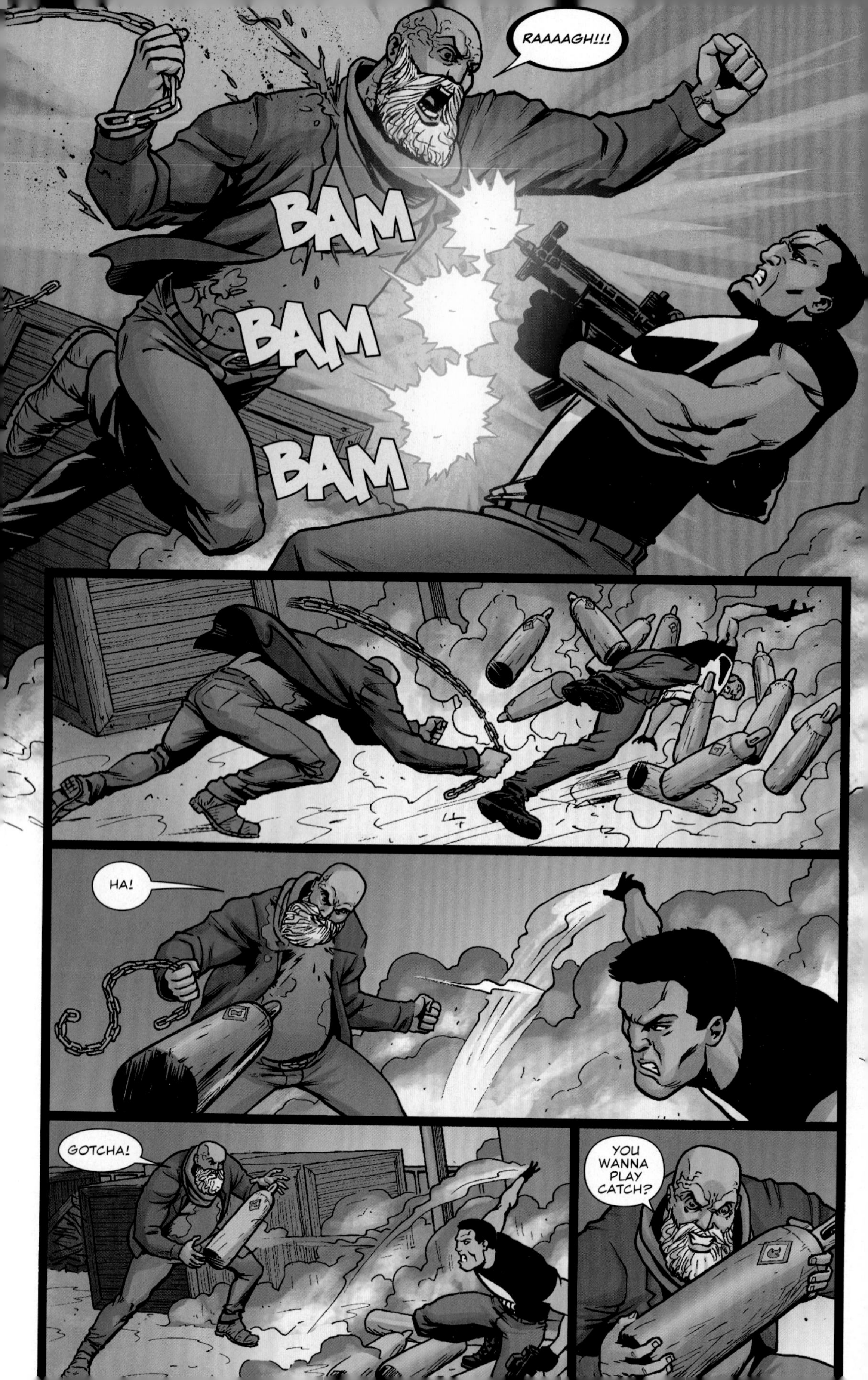
RAAAAGH!!!
BAM
BAM
BAM
HA!
GOTCHA!
YOU WANNA PLAY CATCH?

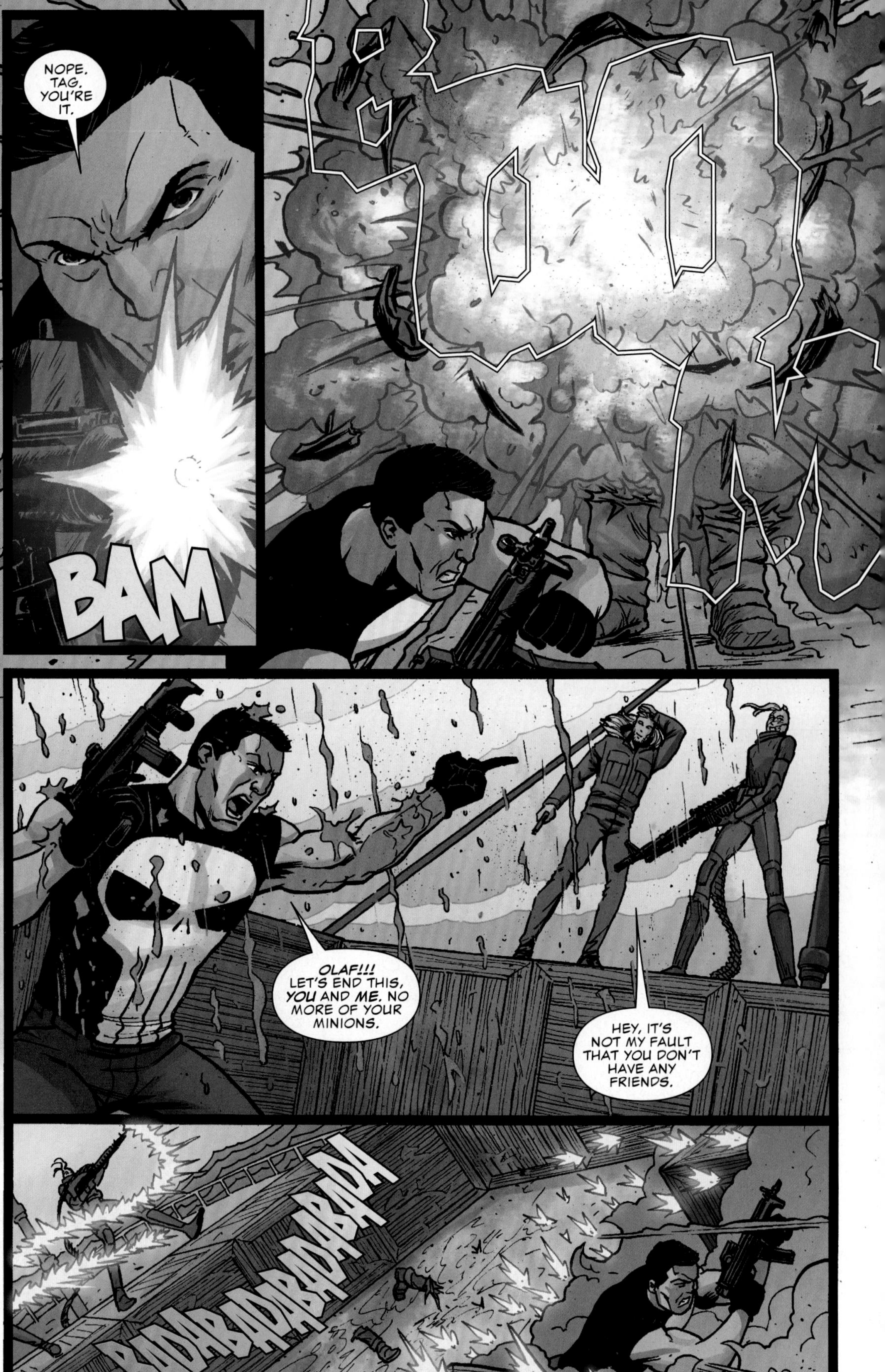
NOPE. TAG. YOU'RE IT.
BAM
OLAF!!! LET'S END THIS, *YOU* AND *ME*. NO MORE OF YOUR MINIONS.
HEY, IT'S NOT MY FAULT THAT YOU DON'T HAVE ANY FRIENDS.
BADABADABADABADA

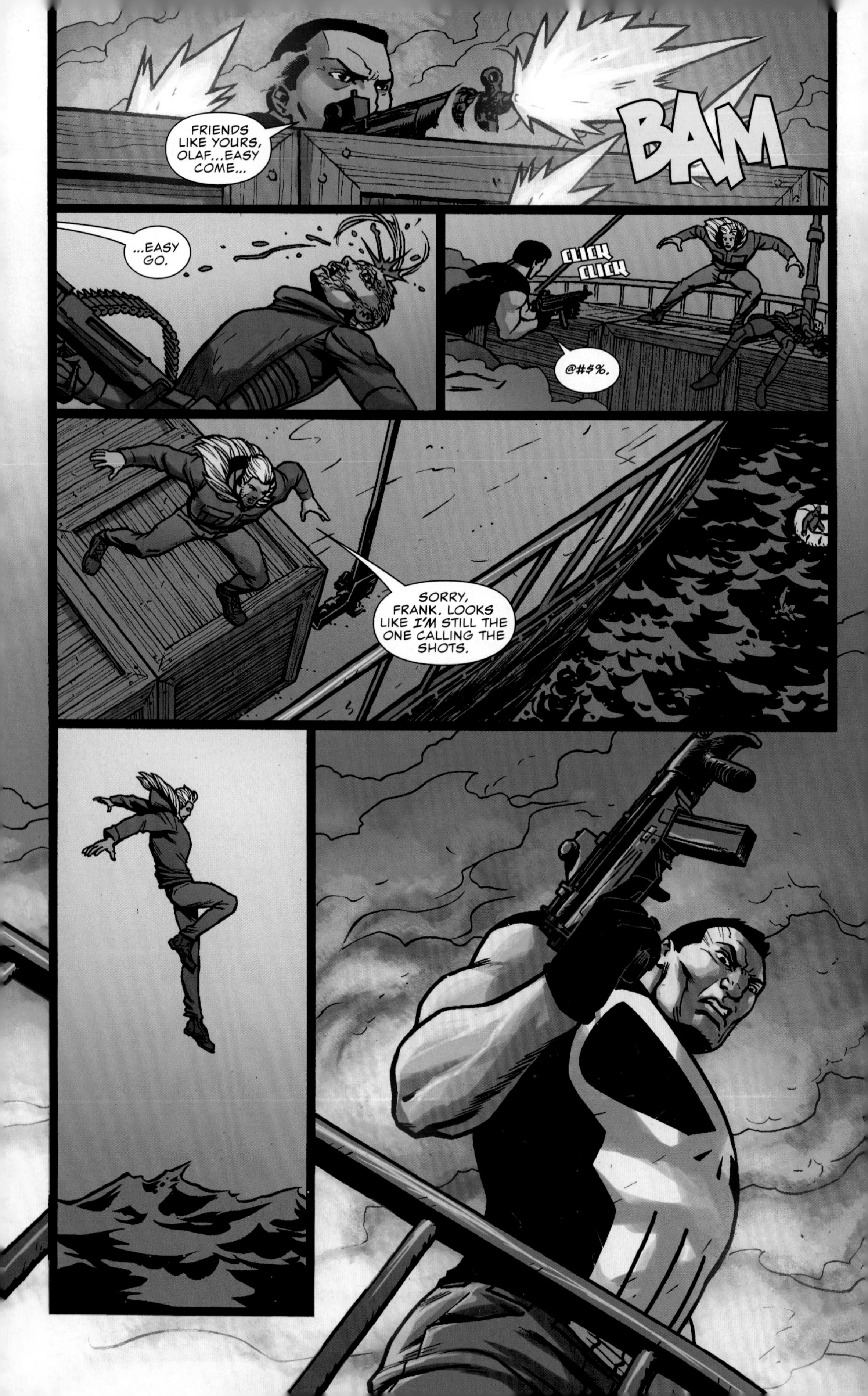
FRIENDS LIKE YOURS, OLAF...EASY COME...
BAM
...EASY GO.
CLICK
CLICK
@#$%.
SORRY, FRANK. LOOKS LIKE I'M STILL THE ONE CALLING THE SHOTS.

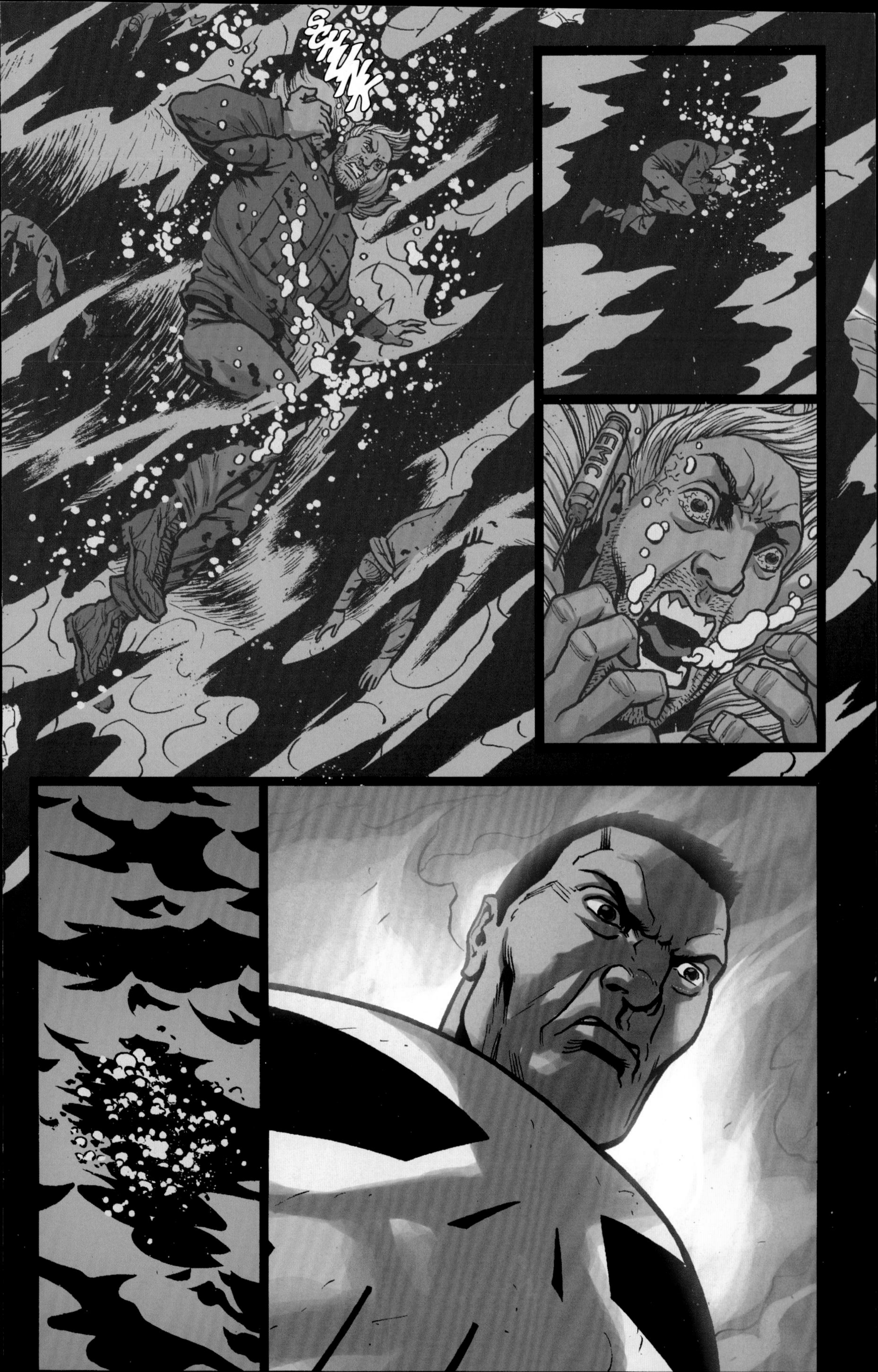
SCHUNK
EMC

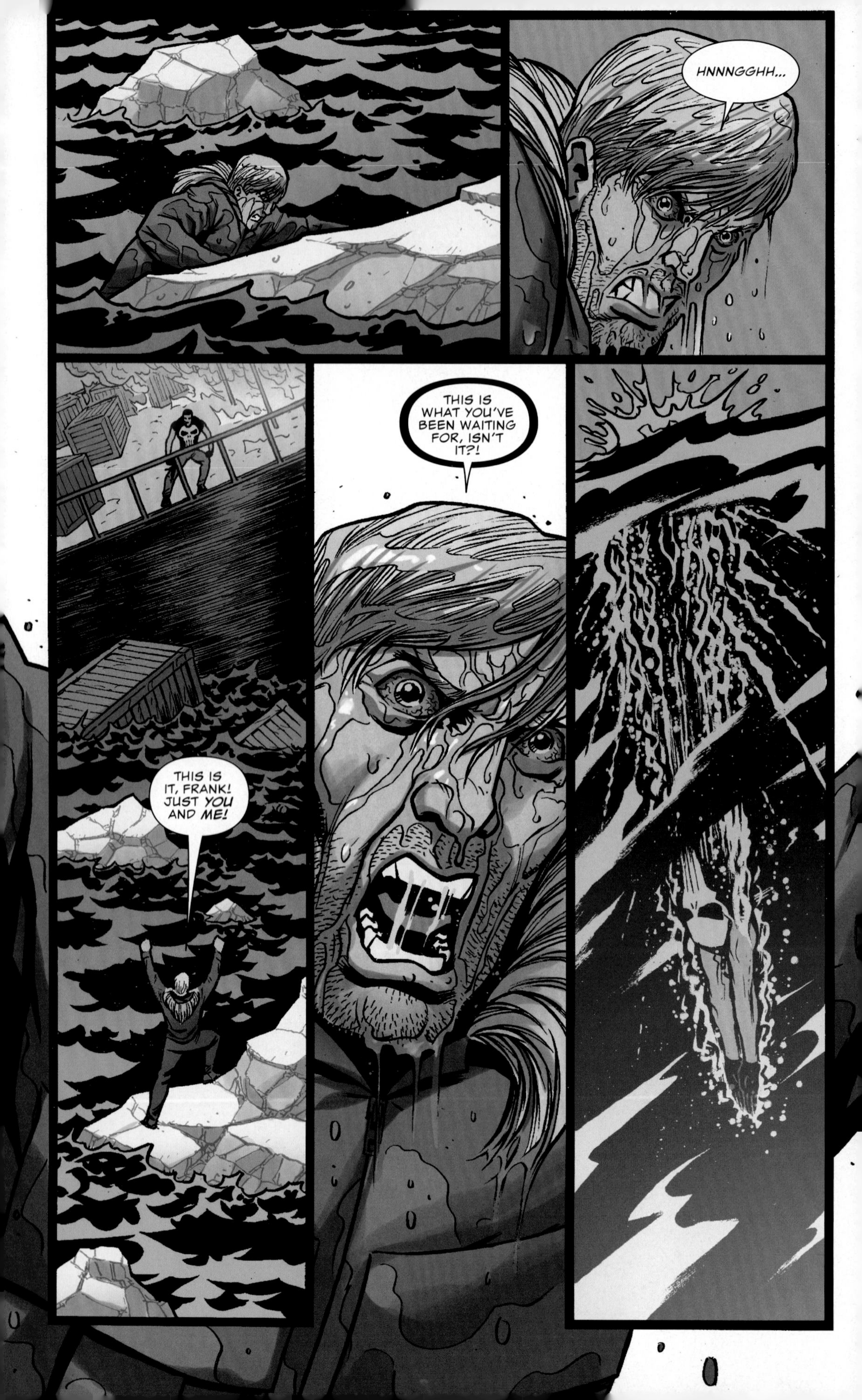
HNNNGGHH...
THIS IS IT, FRANK! JUST YOU AND ME!
THIS IS WHAT YOU'VE BEEN WAITING FOR, ISN'T IT?!

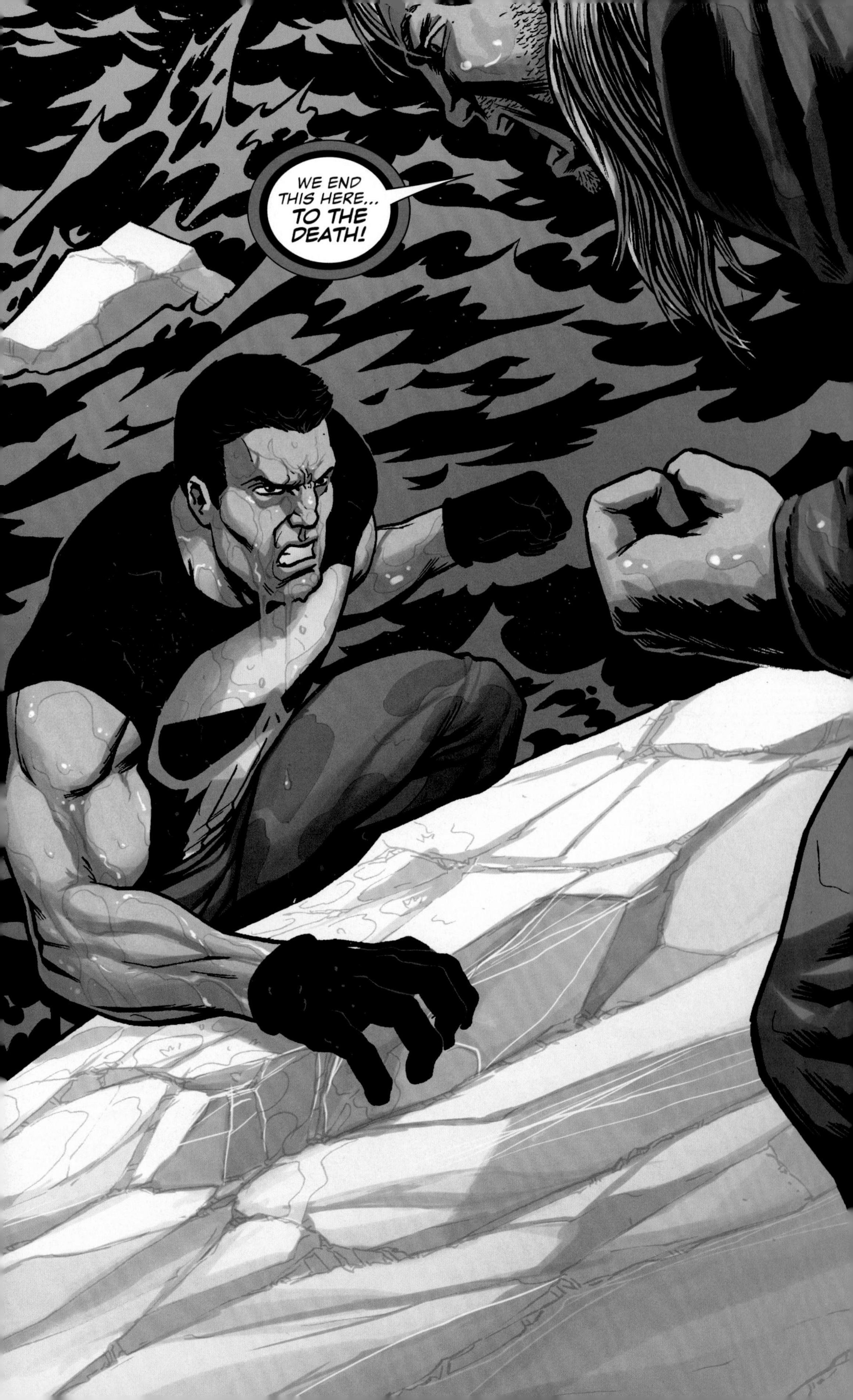
WE END THIS HERE... TO THE DEATH!

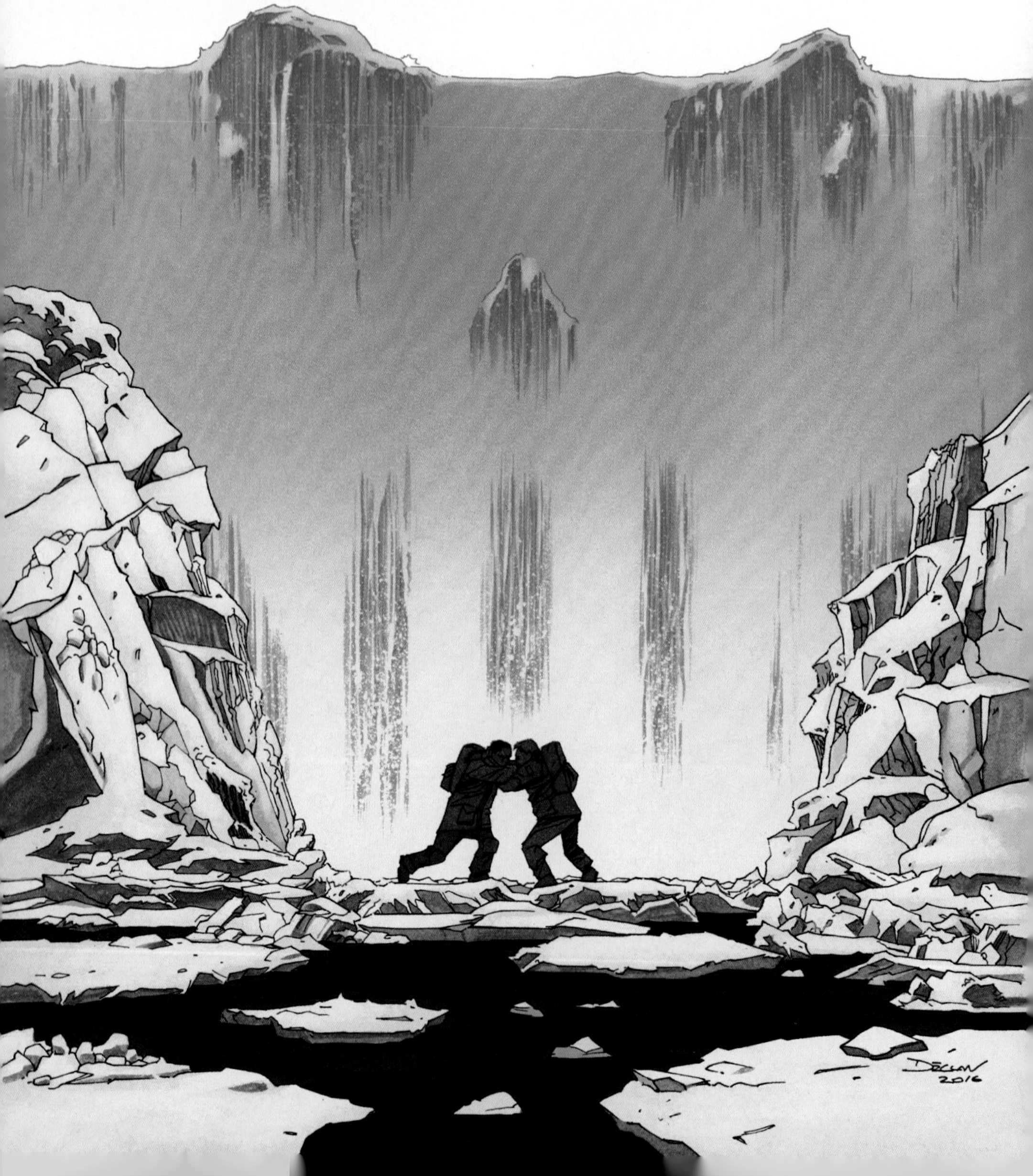
DECLAN
2016

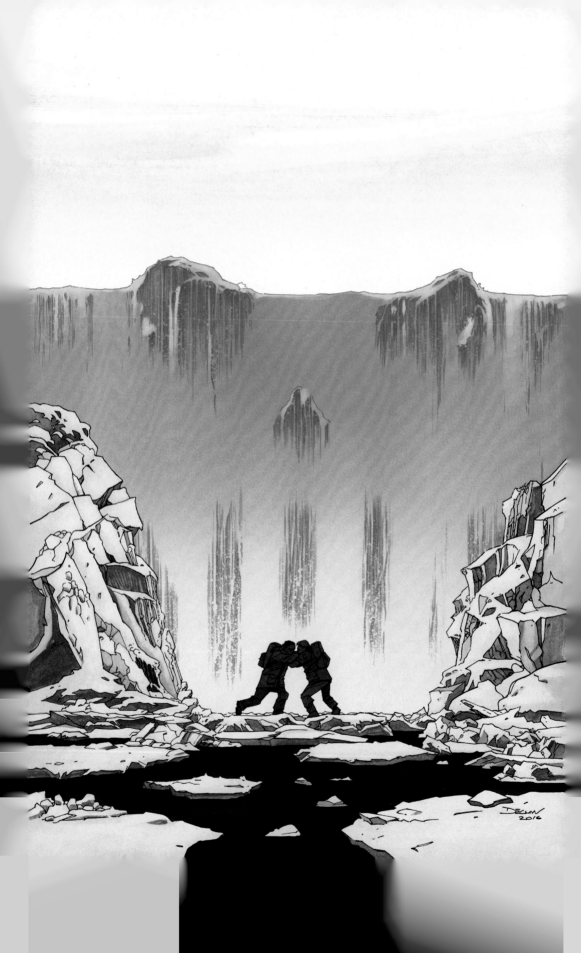

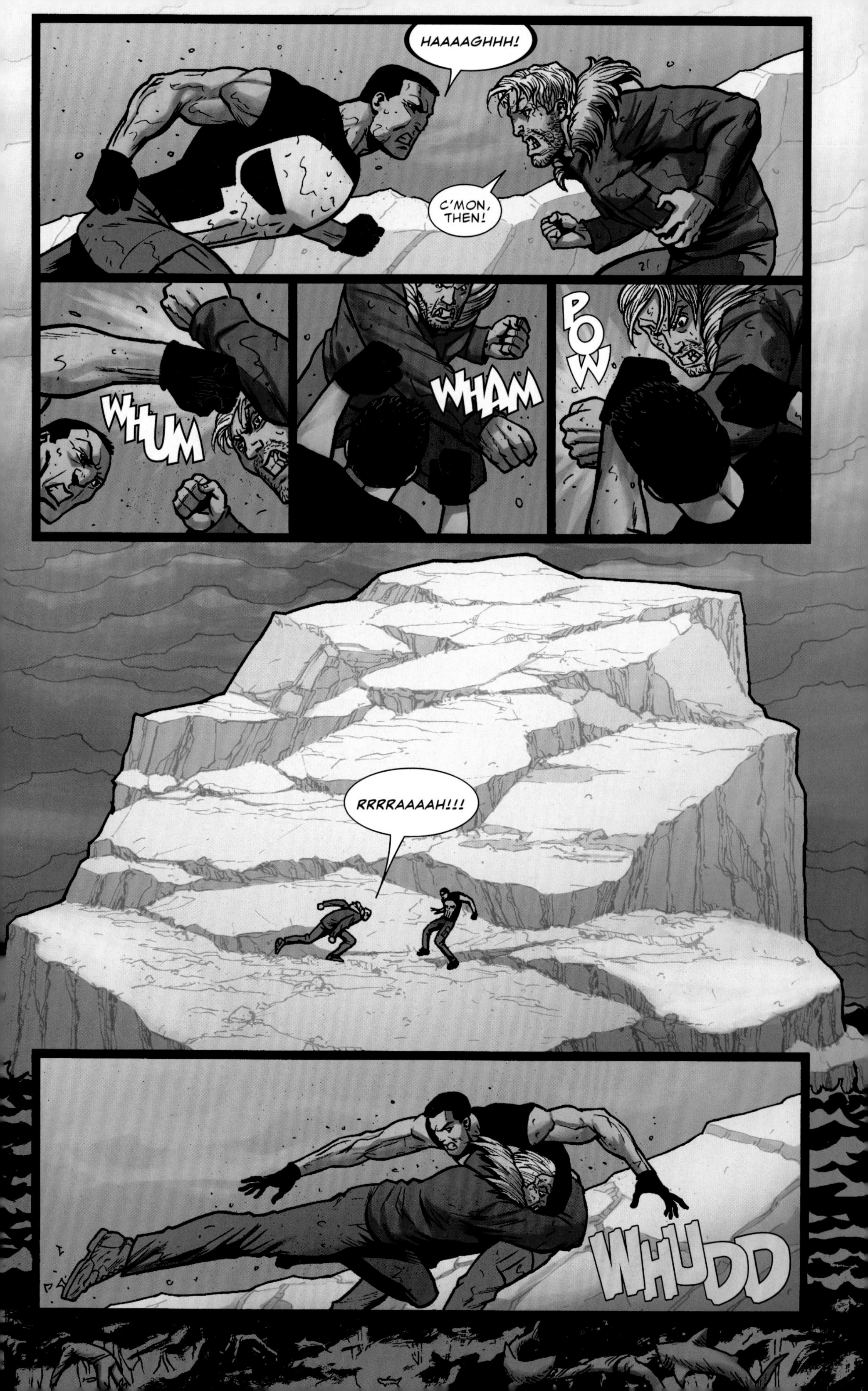
HAAAAGHHH!
C'MON, THEN!
WHUM
WHAM
POW
RRRRAAAAH!!!
WHUDD

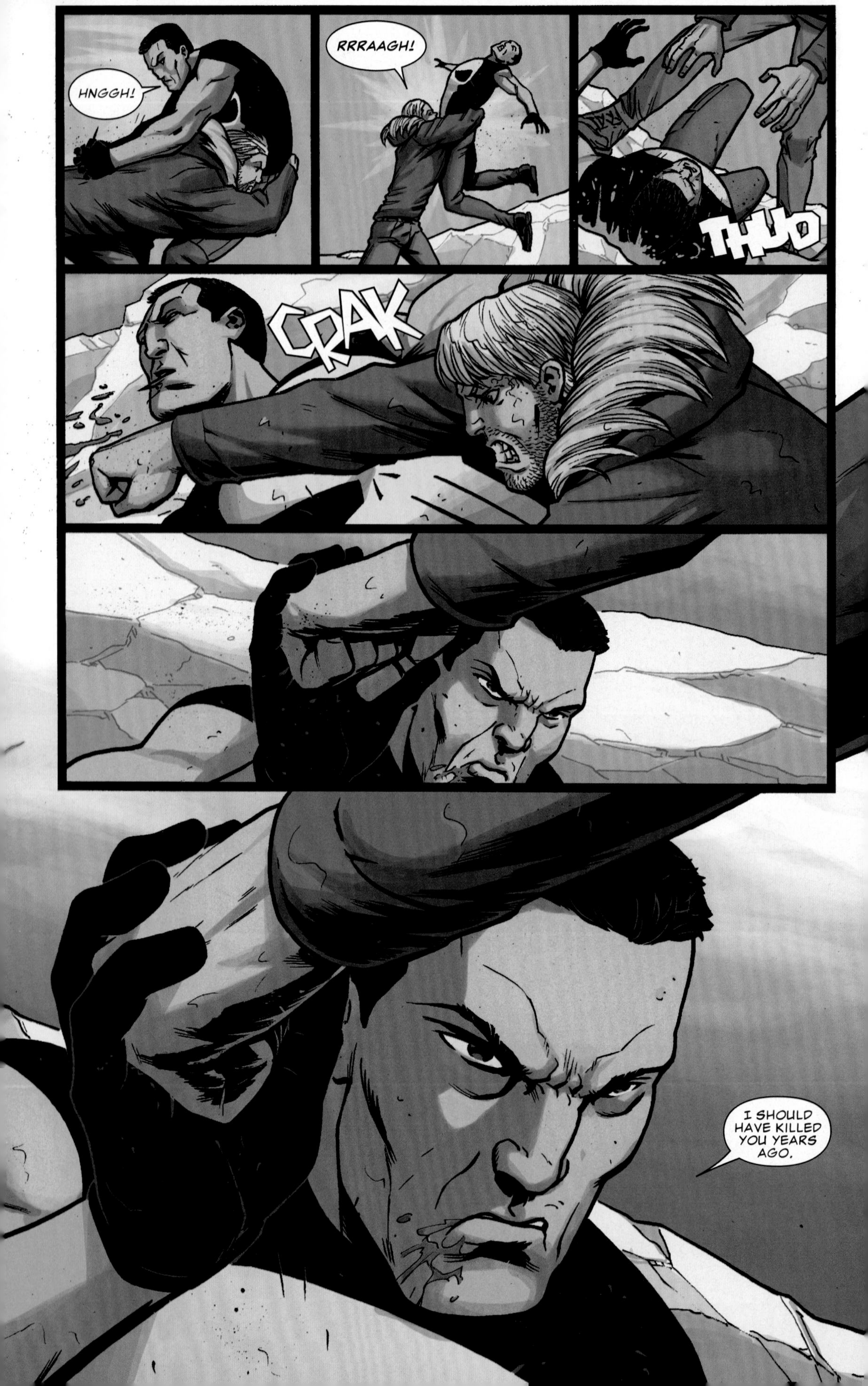
HNGGH!
RRRAAGH!
THUD
CRAK
I SHOULD HAVE KILLED YOU YEARS AGO.

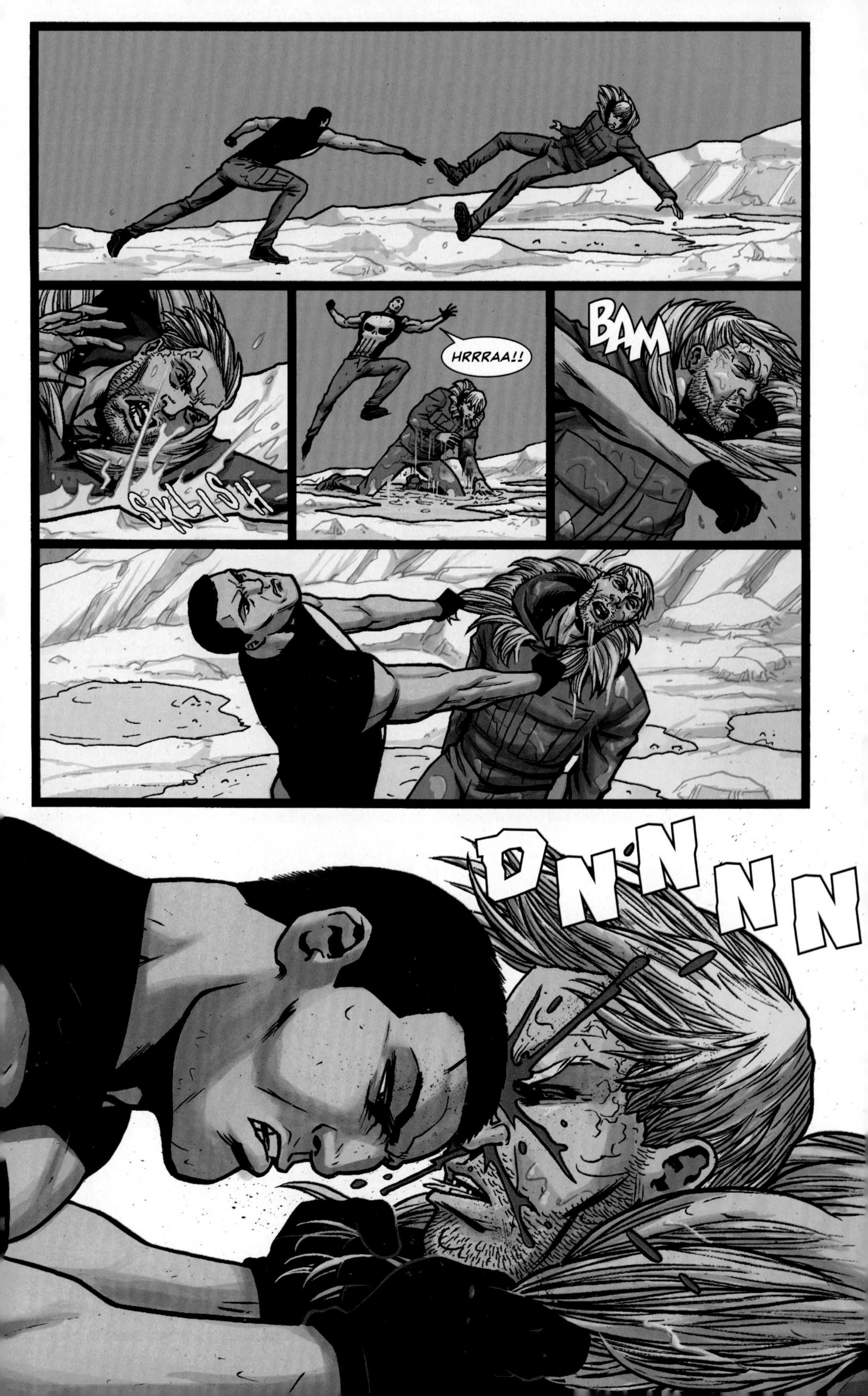
SKLISH
HRRRAA!!
BAM
DNNNNN

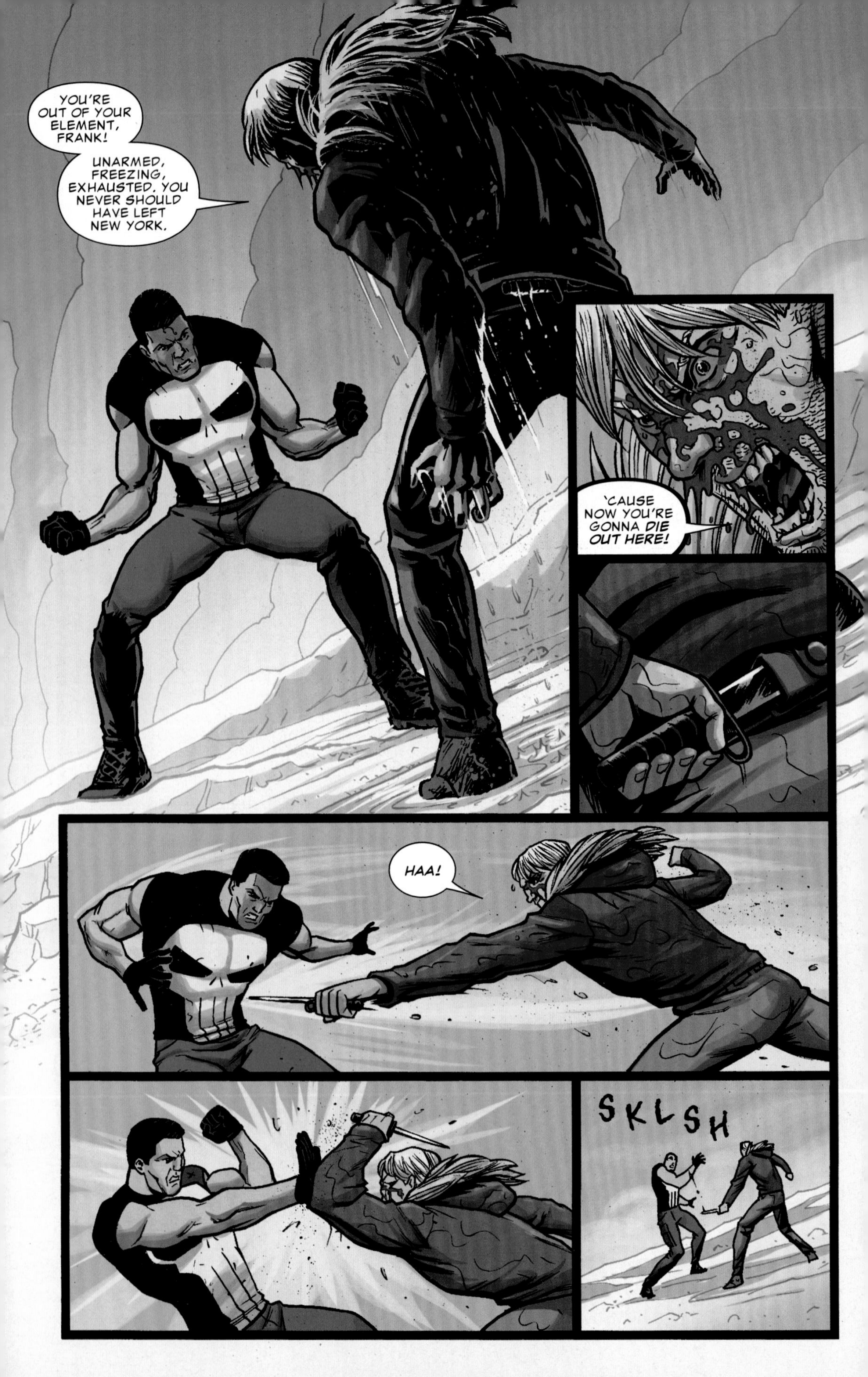
YOU'RE OUT OF YOUR ELEMENT, FRANK!
UNARMED, FREEZING, EXHAUSTED. YOU NEVER SHOULD HAVE LEFT NEW YORK.
'CAUSE NOW YOU'RE GONNA *DIE OUT HERE!*
HAA!
SKLSH

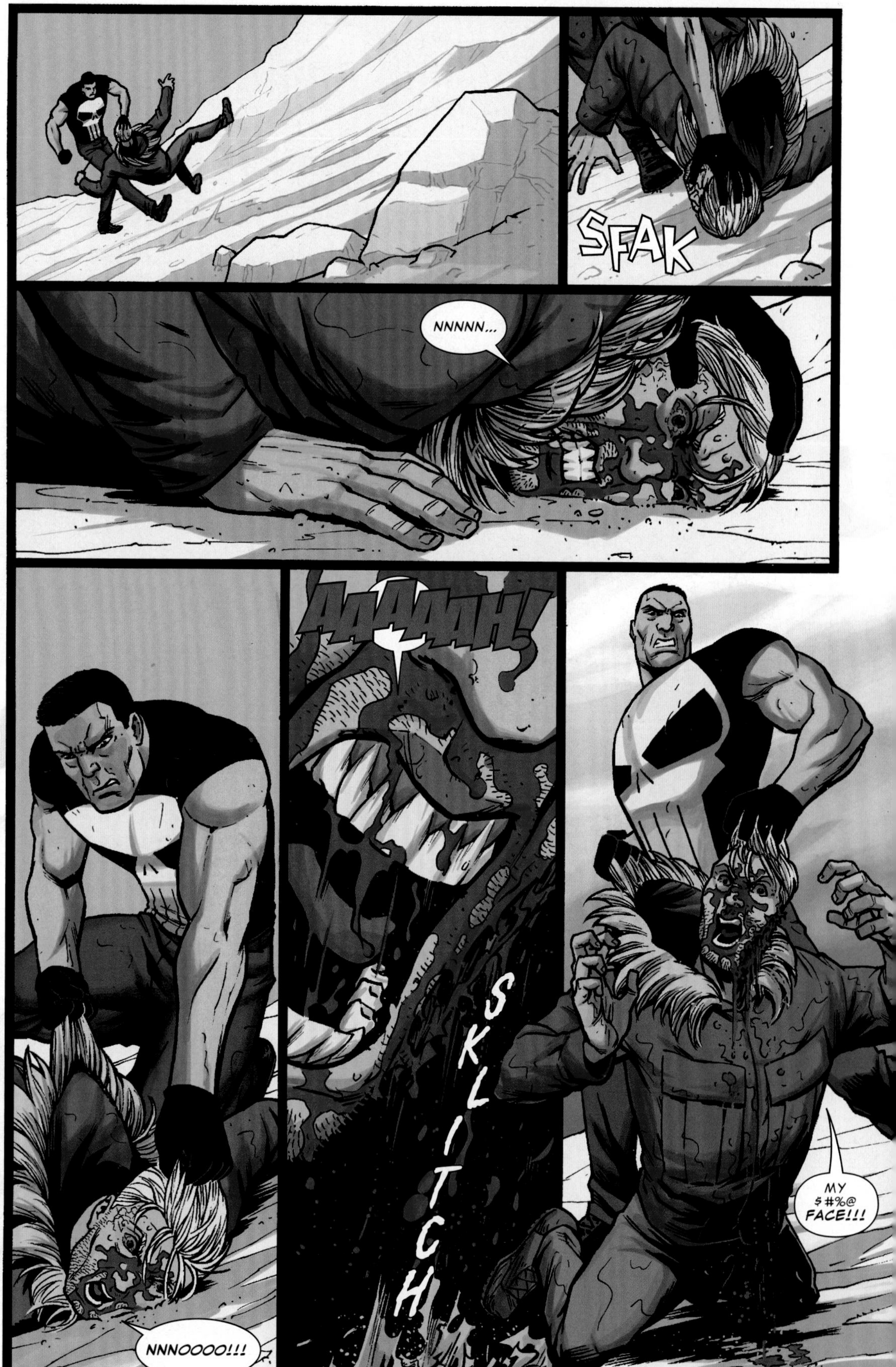
SFAK
NNNNN...
AAAAAH!
SKLITCH!
NNNOOOO!!!
MY $#%@ FACE!!!

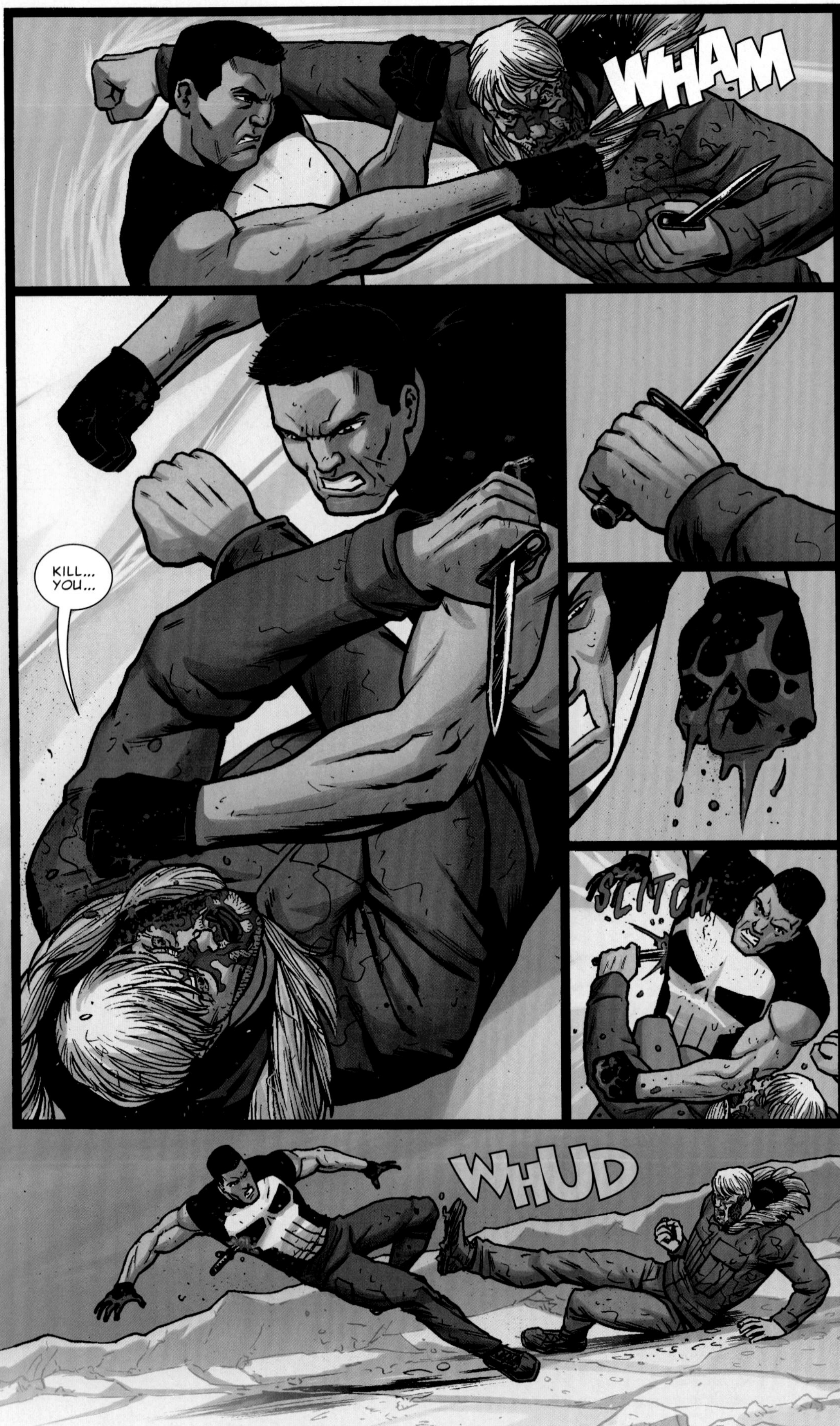
WHAM
KILL... YOU...
SLITCH
WHUD

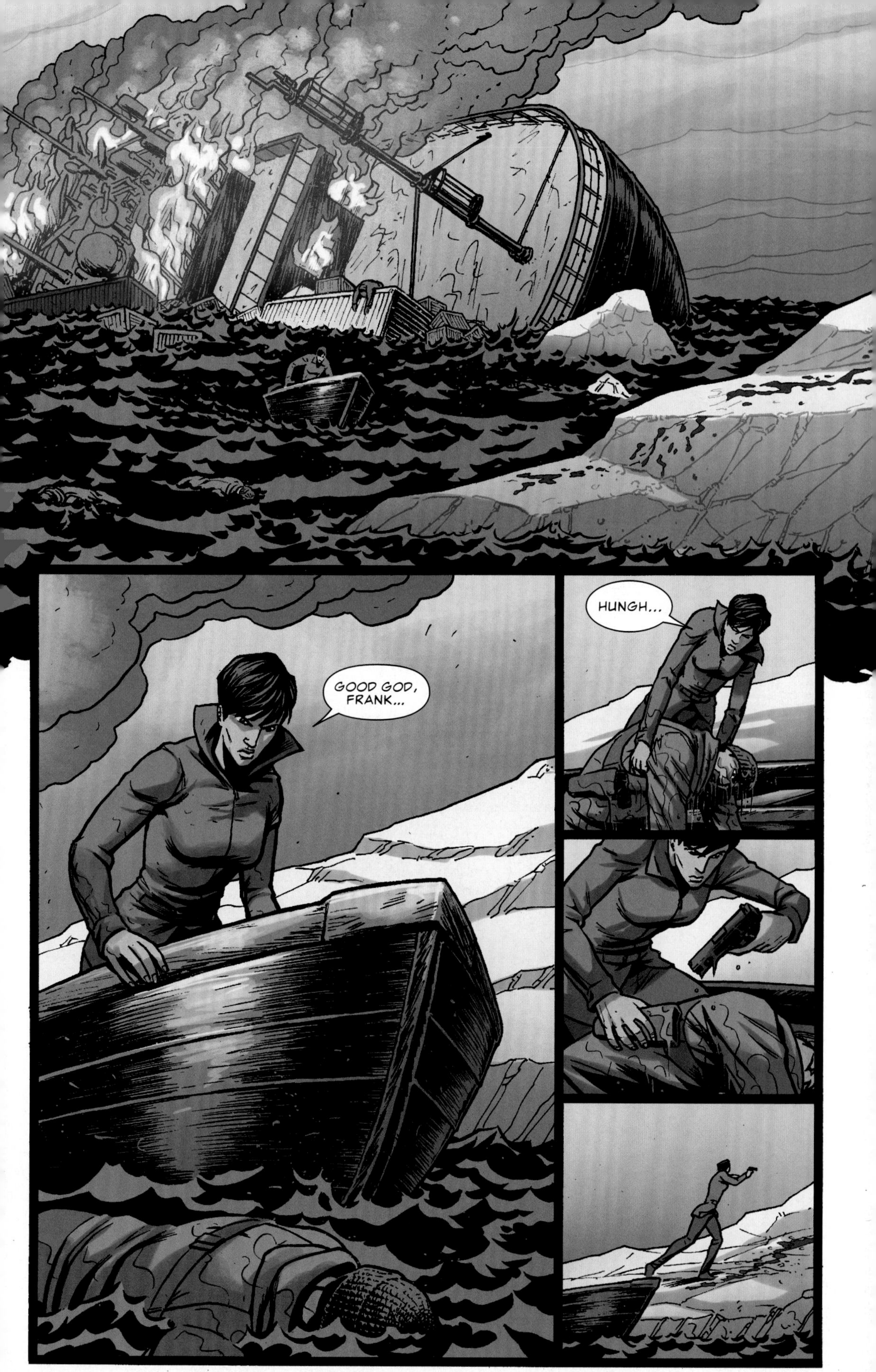
GOOD GOD, FRANK...
HUNGH...

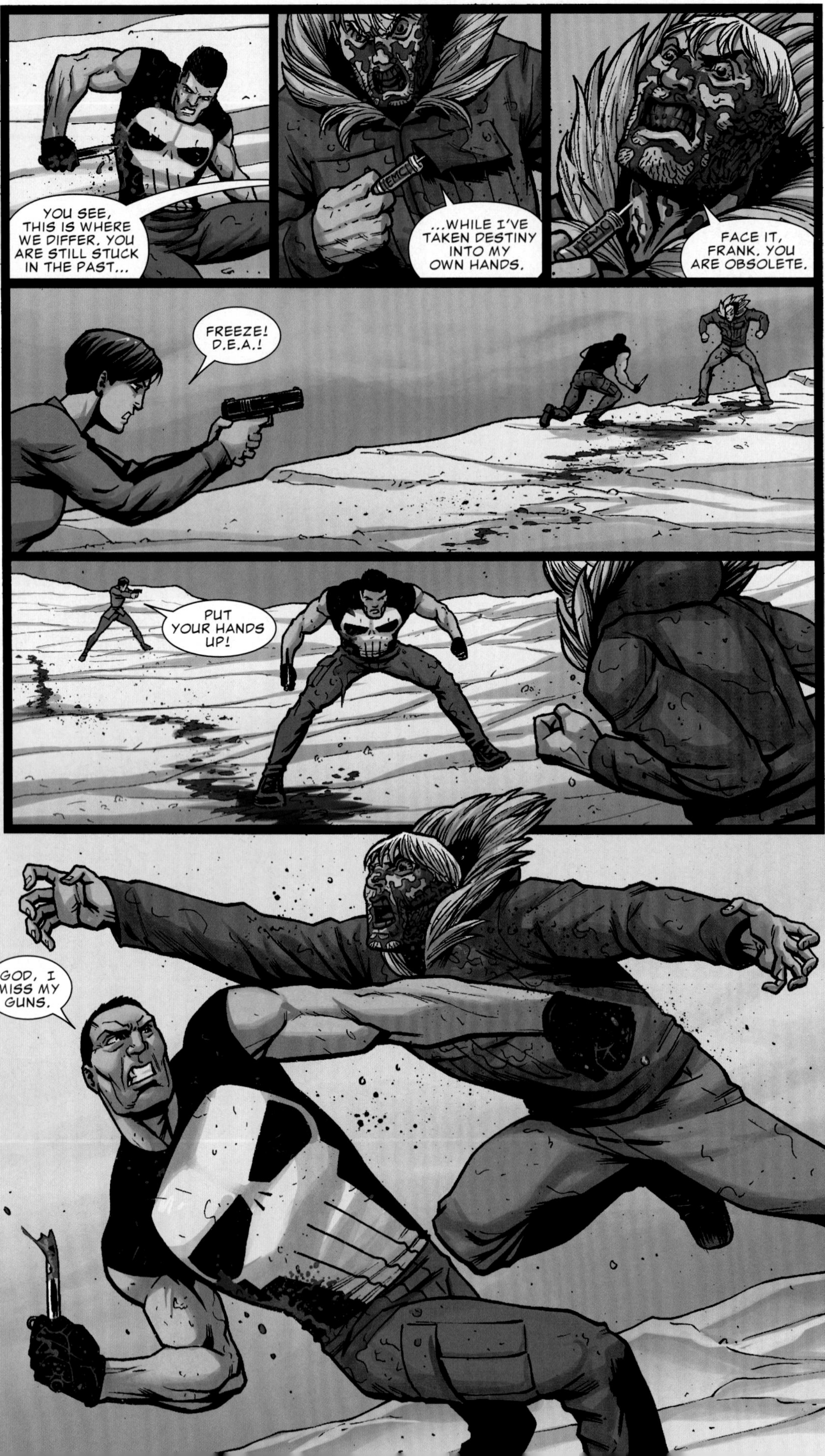
YOU SEE, THIS IS WHERE WE DIFFER. YOU ARE STILL STUCK IN THE PAST...
HEMO
...WHILE I'VE TAKEN DESTINY INTO MY OWN HANDS.
HEMO
FACE IT, FRANK. YOU ARE OBSOLETE.
FREEZE! D.E.A.!
PUT YOUR HANDS UP!
GOD, I MISS MY GUNS.

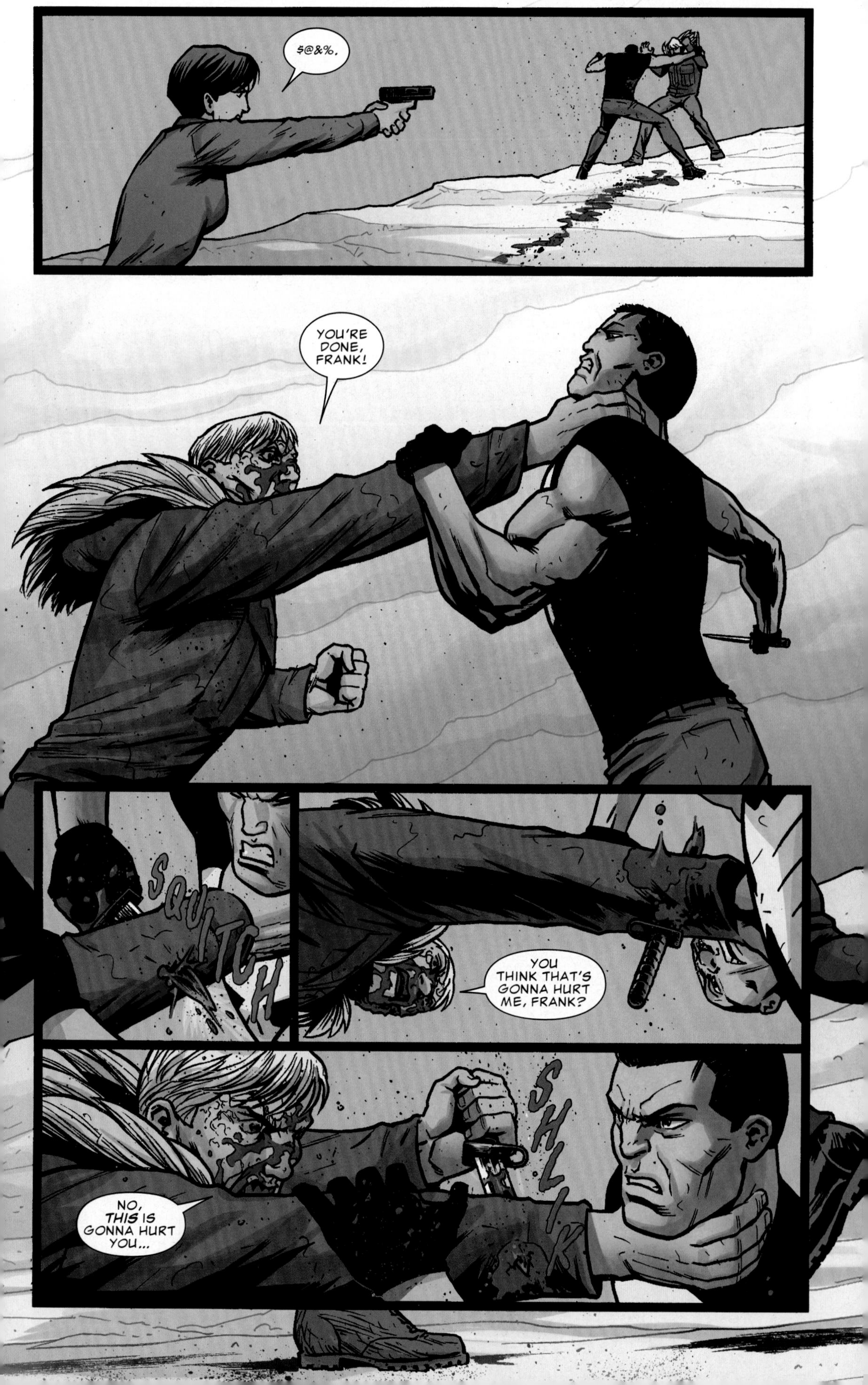
$@&%.
YOU'RE DONE, FRANK!
SQUITCH
YOU THINK THAT'S GONNA HURT ME, FRANK?
SHLIK
NO, THIS IS GONNA HURT YOU...

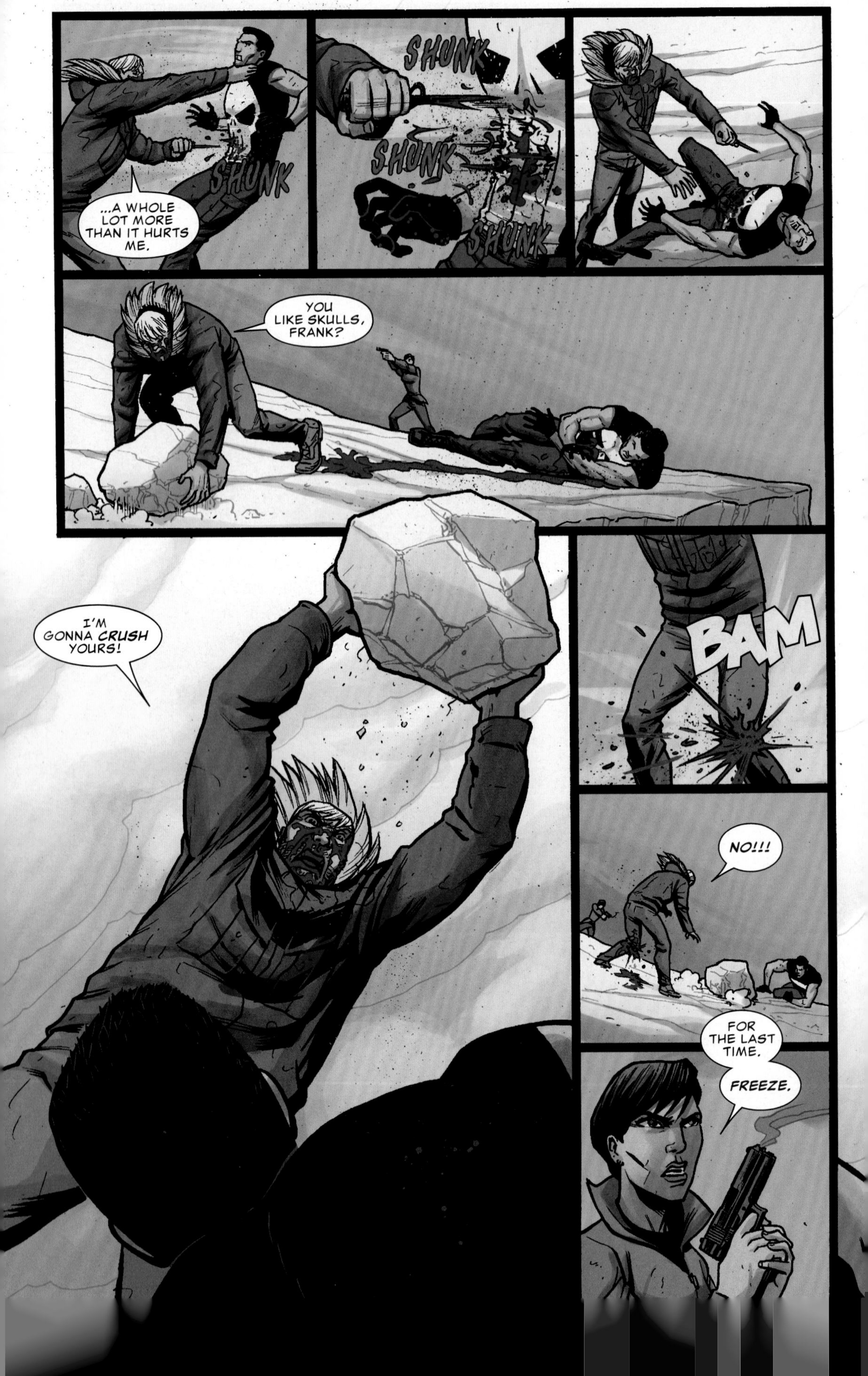
SHUNK
...A WHOLE LOT MORE THAN IT HURTS ME.
SHUNK
SHUNK
SHUNK
YOU LIKE SKULLS, FRANK?
I'M GONNA CRUSH YOURS!
BAM
NO!!!
FOR THE LAST TIME.
FREEZE.

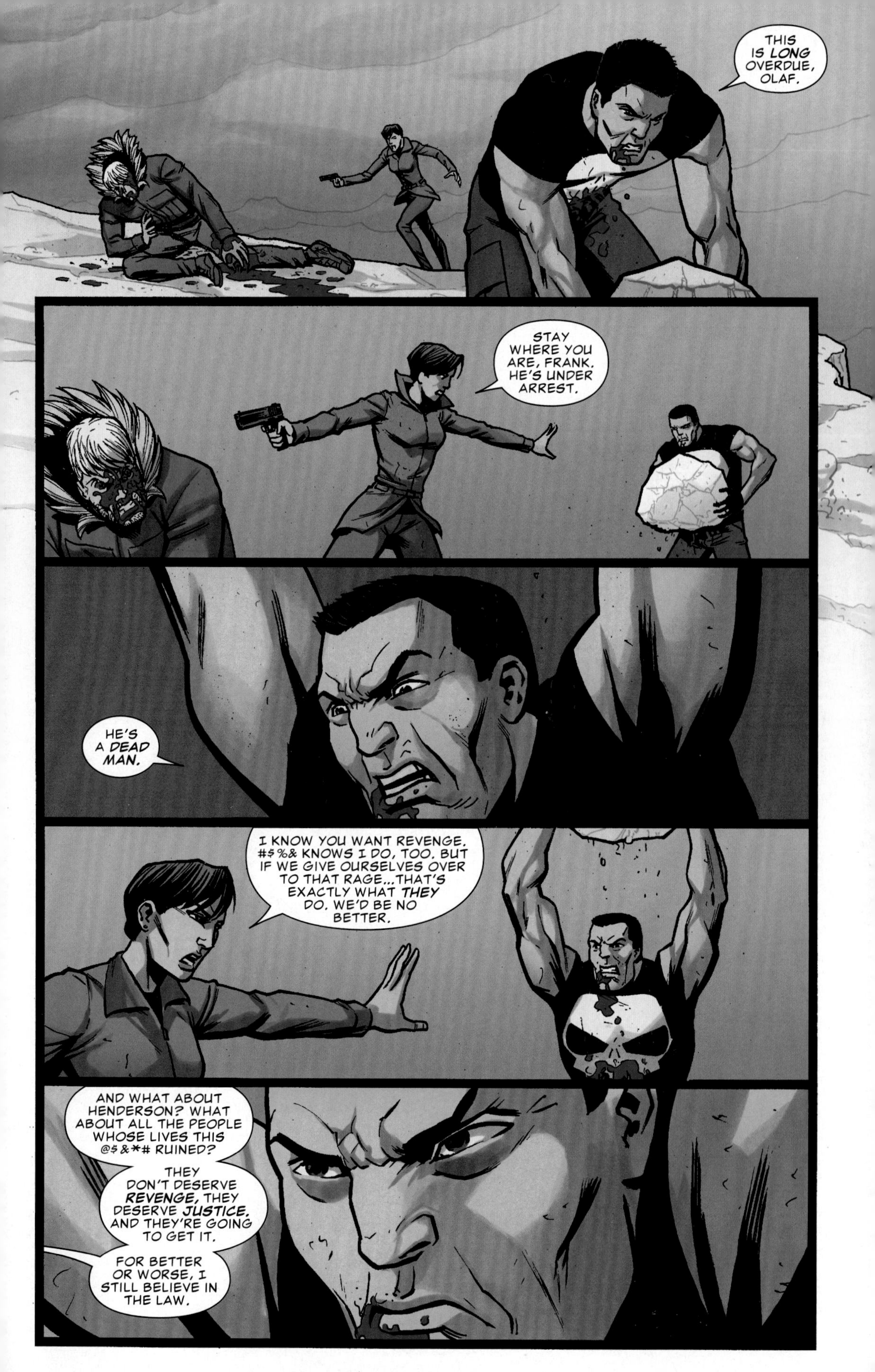

THIS IS LONG OVERDUE, OLAF.
STAY WHERE YOU ARE, FRANK. HE'S UNDER ARREST.
HE'S A DEAD MAN.
I KNOW YOU WANT REVENGE. #$%& KNOWS I DO, TOO. BUT IF WE GIVE OURSELVES OVER TO THAT RAGE...THAT'S EXACTLY WHAT THEY DO. WE'D BE NO BETTER.
AND WHAT ABOUT HENDERSON? WHAT ABOUT ALL THE PEOPLE WHOSE LIVES THIS @$&*# RUINED?
THEY DON'T DESERVE REVENGE, THEY DESERVE JUSTICE. AND THEY'RE GOING TO GET IT.
FOR BETTER OR WORSE, I STILL BELIEVE IN THE LAW.

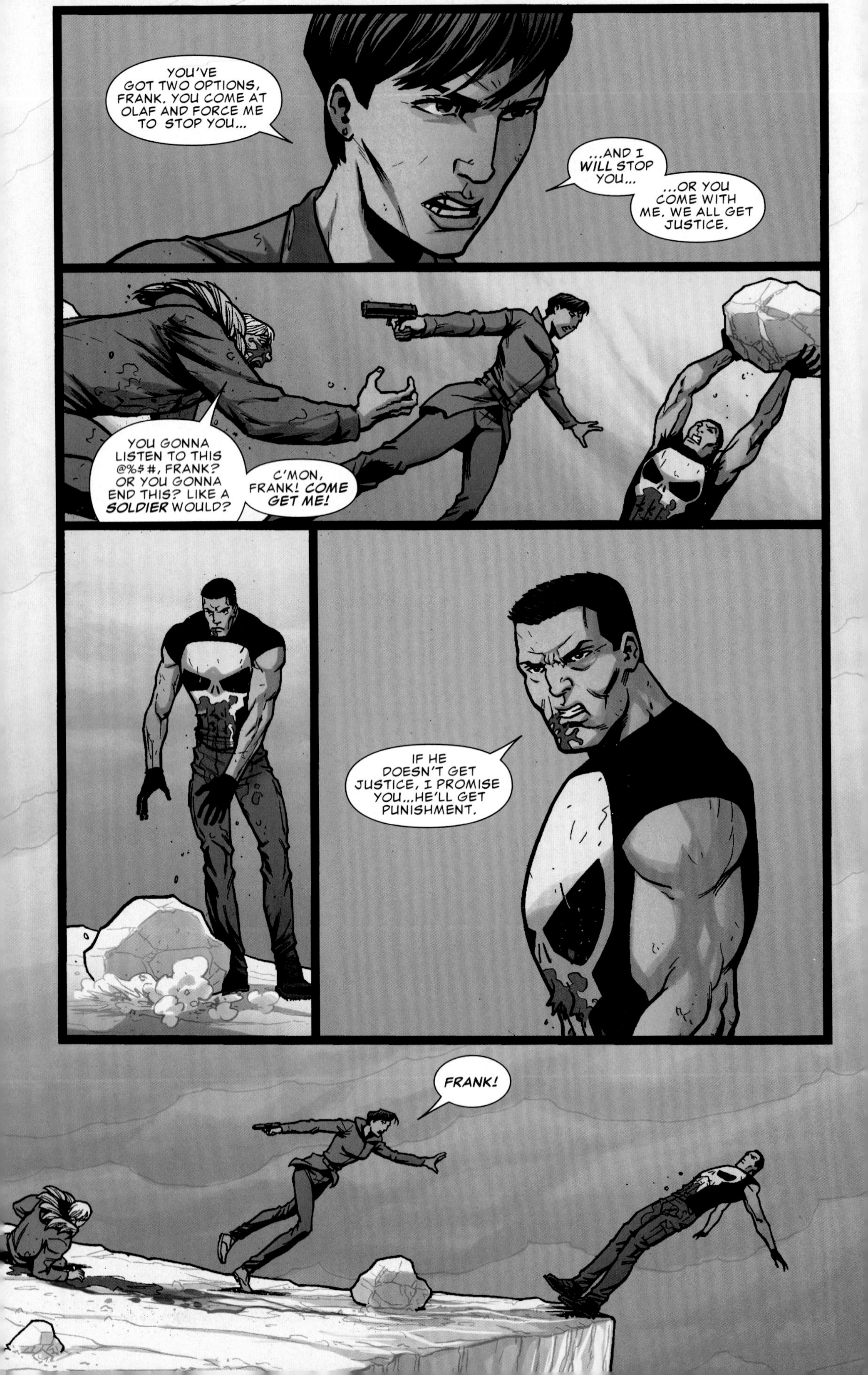
YOU'VE GOT TWO OPTIONS, FRANK. YOU COME AT OLAF AND FORCE ME TO STOP YOU...
...AND I WILL STOP YOU...
...OR YOU COME WITH ME. WE ALL GET JUSTICE.
YOU GONNA LISTEN TO THIS @%$#, FRANK? OR YOU GONNA END THIS? LIKE A SOLDIER WOULD?
C'MON, FRANK! COME GET ME!
IF HE DOESN'T GET JUSTICE, I PROMISE YOU...HE'LL GET PUNISHMENT.
FRANK!

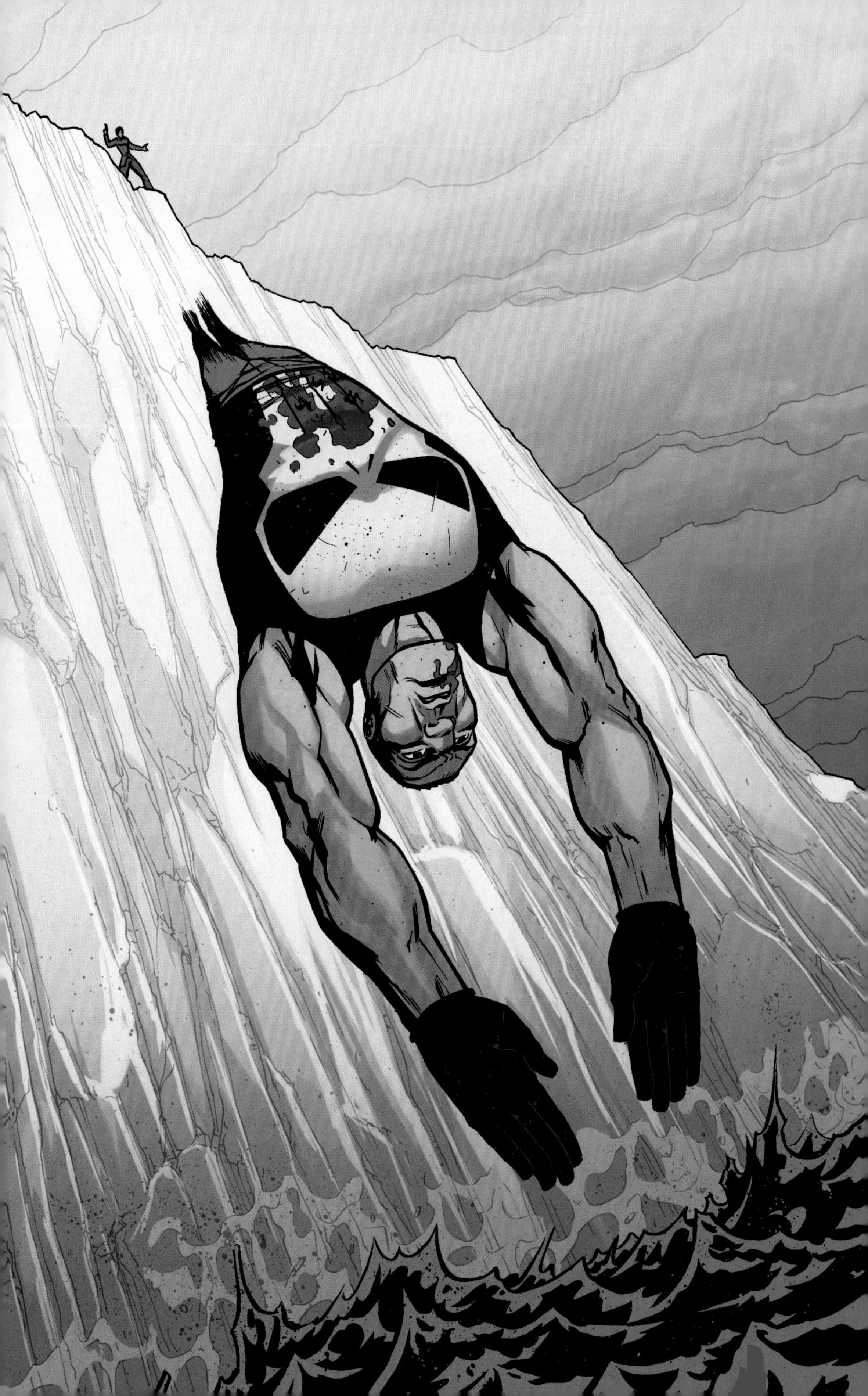

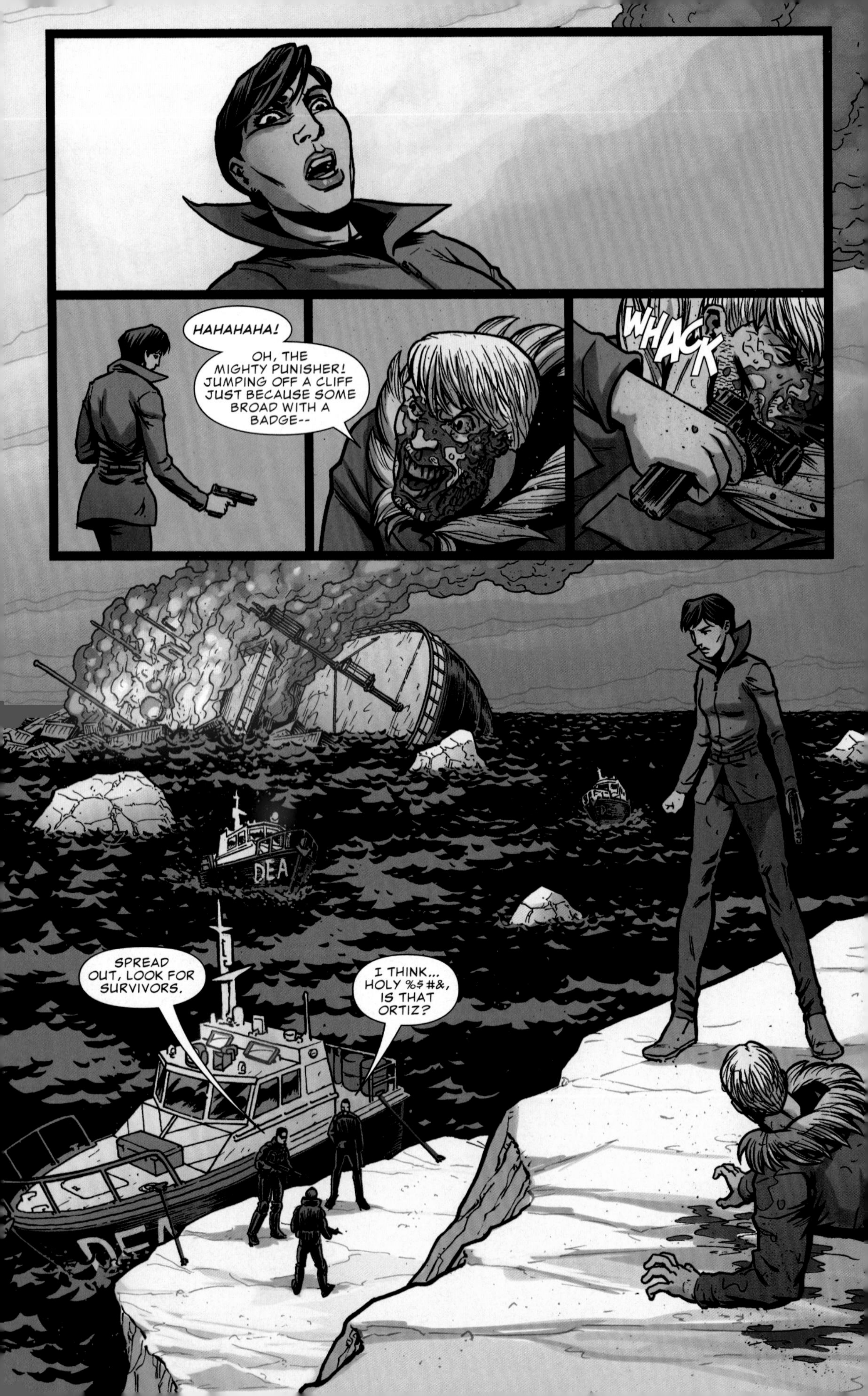
HAHAHAHA!
OH, THE MIGHTY PUNISHER! JUMPING OFF A CLIFF JUST BECAUSE SOME BROAD WITH A BADGE--
WHACK
DEA
SPREAD OUT, LOOK FOR SURVIVORS.
I THINK... HOLY %$#&, IS THAT ORTIZ?
DEA

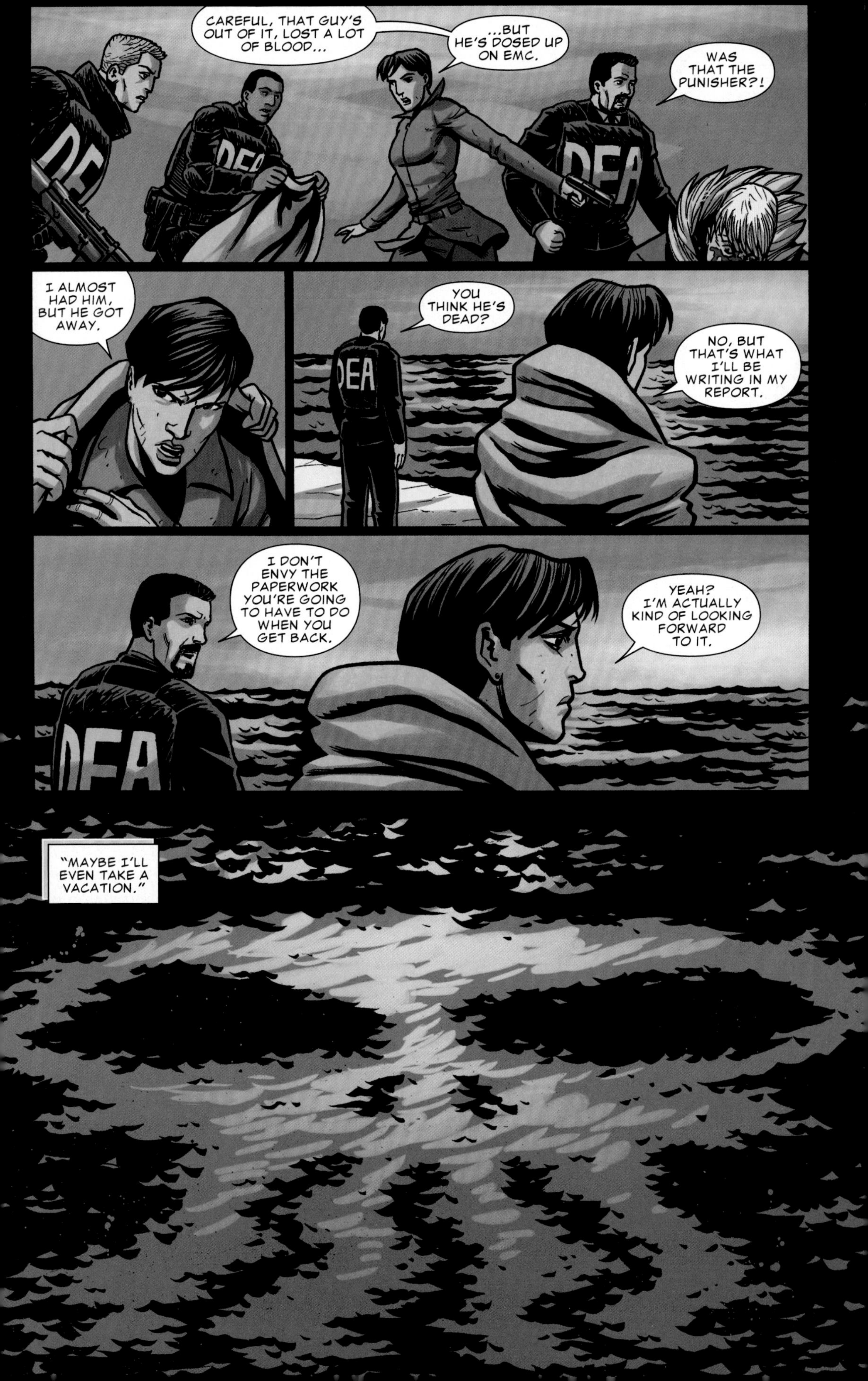
CAREFUL, THAT GUY'S OUT OF IT, LOST A LOT OF BLOOD...
...BUT HE'S DOSED UP ON EMC.
WAS THAT THE PUNISHER?!
I ALMOST HAD HIM, BUT HE GOT AWAY.
YOU THINK HE'S DEAD?
NO, BUT THAT'S WHAT I'LL BE WRITING IN MY REPORT.
I DON'T ENVY THE PAPERWORK YOU'RE GOING TO HAVE TO DO WHEN YOU GET BACK.
YEAH? I'M ACTUALLY KIND OF LOOKING FORWARD TO IT.
"MAYBE I'LL EVEN TAKE A VACATION."

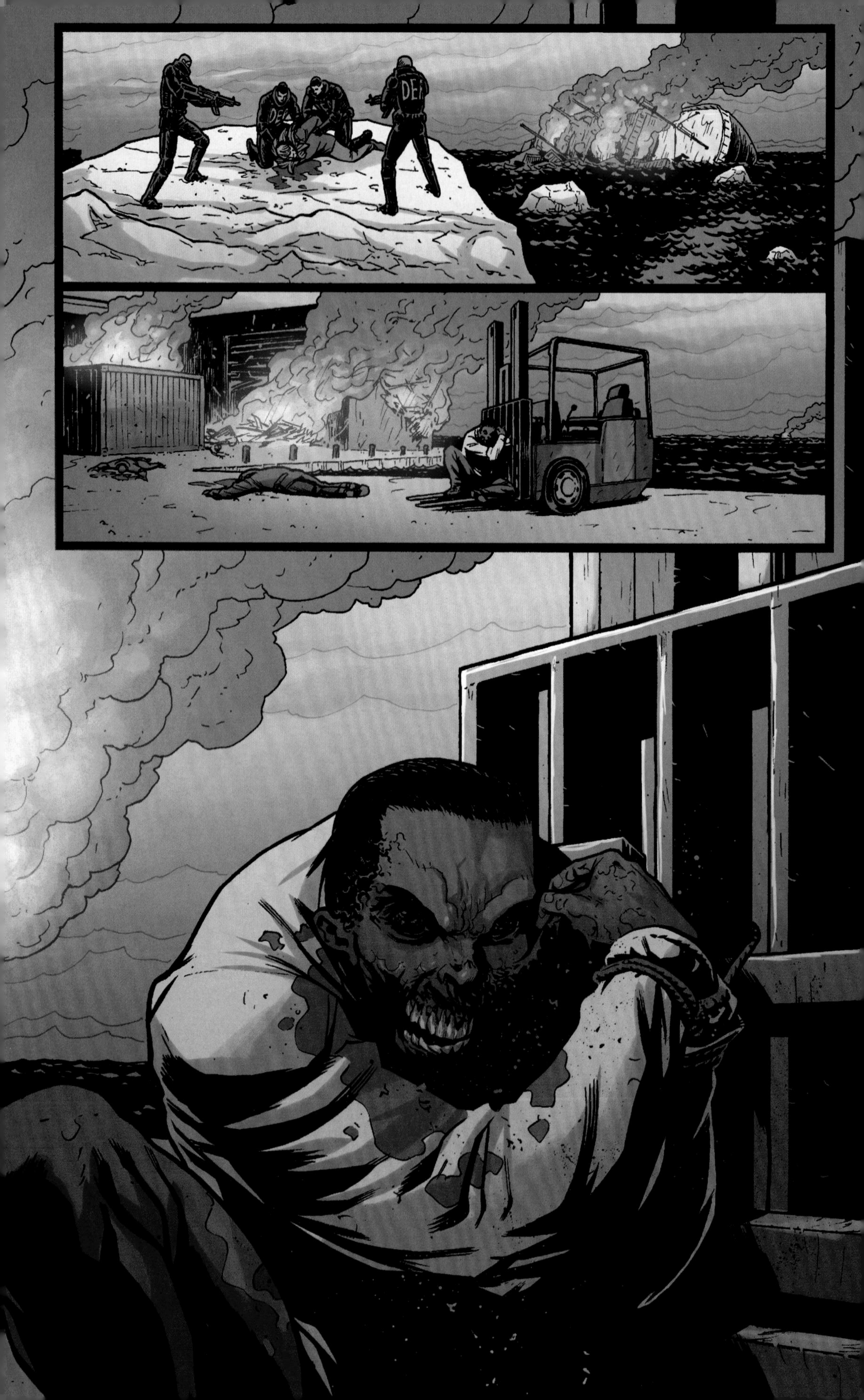
DEA

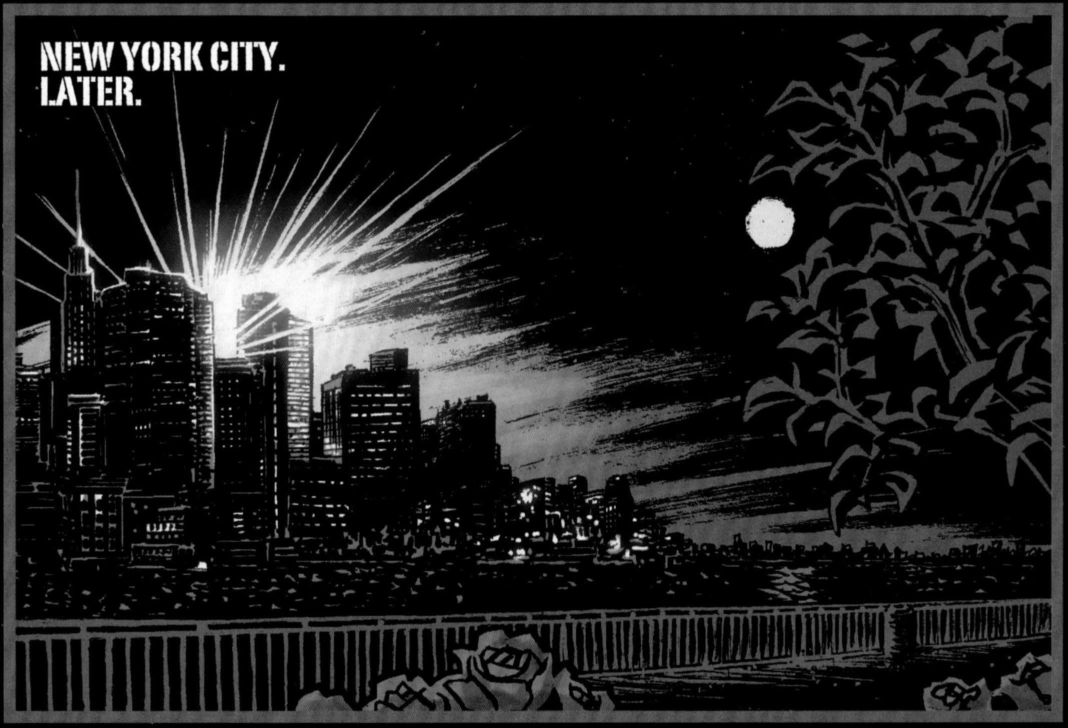
NEW YORK CITY.
LATER.

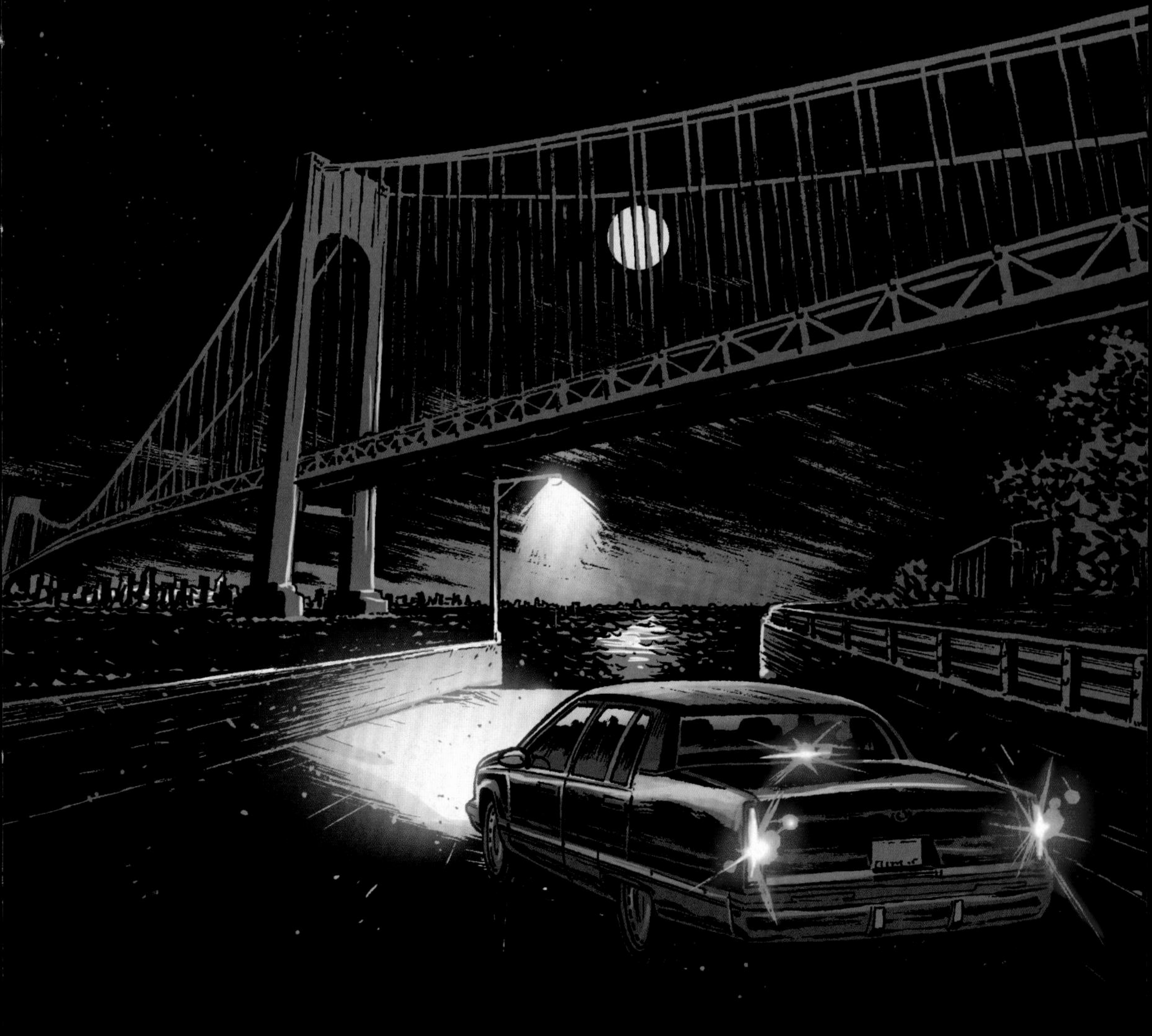

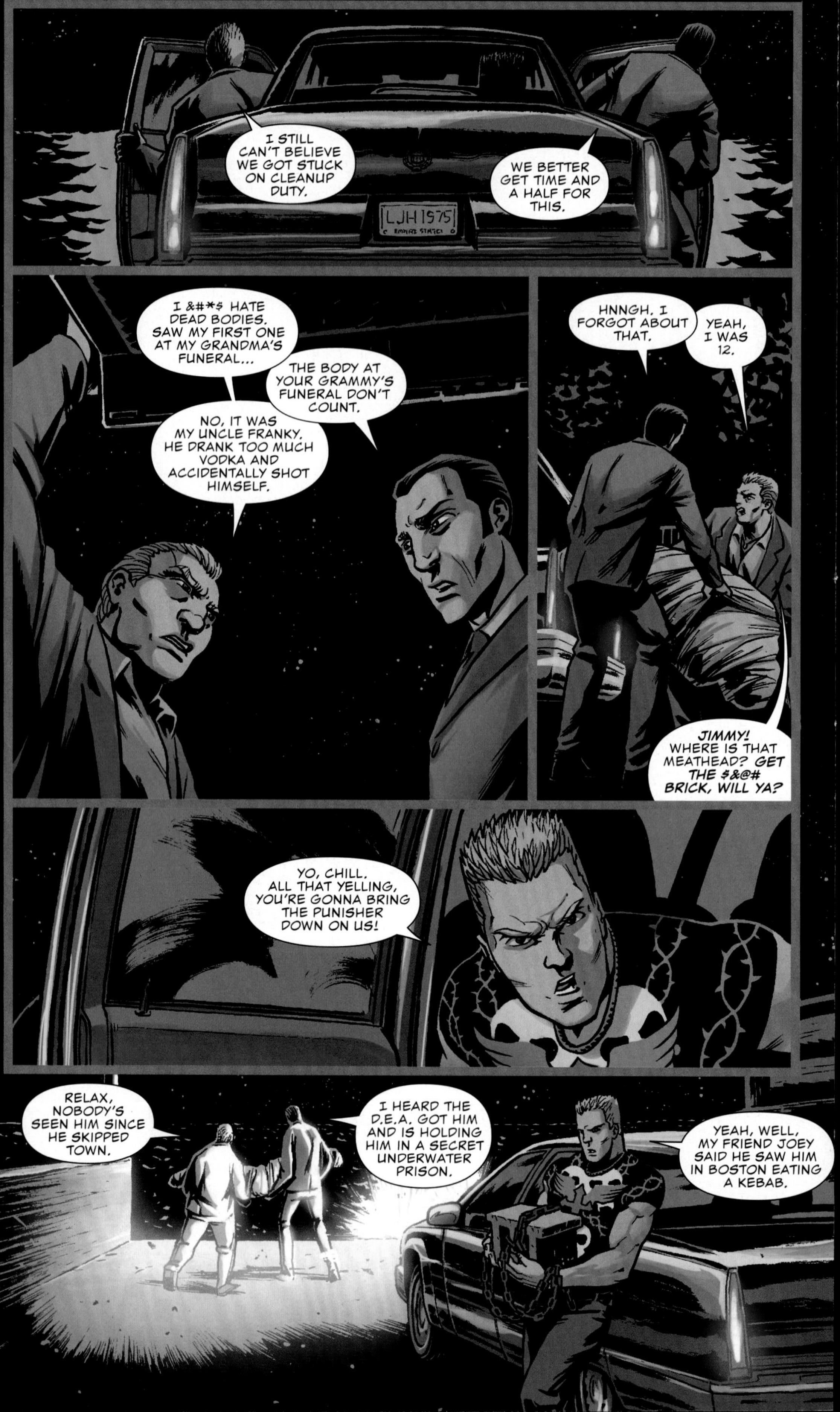
I STILL CAN'T BELIEVE WE GOT STUCK ON CLEANUP DUTY.
WE BETTER GET TIME AND A HALF FOR THIS.
LJH 1975
I &#*$ HATE DEAD BODIES. SAW MY FIRST ONE AT MY GRANDMA'S FUNERAL...
THE BODY AT YOUR GRAMMY'S FUNERAL DON'T COUNT.
NO, IT WAS MY UNCLE FRANKY. HE DRANK TOO MUCH VODKA AND ACCIDENTALLY SHOT HIMSELF.
HNNGH. I FORGOT ABOUT THAT.
YEAH, I WAS 12.
JIMMY! WHERE IS THAT MEATHEAD? GET THE $&@# BRICK, WILL YA?
YO, CHILL. ALL THAT YELLING, YOU'RE GONNA BRING THE PUNISHER DOWN ON US!
RELAX, NOBODY'S SEEN HIM SINCE HE SKIPPED TOWN.
I HEARD THE D.E.A. GOT HIM AND IS HOLDING HIM IN A SECRET UNDERWATER PRISON.
YEAH, WELL, MY FRIEND JOEY SAID HE SAW HIM IN BOSTON EATING A KEBAB.

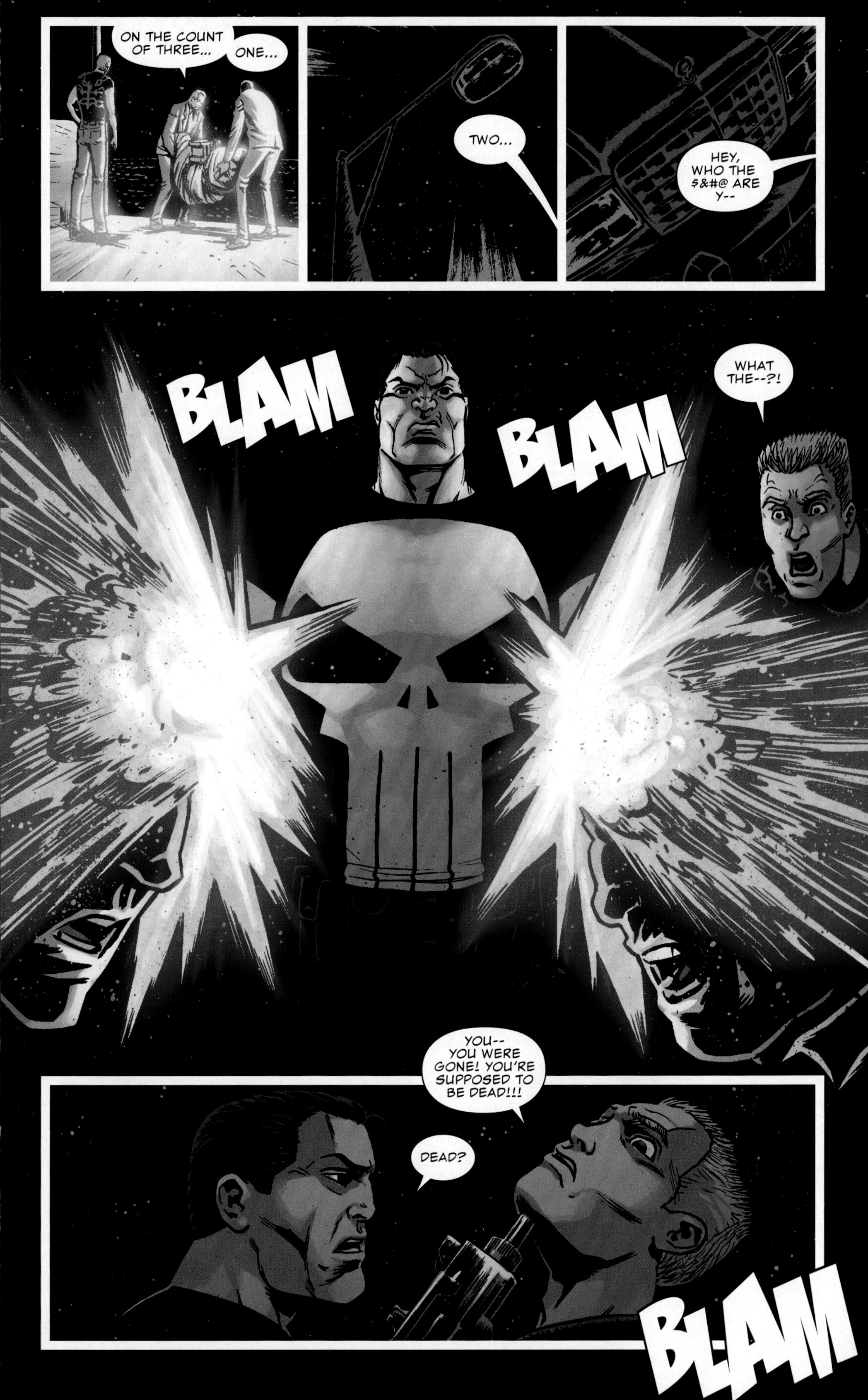
ON THE COUNT OF THREE...
ONE...
TWO...
HEY, WHO THE $&#@ ARE Y--
BLAM
BLAM
WHAT THE--?!
YOU-- YOU WERE GONE! YOU'RE SUPPOSED TO BE DEAD!!!
DEAD?
BLAM

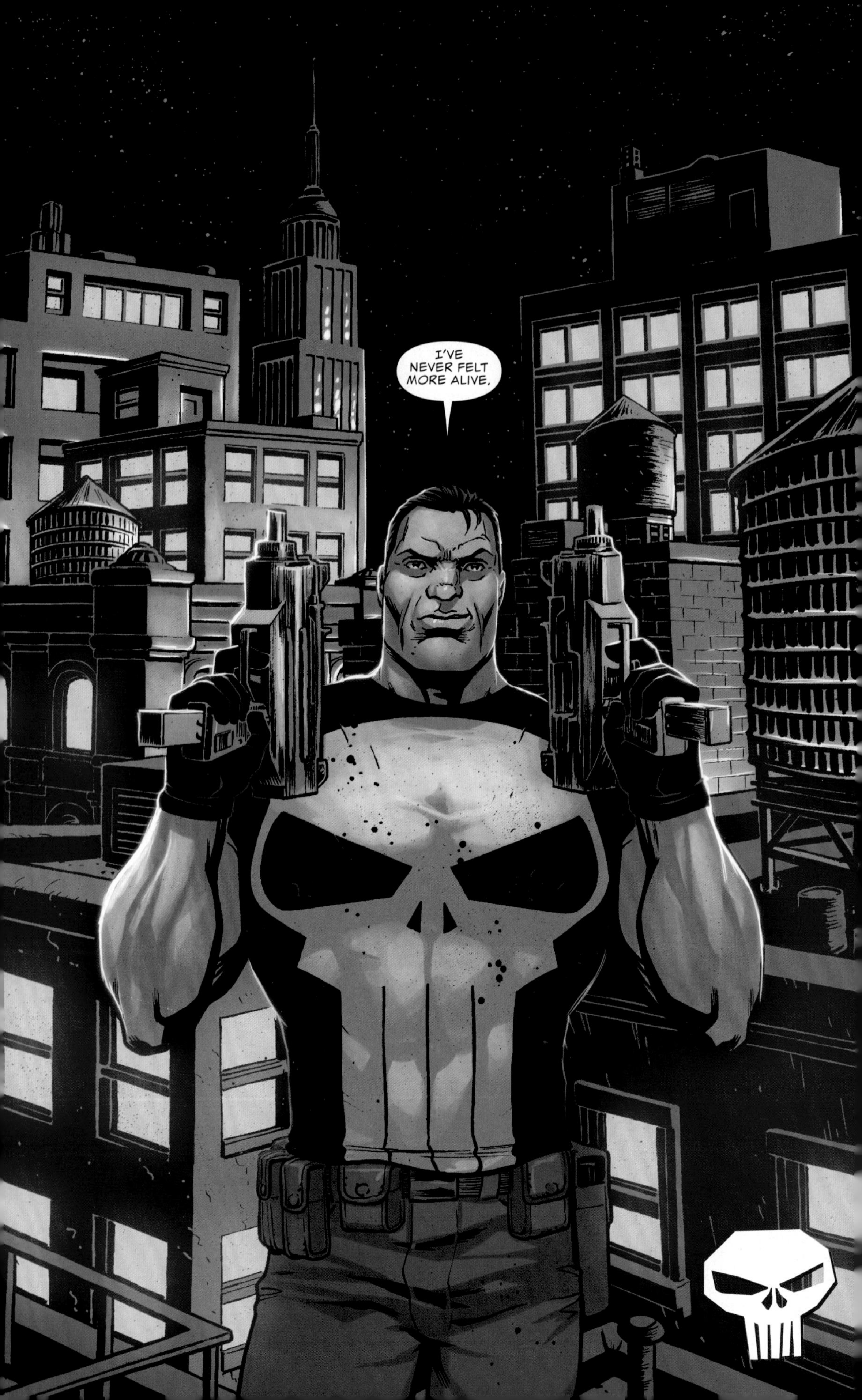
I'VE NEVER FELT MORE ALIVE.

PUBLISH OR PUNISH

Write to mheroes@marvel.com and mark your letters "OKAY TO PRINT."

Hello out there, Frank-o-philes!

Usually we'd have a letters page here, but I wanted to take a moment and do something a bit different. As many of you may already know, Steve Dillon, our artist, passed away on October 22nd. I've talked a lot about Steve's work in these letters pages, but I just wanted to take a brief moment to talk about Steve as a person.

I don't get starry-eyed around many comic book professionals, but Steve was different. *PREACHER* was one of the first comics I truly loved. As the son of a minister who named me after his favorite John Wayne movie (*BIG JAKE*, check it out!), *PREACHER* was an extremely personal and meaningful piece of art for me from panel one. It's also hilarious, profane, and both wildly irreverent and completely sincere. It meant the world to me.

The first time I worked with Steve was on an issue of Jason Aaron's run on THE INCREDIBLE HULK. While working on that issue, Steve dropped by New York and decided to pop up to the offices. Steve talked in a low, conspiratorial London mumble, and so when he announced himself at the security desk, after a literal game of telephone, our receptionist called me and asked if I was expecting a "Steed Ollin." I said I wasn't, and turned away one of my comics heroes.

Steve called me from a phone across the street, and I ran downstairs, flushed with embarrassment, to get him up into the office. I was anxious as hell, but Steve laughed it off and suggested we meet up after work. After that, whenever Steve was in town he tended to let me know and make some time for us to hang out.

He was a warm, funny, sly, welcoming guy. I was thrilled to bring him back to PUNISHER, a character he'd put an indelible stamp on time and time again. He was having a great time working on this series, and it shows in the beautiful work he'd turn in, page after page. The week before he died, I went to his hotel to pick up art for the final page here, the introduction of the Old Crone. I asked him how he was feeling, and he gave me a side grin and said "Not great, but hopefully I'll feel better once this nasty piece of work stops staring at me." A week later, he was gone. I'll miss him. We all will.

I'd also like to take a moment to thank Matt Horak. When Steve started feeling ill, we reached out to Matt to see if he could help out on a few pages. When Steve passed, those few pages became the bulk of this issue. Steve was a hell of an act to follow, but Matt's pages here are absolutely stellar and pick up right where Steve left off.

We're still getting our feet back under us, but this PUNISHER show will go on. Thanks to all of you who reached out for support and sympathy.

When we were putting together the memorial page that ran in books a few weeks ago, Nick Lowe came around to ask if I had any idea what would be a good memorial image for Steve. Thinking back on Steve and his ability to sell the most wild, weird, outrageous story beats we could throw at him, my immediate thought was Frank punching the polar bear in issue #4 of WELCOME BACK, FRANK. Eventually a much better, more poignant image was found. But now that we've got that out of the way, here's Steve drawing the Punisher punching a polar bear.

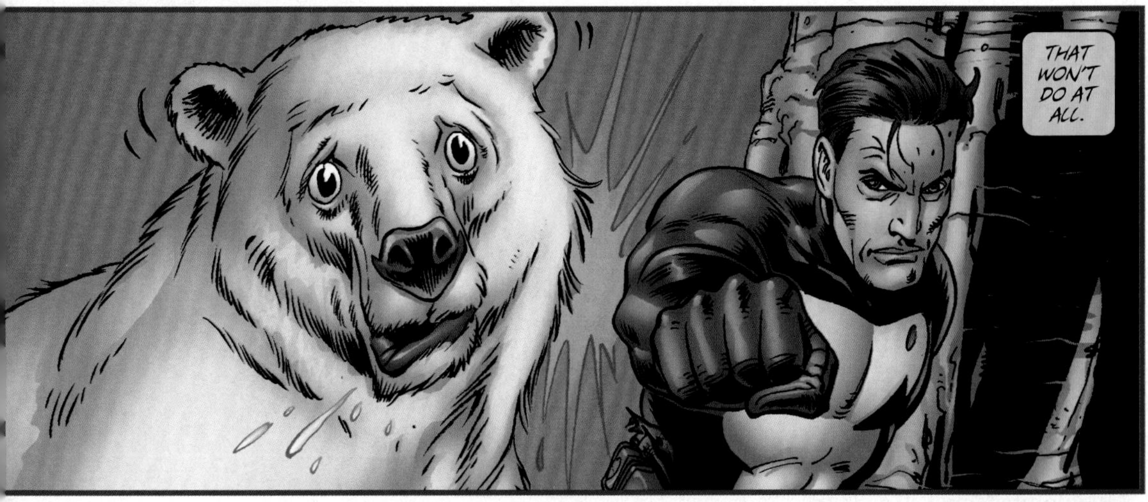
THAT WON'T DO AT ALL.

Here's to you, Steve.
-Jake T.

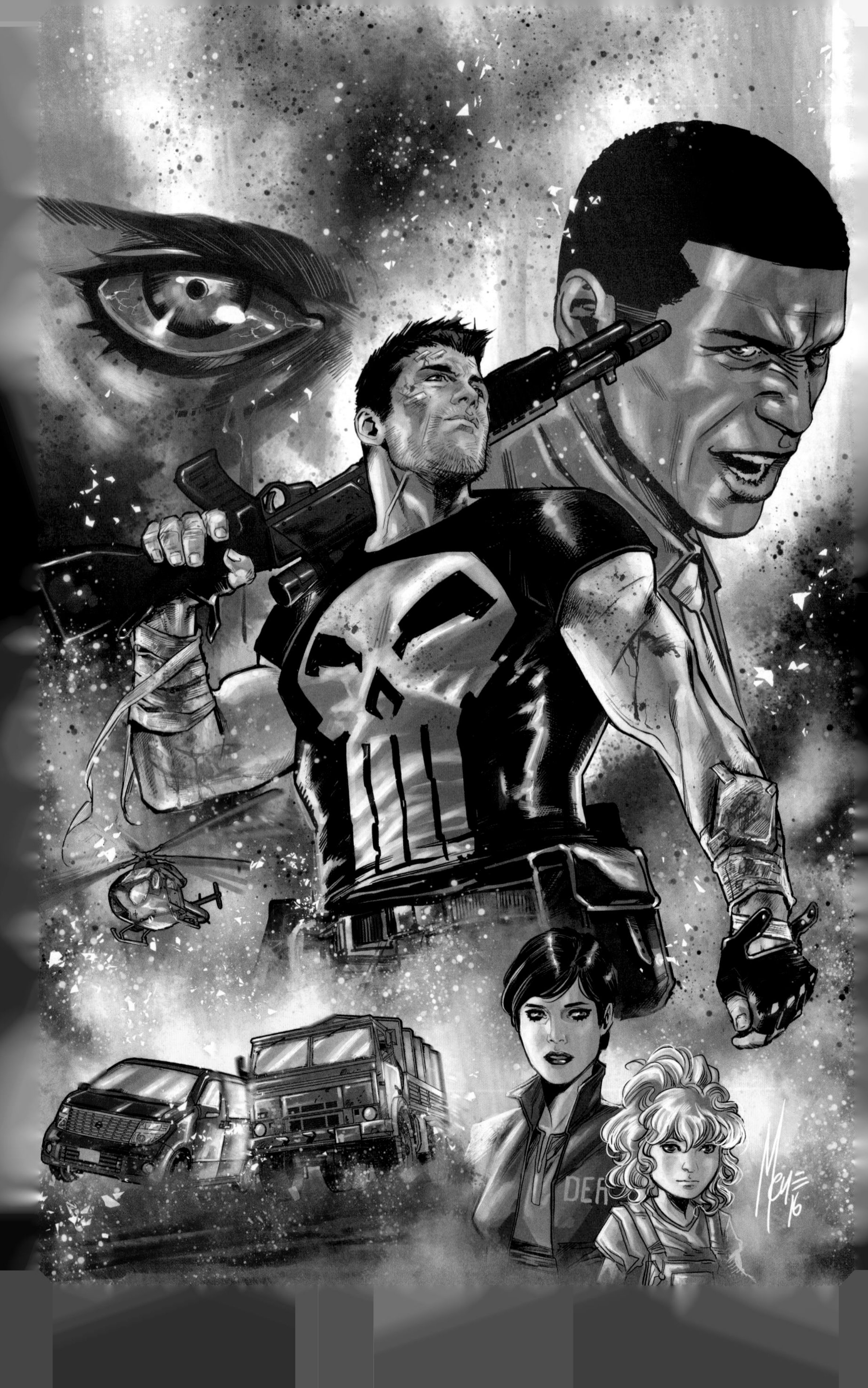
DEA

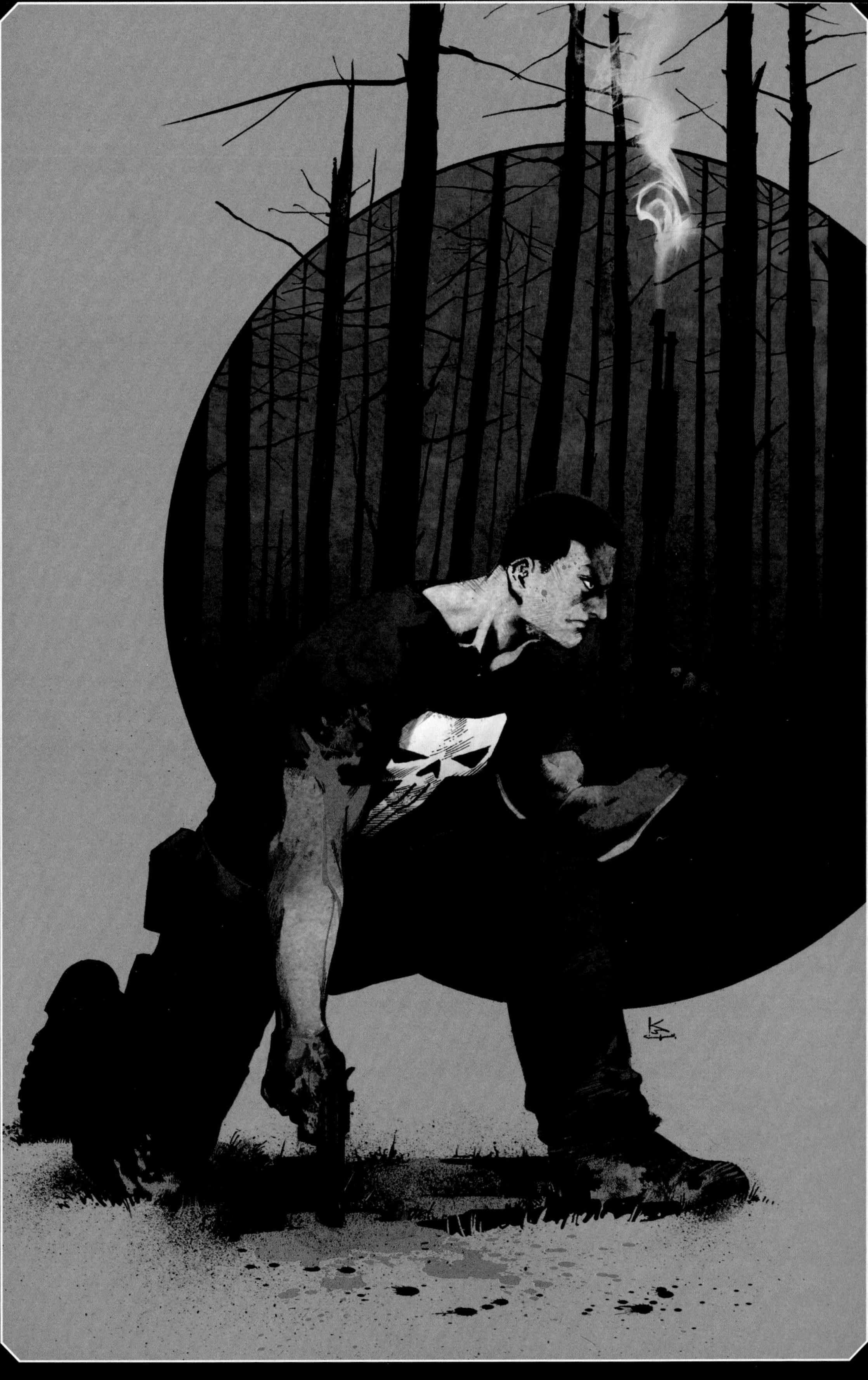

Kamome Shirahama

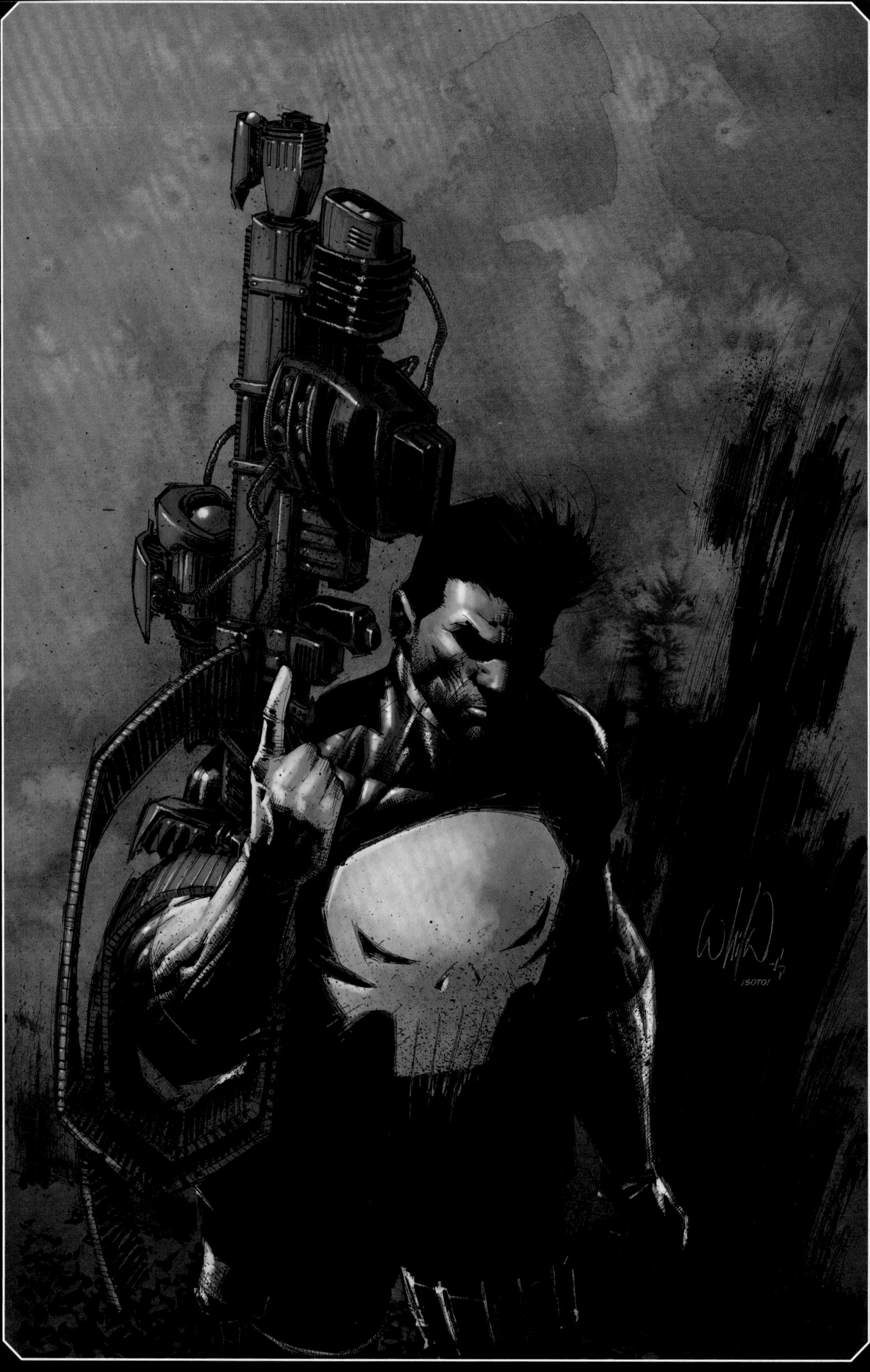
¡SOTO!

Whilce Portacio

No. 7 variant

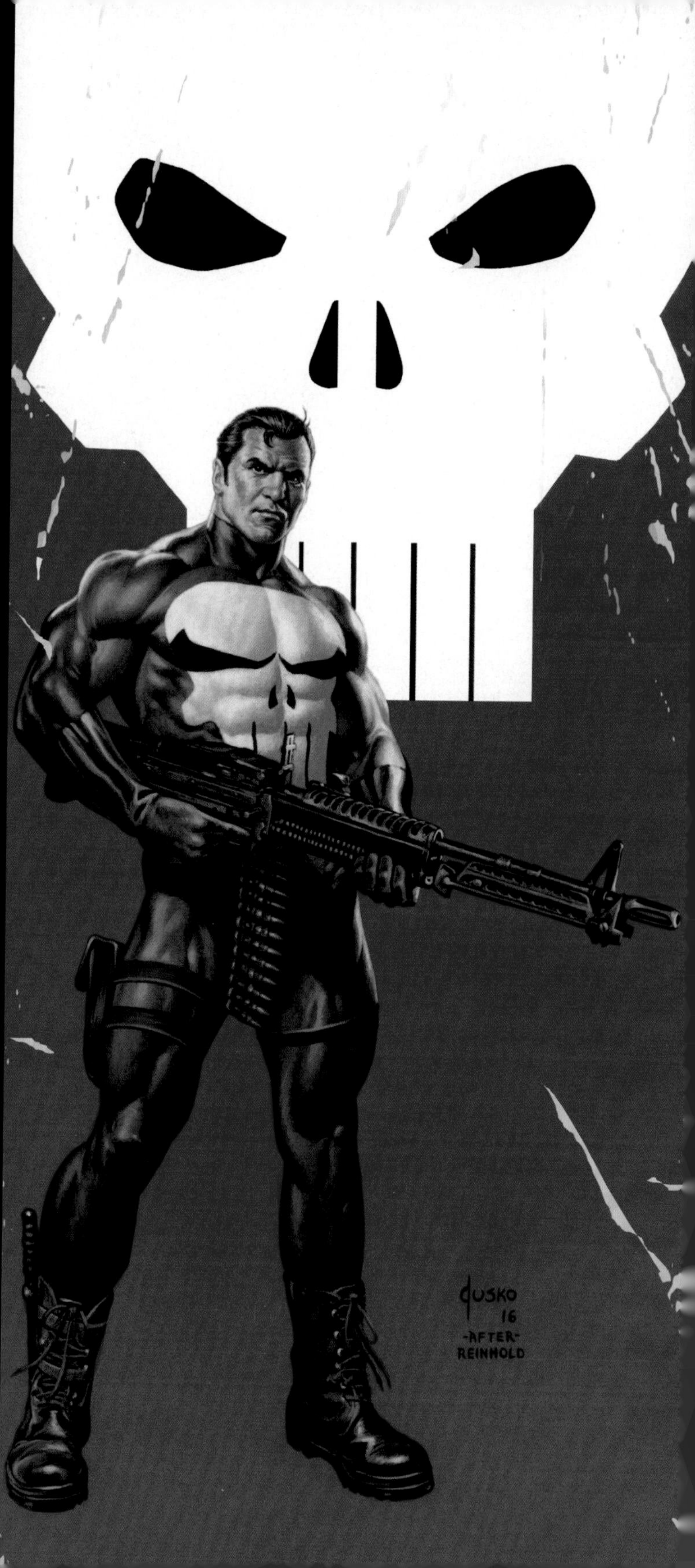
JUSKO
16
-AFTER-
REINHOLD